HIGHER EDUCATION IN THE INTERNET AGE

Libraries Creating a Strategic Edge

Patricia Senn Breivik and E. Gordon Gee

A fully updated and revised edition of Patricia Senn Breivik and E. Gordon Gee's previous, award-winning 1989 book for the ACE Series entitled *Information Literacy: Revolution in the Library*.

AMERICAN COUNCIL ON EDUCATION
PRAEGER
Series on Higher Education
Westport, Connecticut • London

Library of Congress Cataloging-in-Publication Data

Breivik, Patricia Senn.
    Higher education in the Internet age : libraries creating a strategic edge /
Patricia Senn Breivik and E. Gordon Gee.
        p.   cm.—(ACE/Praeger series on higher education)
    Rev. ed. of: Information literacy : revolution in the library. c1989.
    Includes bibliographical references and index.
    ISBN 0–275–98194–0 (alk. paper).
        1. Academic libraries—Technological innovations.   2. Information literacy—
Study and teaching (Higher)   3. Library orientation for college students.
4. Libraries and the Internet.   5. Libraries and colleges.   6. Internet in higher
education.   7. Information society.   I. Gee, E. Gordon (Elwood Gordon), 1944-
II. Breivik, Patricia Senn. Information literacy.   III. Title.   IV. American Council
on Education/Praeger series on higher education
    Z675.U5B816   2006
    027.70285'4678—dc22   2005032674

British Library Cataloguing in Publication Data is available.

Library of Congress Catalog Card Number: 2005032674
ISBN: 0–275–98194–0

First published in 2006

Praeger Publishers, 88 Post Road West, Westport, CT 06881
An imprint of Greenwood Publishing Group, Inc.
www.praeger.com

Printed in the United States of America

The paper used in this book complies with the
Permanent Paper Standard issued by the National
Information Standards Organization (Z39.48–1984).

10 9 8 7 6 5 4 3 2 1

This book is dedicated to our children, Rebekah and Kenneth,
and to students everywhere.

CONTENTS

COMMENTARIES AND CASE STUDIES

PREFACE

When we undertook to write our earlier book, there was a clarion call for major improvement in learning at both the K–12 and higher education levels. Our intent then was to assist in the response to that call by encouraging campus leaders to make better use of their academic libraries in enhancing undergraduate learning. With the emerging presence of the information age, it seemed common sense to us—though we did seem to be among the small but worthy minority—that since current and all future generations of students would live and work in an information-overloaded society, presidents and other academic leaders should use their campus libraries as a strategic resource in addressing undergraduate learning as well as other campus priorities.

Now, more than fifteen years later, there is no clarion call in education, but the academic environment has been unalterably changed by the presence of the Internet, and we find our original intent even more relevant. Because the library is a major information resource investment, it simply makes good old-fashioned common sense that the library should be used as a primary strategic tool in addressing campus priorities. Indeed, at a time of funding scarcity, it would be shortsighted not to take a fresh look at how library resources and services can better contribute to these priorities.

In particular, we strongly maintain that library resources and services have an especially important role to play in student learning and in preparing students for lifelong learning. This was the key concept in our earlier book, and we find that the remarkable growth of the information literacy movement of the past fifteen years adds a compelling reason in support of that concept. The academy is learning that advances in information technology are of little value without concern for the information available through nearly ubiquitous technology and for the need to empower people to access, evaluate, and effectively use that information. When these concerns are taken seriously, there is at last hope for closing the information divide or, as is erroneously called by many, the digital divide.

An examination of the references for this book will evidence a gap in dates. Many citations—particularly those dealing with technology—required being as current as possible. However, where an idea or concept remained as valid today as when we originally stated it, we declined to use more recent substitutes, preferring to emphasize that the key issues remain the same even with the significant changes in the academic environment.

As in our earlier book, we heavily cite efforts with which we have been directly involved, because they provide concrete examples of what is possible and because they are a matter of pride. We apologize where outstanding examples of innovative contributions by libraries in support of campus priorities have been omitted and hope that this publication will encourage better publicity for such undertakings.

Patricia Senn Breivik
University Library Dean
San José State University Library

E. Gordon Gee
Chancellor
Vanderbilt University

EXCERPT FROM
1989 PREFACE

With heavy demands facing academic administrators today, no president lightly undertakes a book commitment. Academic administrators can but seldom spare the time to deal with academic issues. We see the problems, and we serve on national committees and commissions to document academic shortcomings, yet rarely do we move beyond exploring the issues to researching and documenting new alternatives.

The current concerns regarding the quality of education, however, pose a challenge too important for normal responses. Because of our experiences, education, and commitment to the future of institutions and country, academic administrators have a special contribution to make to the current search for excellence. Beyond the attempts we make to guide our own institutions, sharing our ideas and the outcomes of our efforts with one another may help us to guide the evolution of higher education.

This book is a contribution to this larger dialogue. It is about a new partnership in higher education, a partnership between a president and a university librarian committed to quality education in the information age. The particular partnership that inspired this book started in 1985 at the University of Colorado (CU). The issues the partnership was formed to address arose much earlier.

In the late 1970s, CU responded to the coming of the information society by requiring undergraduates to take computer-literacy courses. To a large extent these courses emphasized computer programming. This approach was a common one, followed by colleges and universities across the country. It was also, as became clear in the next several years, an inadequate response to a broader need for information-literate citizens. Realizing the limitations of the computer-literacy approach, librarians on the three general campuses of CU produced a thought paper in 1982 raising the broader issue of information literacy and emphasizing the role of libraries, but their effort was ignored. Libraries seemed passé; computers were new and exciting.

By the time I became president of the University of Colorado in 1985, academic administrators who supported reform in undergraduate education were acknowledging that computer literacy, as initially defined, had proven inadequate as a response to the new information technologies. It was time to take a fresh look at literacy at CU. My experience in legal education had taught me to distinguish between schools that have students focus on "black letter" law and the better law schools, which challenge their graduates to understand how to locate and apply legal principles to the cases or controversies at hand. This shaped my concept of information literacy. Without active learning skills such as the better law schools were teaching, CU students in any discipline were in danger of being overwhelmed by information they did not know how to use.

During my first year as president of CU, my attention was split among many demands. I was fortunate, however, to have on my staff as a part-time special assistant Dr. Patricia Senn Breivik, who also served as director of the library on the Denver campus of the University of Colorado. As will happen when two people work together, our common areas of interest began to surface. She has a long-standing interest in information literacy because of her experiences at Brooklyn College during the summer of 1970, when open admissions began. Her doctoral work involved a controlled experiment to see if information-handling skills could help academically disadvantaged students to survive in the competitive college environment. A decade later, Dr. Breivik coauthored the thought paper on information literacy at CU. By then her views of computer literacy had been confirmed by experience at CU, and thus she found me a more receptive audience.

As we studied the education reform reports, we found to our surprise that references to libraries were exceedingly rare. Although we lived in an information society, no one seemed to think that libraries had anything to do with quality education. Dr. Breivik's and my first serious joint effort to address this omission was to work with Columbia University in organizing a national symposium entitled "Libraries and the Search for Academic Excellence." Held at Columbia University's Arden House in March 1987, the symposium brought together seventy-two people: higher education faculty and administrators; library educators; and a scattering of representatives from business, government, and educational associations. To our knowledge it was the first higher education meeting to focus on the role of libraries in attaining desired educational objectives. By the end of the meeting, we knew we were on the right track. Libraries do have a unique role to play in the search for academic excellence—the trouble is, most academic administrators do not know this. They do not plan for or even think about an active educational role for academic libraries.

The symposium was covered in the July/August 1987 issue of *Change.* Shortly before the symposium was held, Dr. Ernest L. Boyer's report, *College: The Undergraduate Experience,* had also underscored the importance of libraries. I was now faced with the challenge of using the library system at CU as an active partner in the search for excellence—of practicing what I preached. What could I do within CU to implement that concept? This book documents some early efforts and presents a unified vision of what I believe can and should be done in the future. Its coauthorship is an expression of the partnership between the president and the university librarian—a partnership that I believe may become one of the key factors in promoting quality education today.

Dr. Breivik and I believe that quality education in the information age requires that students become effective information consumers who are able to locate pertinent information for any need in their personal or professional lives. We believe quality education means an active education that helps students develop a pattern of lifelong learning. This is a book of advocacy. It is not, however, a book of advocacy for libraries per se but rather of advocacy for the quality of learning, research, and service that can occur on campuses where more imaginative use is made of academic libraries.

E. Gordon Gee

ACKNOWLEDGMENTS

We gratefully acknowledge the continued interest of the American Council on Education in this important topic and the support of our families and colleagues—many of whom made contributions to this volume either directly or through the generous sharing of their ideas.

We are indebted to Louis Albert, Barbara Cambridge, Robert Caret, Oswald Ratteray, Gordon Smith, and Ralph Wolff for taking precious time from very busy schedules to share their thoughtful considerations on key issues addressed in this book. Additional thanks go to Margaret Auer and Camilla Benbow for the true-life case studies they provided.

We also wish to express our appreciation to Mary Ager, Patricia Hernas, and Laura M. Miller for their contributions toward preparing this manuscript for publication—but especially our thanks go to Jean Amaral for her dedication and work in researching for and text management of the contents.

CHAPTER 1

A New Look at Libraries and the Internet

The critical lack of financial resources is an almost universal challenge across all segments of higher education today. As painful as the responses are that campuses are making to current limitations, there can be a positive outcome if we seriously reevaluate business as usual on campuses. A statement by one national leader offers reassurance. Gordon Davies, director of the Collaborative for Higher Education Policy, in 2003 said: "The bad news is, money is scarce. The good news is, that's when the most substantive change happens."[1] This would certainly be one of those times.

What is significantly different today are neither the problems nor issues confronting higher education, but the full-scale arrival of the Internet and its inherent age of information. Today, most people have a vague and uncomfortable awareness of information overload set against a shrinking global community. Too often such awareness is slow to result in changes in how learning takes place or business is done on campuses. Instead, this awareness is more likely to result in creating chief information officer (CIO) positions and making large investments in technology than in reexamining the role of libraries—the primary campus access point to most information.

This widespread failure of the academic community to recognize or take advantage of the enormous potential of libraries is lamentable. Despite significant changes in library resources and information technology, most people, if they give any thought to libraries at all, tend to view them in simplistic terms. Most faculty members are happy if the library provides the journals they want (preferably now in electronic format) and makes it easy for them to put materials on reserve. Students are primarily concerned with the hours the library is open. Some administrators may continue to refer to libraries as the heart of the university, but they largely ignore them—just as they ignore their physical hearts—unless a problem (such as a bad accreditation report) attracts their attention. Because everybody "knows" what a library is, hardly anyone thinks about what a library could do or asks how it could address current institutional needs and priorities. The challenge for administrators is to see libraries not merely as ends in themselves (libraries are frequently presented as self-contained units in academic plans and accreditation reports), but as strategic tools in achieving campus goals and priorities.

EXPANDING ROLE FOR LIBRARIES IN THE INFORMATION SOCIETY

This book is dedicated to the concept that, in today's information society, the active involvement and support of the academic library staff and resources will be a key to students' acquiring lifelong learning abilities and faculty achieving greater research productivity. Libraries can also be strategic tools in enhancing community service and in supporting other important priorities, such as student recruitment and globalization of the curriculum. To persist in a traditional narrow view of libraries in the information age is to weaken most campus efforts, particularly in the crucial area of information literacy. Within the differing environments of more than 3,000 U.S. colleges and universities, the contributions of active libraries can range from institution-specific planning support to broader efforts to address the societal problems of the information age. In partnership with academic administrators and classroom faculty, librarians can enhance instruction, research, and service while supporting the eventual transformation of higher education.

An analogy may help elucidate how this can work. Your campus library is like a computer network. In all likelihood, you were not personally involved in the design or the assembling of campus network hardware and software, nor did you enter the data. Yet that network is a very powerful tool in your work as an academic administrator. It assists you in tackling a multitude of campus projects and problems. You provide the leadership, identify the issues to be addressed, and direct the staff to provide the statistical analyses and other information you need. Of course, you could conceivably ignore the capabilities of campus computer technologies and networks altogether. You could restrict your staff to type-

writers and calculators. The computer could just sit there as an idle fix-
ture, conveying the image of an up-to-date and efficiently run administrative office without actually helping it to function effectively.

Your library can sit there too, or it can be a powerful tool for addressing campus projects and problems. Most likely you have had little or no
personal involvement in the guiding, equipping, or staffing of the library.
You may not clearly understand how the library operates; yet, if you provide the vision and the leadership, library personnel and resources can
be integrated into everyday decision-making and can help you accomplish your goals. Of course, you could simply ignore the library. It will be
properly ornamental when prospective students and their parents tour
the campus and when accreditation teams come to visit. Nothing terri-
ble will happen, but are you willing to pass up the contributions your library can make toward achieving campus priorities?

In times of limited financial resources, no administrator can sensibly
forgo exploiting any campus resource—much less one as large, as expensive, and as potentially powerful as the library. The library plays a
crucial role in an information society—connecting, integrating, and
managing informational resources—and nowhere has technology been
more empowering than in library operations and services. The value of
the library for the academic administrator is not less than in pre-Internet
days, but far greater.

Before academic leaders can make effective and efficient use of this
tool, however, a new partnership must blossom among academic administrators, faculty, and librarians. Most academics—and, indeed, many librarians—have very firm, but limited, ideas of how library personnel and
resources can be used to accomplish campus priorities. Only vision and
leadership on the part of presidents, academic vice presidents, and heads
of libraries can create the necessary climate for academics to take a new
look at their libraries and to integrate them into all aspects of campus
life.

EARLY PRESIDENTIAL VISIONS OF THE LIBRARY'S CENTRAL ROLE IN EDUCATION

We are not the first educators to call for an expanded role for academic
libraries, and others keep emerging. Although our predecessors did not
foresee all of the special contributions libraries could make in today's
world, their ideas and their visions provide the foundation for this book
and for the projects we discuss, and we have added more recent presidential visions as well.

Historically, no president has championed the role of libraries and reading in quality undergraduate education more than Henry M. Wriston, who served as president at Lawrence University (1925–1937) and at Brown University (1937–1955). In his autobiography, Wriston wrote, "The classroom is only one of the places where the educative process takes place, and it is by no means always the most important."[2] Wriston singled out libraries and student life as the two areas in which a president could best influence the quality of education. His broad assumption in regard to the library was that the "best teachers and scholars make the fullest and most varied use of libraries and stimulate their students to do likewise."[3]

Wriston's personal involvement with libraries was most noticeable to people beyond his own campuses through his role within the Association of American Colleges. In 1937, under Wriston's leadership, the association commissioned Harvie Branscomb, director of libraries at Duke University, to study the relationship between library use and academic performance. This study was the basis for *Teaching with Books*, published in 1940. Although now outdated on library administrative issues, the book addresses the role of libraries in instruction very well. "The task which the directors approved and which I undertook was . . . a consideration of the extent to which the efforts of the college library are integrated with those of the institution as a whole. In other words, this project undertook to study the college library from the standpoint of its educational effectiveness rather than its administrative efficiency."[4]

Wriston's and Branscomb's concepts of how libraries can support educational quality (further explored in chapter 3) have had a lasting influence. The basic questions they raised are the same we raise today:

- How is the library integrated into campus "initiatives"?
- What is the educational effectiveness of the library?

Several decades after these farsighted educators called attention to instructionally underutilized libraries, the 1972 report of the Carnegie Commission on Higher Education echoed their call for a new look at libraries in the learning process.

> The library, by whatever name, should occupy a central role in the instructional resources of educational institutions. Its personnel should be available not only for guidance to materials held in the collections of the campus, but also should, when qualified by subject-matter ex-

pertise, be utilized as instructors. We also believe that nonprint information, illustrations, and instructional software components should be maintained as part of a unified informational-instructional resource that is cataloged and stored in ways that facilitate convenient retrieval as needed by students and faculty members.[5]

Five years after *Teaching with Books* was published, Virgil M. Hancher, president of the State University of Iowa, echoed its themes when he outlined the philosophical foundation for the new Iowa State library in the introduction to his thought paper, "The Library as a Teaching Instrument."

> I am especially interested in this library building because it will be more than just another building, or even another store-house for books. I visualize it as a great study center for the campus—a workshop where faculty researchers in many departments can study in convenient and stimulating quarters in close association with graduate students—a new kind of home for the College of Liberal Arts, a base that will give personality to and unify many of the now scattered activities of that college—a center where new methods of teaching and new faculty-student relationships may emerge—a center where students may develop a greater appreciation for the knowledge and wisdom that come from direct and positive participation in research.
>
> Most important of all, I foresee an educational program emerging from this center that should give our students a better understanding of their heritage, a more sober realization of the problems that will confront them as adults, and a more realistic understanding of what they must do to solve these problems.[6]

Many years after Hancher's observations on the construction of the new Iowa library, the introduction of high technology into information management inspired new and very different views of how libraries should be physically constructed. Yet regardless of what design they choose, presidents who speak of libraries as central to the learning process have carried on Wriston's ideas, recasting his themes in the language of the computer age. For example, in a 1983 speech, Clarkson's President Robert A. Plane was prophetic in his vision for the new Clarkson library.

> When our network system is complete, the library will become a node or hub linking all parts of the campus together. Once all parts

of the campus are so linked with information flowing freely between all points, it becomes relatively uninteresting as to where the information originates. By linking our network to external databases, one may never know whose holdings are being utilized. At that point, we will indeed have elevated information access to top library priority. However, just to ensure that we understand the distinction between gaining information and learning, I am pleased that we will always have, right in our library, both classrooms and a commons area for person-to-person discussions and true learning.[7]

In following years, other presidents of major universities stressed the importance of libraries in providing quality education. In a 1986 speech to a conference on telecommunications and higher education, President Richard L. Van Horn of the University of Houston suggested that all use of technology should be approached in the same way that higher education approaches libraries. Both, he stressed, are concerned with providing access to information. He further urged that learning across the curriculum should be modeled after learning in the library.

One of the valuable aspects of a library is that libraries are not organized along course lines. Universities should give students at least some exposure to problem-solving that is not course oriented. Business leaders who hire our students say that when those students get out on the job, they often do not know how to address complex problems. In the university, they are in a physics or an English course. So, if they see a problem, it is a physics problem or an English problem. Out on the job, a problem is just a problem. It does not fit anywhere, and students find that difficult. We should reinforce in students the notion that learning is really not related to courses. Courses are an administrative convenience that help use faculty and student time effectively, but they have little to do with the way the world is structured.[8]

Van Horn suggested that a more unstructured environment, more "independent activity," and a greater focus on student use of libraries would better prepare students for the environment they will enter upon graduation. These are among the elements that President William G. Bowen also mentioned as important in his 1985 Princeton University report devoted to the Princeton library. He notes the "emphasis on independent study, an atmosphere of free thought, and the integration of the library into teaching and course work . . . have guided the development of Princeton's library into modern times."[9] Bowen further articulates Princeton's philosophy on the role of the library and its staff as active participants in the learning process by quoting William S. Dix, head librarian at Princeton from 1953 to 1975.

> As the relative size of personal book collections continues to decline and as public and institutional library resources become progressively richer, the knowledge of how to make effective use of a complex library as an adjunct of private life and professional career must become a more vital part of the education of the Princeton student. Much of this knowledge is gained through formal course work, in support of which the library staff works in close collaboration with the teaching faculty, but a substantial part of it is the independent responsibility of the reference librarian in his teaching role.[10]

Presidents who share the views of Van Horn and Bowen about the role of libraries in education have sometimes been inspired by the vision of a librarian. An innovative librarian can do much to influence a president's view of the academic library, as librarian Patricia Knapp's career clearly illustrates. Knapp had such a strong and attractive vision of the library as a center for learning that she decisively influenced the views of two men who later became university presidents.

In the early 1960s, as director of the Montieth Project at Wayne State University, Patricia Knapp tried to implement the university's plan to have its experimental Montieth College undertake a more active learning process. Faculty members were to serve as facilitators of learning by making more dynamic use of resource materials instead of relying solely on textbooks, reading lists, and reserve materials. Housed within a new experimental college, the project ultimately failed because of the unwillingness of faculty members to transcend traditional teaching methods.[11] Yet her efforts were noticed by both Robert Spencer and Franklin W. Wallin, who drew upon Knapp's example.

Robert Spencer became the founding president of Sangamon State University (SSU) in Springfield, Illinois, where he sought to create a "teaching library." The first building at SSU was the library, and in 1977, Spencer invited representatives from four other institutions to attend a leadership conference on the instructional role of academic libraries. One of the four institutions involved was Earlham College, which today is nationally known for its active information literacy program. Strong support for the development of the Earlham program was provided by President Franklin W. Wallin, who had also been influenced by Knapp's work at Wayne State.

The common thread that runs throughout the words and actions of these college and university presidents is their understanding of the li-

brary as a dynamic center of learning that enhances the quality of undergraduate education and better prepares students for living and working in the real world. We are happy to note that this understanding is
gaining an increasing number of proponents among higher education
leaders and is now a matter of global concern.[12]

Yet the attitude of many administrators displays the kind of ambiguity
described by University of Virginia President Robert M. O'Neil in 1982:

> It [the library] is the center of research and a key to a university's
> scholarly distinction. It is a mounting and at times uncontrollable
> drain on the university's budget. It is a window to the community—
> both the academic community and the general citizenry. It is the
> most dependable link with other institutions of higher learning. It
> can be an administrative headache and at times a battleground of
> personnel policies. It is the source of greatest promise and greatest
> problems in the use of new technologies. It is the key to develop-
> ment of new academic programs and the strength of existing pro-
> grams. It is all of these elements and many more. The university
> library is, in short, a source of pride and a source of problems.[13]

The typical underutilization of libraries is usually caused by undue
focus on the problems and a lack of vision. A conference of librarians
and academic administrators at the University of California–Los Angeles in 1981 concluded that the "academic research library is treated as a
peripheral aspect of university planning . . . despite the repeated refrain
that the library is the heart of the university."[14] As a distinguished academic librarian in New England wrote in response to a survey of library
directors, the "most pervasive attitude toward the library that I've en-
countered is benign neglect. Nothing overtly subversive, nothing openly
hostile, just a certain amount of indifference, impatience, and a lack of
understanding of the complexity of library activity and of the importance
of the library as a means for academic excellence."[15]

MORE RECENT VISIONS

Since our earlier book, additional visions for academic libraries have
emerged that offer more dynamic uses of libraries. The number of educational leaders who envision libraries as critical resources in achieving
desired student learning outcomes has also significantly increased, and

visions for academic libraries in support of campus service missions are increasingly being articulated.

The building of two new libraries half a continent apart provided opportunities to make more dynamic use of libraries. Years of hard work finally paid off in 1995 when Wayne State University (WSU) received funding from the legislature to build an undergraduate library. Part of the initial challenge was that only President David Adamany wanted it! By and large, undergraduate libraries on research campuses had failed to make a positive impact on student learning, and almost up until groundbreaking, there was no articulated vision for the role the new library would play in relation to the four existing research libraries on campus.

But Adamany's commitment to the library was based on WSU's clear commitment to first-generation college students, and a series of focus groups initiated by new library leadership—including some outside consultants with expertise in retention of at-risk students—eventually developed a mission statement for the new library. The library was to promote the retention and academic success of freshmen and sophomores. This mission, unusual for a library, significantly impacted the internal design of the building, the services offered, and the staff engaged.

Once opened in 1997, the success of the library was quickly evidenced by its high rate of usage. It was, in fact, so popular that the existing general computing labs experienced such a significant drop in usage that they were closed and their student budgets transferred to the library. Moreover, a couple of years later, the desire of the incoming president, Irvin R. Reid, for a Student Success Center was met with the happy news that the campus was more than halfway there with the David Adamany Undergraduate Library. (More information on this library is provided in chapter 7.)

At about the same time on another large urban campus on the West Coast, San José State University (SJSU) President Robert L. Caret was confronted with a very different challenge. Committed to having SJSU intrinsically engaged in its community in the heart of Silicon Valley, Caret and then-San José Mayor Susan Hammer decided to build a joint library, combining the university library with the city's downtown main library. When the project was announced at a mayor's press conference, initial campus response was highly negative and quickly sparked a SOUL (Save Our University Library) campaign in which faculty and library staff participated. After months of working with campus leadership, the Academic Senate voted to support the project.

The library, which integrates all major service units and allows full use of all materials by campus and community alike, opened on August 1,

2003. Over 21,000 people participated in the grand opening celebrations on August 16, and the 1,000,000th visitor was celebrated on December 1 of that year. Campus personnel quickly began to use the new library for pleasure as well as for scholarship, and during the first ten months of operations, academic patron checkouts of materials increased by more than 100 percent. Overnight, the library became a destination site for the city, and its success quickly led to approaches by city leadership as to other possible joint projects with the university. (More information on this library is provided in chapter 7.)

Besides presidents, other leaders in higher education are increasingly promoting libraries to contribute to achieving campus goals, particularly as they relate to student learning and information literacy. Years before its library opened, San José State University was participating in California State University (CSU) initiatives on information literacy. One of the driving forces behind the initial systemwide effort was Dr. Lorie Roth, a former English professor by then on staff at the CSU system office. Roth is fond of telling how she became an information literacy champion in a garbage can, describing the event as follows:

> Amazing as it may seem, I first became concerned about the topic of information literacy by sifting through garbage cans. Before I became a full-time administrator in the Office of the Chancellor at the California State University, I was an English professor. And since English professors are dependent on printed materials for their very livelihood, I have always spent a lot of time in the library. One day, about three years ago, I went to the campus library to get an orientation in the use of computer databases. . . .
>
> As the librarian explained to me the features of computerized information retrieval, she launched into a complaint that students did not have the skills they needed to be able to use the databases. She then reached into the trash can beside her and pulled out a fistful of computer print-outs. . . . The print-outs recorded every decision made by the students as they conducted the computerized library research—as well as the result of that decision.
>
> As I examined these vestiges of the students' work—and gained glimpses of the thought processes that lay behind this tangible evidence of their skills—I was disheartened more profoundly than I ever before had been in my career. For it was absolutely clear to me that the students who had been sitting at these terminals, these college students who were conducting library research—didn't have the faintest idea of what they were doing. . . .
>
> As I sat there, surrounded by the detritus from the trash cans, paging through these print-outs, I tried to reconstruct what kind of

thought processes these students were using. I finally arrived at the conclusion that, in fact, there was no process; that there was no logical, clear, systematic inquiry; that the students at my university did not, in fact, have the skills necessary to find the information they needed. And I thought that I as a teacher had failed, and that we as a collective faculty had not done right by our students by allowing them to be information illiterates in the Age of Information.

There before me on the table I had tangible evidence that students did not know how to find information. If they didn't know how to find it, could I have any confidence that they knew how to evaluate the information? Or how to use the information in a responsible manner? That's when I became a convert, on the spot—not even just a convert, but more like a zealot—on the topic of information competence—and how important it is for survival in today's world.[16]

Thanks in part to Roth's commitment to information literacy, CSU has established systemwide standards, initiated assessment strategies, and provided seed money for faculty/librarian projects to integrate information literacy into the curriculum.

This CSU leadership role in information literacy also caused the Educational Testing Service (ETS) to ask CSU to partner in its information and communications technology (ICT) skills assessment initiative. Unlike many ICT skills efforts, this assessment fully integrates information literacy and critical-thinking skills along with more technical skills. A December 2003 press release outlined the purpose and scope of the project:

> "To succeed in today's information-based economy, students need to know how to use technology to create and transform information," says ETS President Kurt Landgraf. "ETS is collaborating with these forward-looking universities to offer the promise of a suite of assessments that measure not just knowledge of technology, but the ability to apply technology to solve problems while in college and to help all students learn the ICT literacy skills that they will need to compete for jobs and thrive in the workforce."
>
> ETS and charter colleges and universities will use cutting-edge measurement techniques that are technology-delivered and scenario-based to accurately assess these skills. Dr. Ilene F. Rockman, CSU Manager of Information Competence and Systemwide Library Initiatives, indicates, "We as college and university educators are increasingly asking our students to successfully demonstrate their ICT literacy skills within a technologically-rich teaching and learning environment. After examining the status of assessment instruments currently

available or in development, there is none more comprehensive or dis-
tinctive than this performance-based, web-based, holistic assessment
tool envisioned and anticipated by ETS and this consortium.[17]

Other sources of strong support for libraries as central to the learning
process and especially to information literacy abilities over the past decade
have been two regional accreditation agencies. The involvement of the
Middle States Commission on Higher Education (MSCHE) in information literacy began with Howard Simmons, who was its executive director from 1988 to 1995. In a 1992 article, Simmons raises the question of
why libraries should be of particular concern to accrediting agencies:

> One might ask how and why an accreditation agency became such
> a strong proponent of the centrality of library and information re-
> sources in the total scheme of things? And why would an accredita-
> tion body link information literacy to the improvement of the
> teaching and learning process, especially at the undergraduate level?
> Why is it essential for the Middle States CHE to view bibliographic
> instruction and information literacy as important factors in the as-
> sessment of student learning outcomes and institutional effective-
> ness?[18]

His article then goes on to answer the question.

> Because the Middle States CHE is concerned about the continuous
> improvement of quality, particularly at the undergraduate level, it
> believes that programs to improve the teaching and learning process
> in colleges and universities should include an appropriate emphasis
> on information literacy and other resource-based learning strategies.
> CHE understands that it has a corresponding responsibility to en-
> sure that this emphasis on information literacy through the medium
> of the library—as broadly defined—is realized in self-study and eval-
> uation team reports, institutional assessment program reviews, and
> in accreditation decision making.
>   CHE's concern about the lack of effective programs of biblio-
> graphic instruction and information literacy on some campuses is
> highlighted in annual reports. Not only are these programs seen to
> assist students and faculty in making more effective utilization of in-
> formation sources in the teaching and learning process, but they are
> also considered to be intrinsically and inextricably related to aca-
> demic quality and excellence, student learning, teaching perfor-
> mance and effectiveness, and institutional effectiveness.[19]

The Middle States' leadership role with information literacy continued
after Simmons's departure. In 2003, for example, Middle States issued an

excellent book, entitled *Developing Research & Communication Skills: Guidelines for Information Literacy in the Curriculum*, which documents the essential partnering role between classroom faculty and librarians in the promotion of information literacy.[20]

But while the Middle States CHE has been particularly strong in pragmatic approaches to facilitating the success of information literacy programs, the leadership at the Western Association of Schools and Colleges (WASC) has done a particularly good job of embedding information literacy expectations in its standards. In a 1995 article, WASC executive director Ralph Wolff argued for the need for the accreditation process to transform the mission of the library, stating that none of the standards as yet established for libraries to date was equal to the emerging needs of higher education and an increasingly information-based society. Wolff's vision for future standards remains far beyond considerations on most campuses:

> The Newtonian model of separating the world into independent parts is reaching the end of its usefulness in both higher education and the larger society. The quantum physics model outlines a new approach built around relationships and multiple roles and gives form to the fundamentally changing character of knowledge and the learning process. The mission of the library of the future will be principally a teaching one that is directly linked to the educational mission of the institution. Thus, assessment should be directed primarily at the library's relationship to the teaching and learning functions of the institution. Any evaluation should emphasize how interaction with the library affects or enhances student learning. Through the self-study and visit processes, accreditation can play a useful role in exploring each of these issues and promoting the development of new partnerships throughout the institution.[21]

Commentary: "Accreditation's Shift to Learning-Centeredness: Implications for Information Literacy"

Ralph A. Wolff
Executive Director
Accrediting Commission for Senior Colleges and Universities
Western Association of Schools and Colleges

In the past ten years, regional accreditation has undergone a significant transformation, focusing heavily on the assessment of student learning as a central element of the accrediting process. Presidents and provosts need to be aware of these changes since they require thinking about accreditation long before the next visit takes place, especially the new approaches accrediting agencies are taking with respect to information literacy.

Regional accreditation plays a key role in defining and evaluating institutional quality in the United States through the articulation of accrediting standards and the application of these standards to over 3,000 higher education institutions in the United States. Organized into six regions and seven accrediting commissions, since 2001, six of the seven commissions have developed new accrediting standards, and the seventh (the Northwest Commission) is currently in the process of reviewing its standards. In each case, the new accrediting standards have placed significantly greater emphasis on assessing student learning. Several commissions have also begun to use the phrase "learning-centeredness" to describe their new emphasis and direction.

In 2003, the Council of Regional Accrediting Commissions (C-RAC) developed a Statement of Principles regarding Accreditation and Student Learning, reflecting this new and important emphasis. This Statement of Principles, along with implementing resource guides, was endorsed by all seven accrediting commissions. It states that the role of student learning in accreditation is now to be seen as central to the mission of regional accreditation, as reflected in the first principle addressing what each accrediting agency should expect of itself: "Evaluation of an institution's success in achieving student learning is central to each Commission's function and public charter."

This new emphasis has significant implications for addressing information literacy. Each of the commissions addresses information literacy as a *capacity* issue, reflecting the need for each institution to provide adequate information resources to students and faculty. Such capacity statements are typically found in the standards dealing with libraries and learning resources. An emerging trend of significance is that several commissions now also focus on information literacy as a key learning outcome as well. This provides the basis for a different set of accreditation expectations for institutions. And it provides a set of challenges for accreditation, as will be discussed later.

In articulating information literacy as a core part of institutional capacity, accrediting standards deal with the sufficiency of information resources, assurance of access to information resources, and the provision of training in library research techniques. The New England Association, for example, addresses adequacy of resources in Standard Seven: "The institution demonstrates sufficient and appropriate information resources and services and instructional and information technology and utilizes them to support the fulfillment of its mission." The Southern Association addresses access in its Standard 3.8.2: "The institution ensures that users have access to regular and timely instruction in the use of the library and other learning/information resources." The Community College Commission of the Western Association addresses training in its Standard 2C: "The institution provides ongoing instruction for users of library and other learning support services so that students are able to develop skills in information competency."

The shift to information literacy as a learning outcome began with the Middle States Association emphasis on it as a learning outcome in its "Characteristics of Excellence" and in symposia it conducted as early as 1995. In its current Standard 11, Middle States defines information literacy and then states:

Information literacy is vital to all disciplines and to effective teaching and learning in any institution. Institutions of higher education need to provide students and instructors with the knowledge, skills, and tools to obtain information in many formats and media in order to identify, retrieve, and apply relevant and valid knowledge and information resources to their study, teaching, or research.

Middle States has also published a very useful guidebook on information literacy to support its diffusion throughout all curricula.

Other accrediting agencies have also incorporated information literacy as a key learning outcome. The Senior College Commission of WASC has included information literacy as one of the core competencies expected of all baccalaureate programs (Standard 2.2).

Identifying information as a key learning outcome is reflected in the increasing understanding that learning has become more than fact mastery and that a critical lifelong learning skill will be the ability to sort through and discriminate among an overwhelming array of information and data. As stated by the Higher Learning Commission in its new Standards:

> *Knowledge* is a powerful word, for it speaks to comprehension, application, and synthesis, not just mastery of information. Computers may have introduced the Information Age, but in a short time our definitional language for this new era began to include the term *knowledge worker*. The shift is as important as it is misunderstood.
>
> The knowledge worker will be technologically literate, to be sure, but what is valued is the knowledge worker's capacity to sift and winnow massive amounts of information in order to discover or create new or better understandings of ourselves and the world we live in.

This shift in emphasis to learning-centeredness for information literacy has a number of significant implications for institutions and accrediting agencies.

For Institutions

1. *Treating information literacy as an institutional learning outcome, not just the library's.* Information literacy is a key learning outcome not just for undertaking research, but also as a vital skill for lifelong learning and survival in the twenty-first century. Seen in this light, it underpins all disciplines. Some institutions currently treat information literacy as a basic skill, taught to first-year students as part of library orientation; others extend information literacy to general education; and still others incorporate information literacy outcomes into the major. Accrediting agencies can play a central role in promoting and shaping the fundamental understanding of information literacy as a key institutional learning outcome for all disciplines by applying this broader definition in the accreditation review process.
2. *Addressing information literacy in self-studies.* Past reviews of libraries in self-studies reflected a heavy emphasis on library resources, facilities, and staffing. More recently, however, a review of self-studies for the Senior College Commission of WASC reflects greater identification of information literacy as a learning outcome, but little analysis of the achievement of this outcome.

Much more can be done in the self-study process to study the *achievement of information literacy outcomes* across the institution. Institutions should make assessing the achievement of information literacy skills of graduates across the institution a major focus of self-studies. Such skills are just as important as writing and critical thinking, yet are evaluated far less frequently.

3. *Transforming the role of librarians and faculty to be information literacy assessors.* The role of the librarian has taken on increasing value as information needs expand. At the same time, the librarian's role should not be limited to basic information resource instruction as part of first-year orientation or a basic course. Librarians need to be working closely with faculty to create specific information literacy learning outcomes for general education and each of the disciplines, as well as methods of assessment of their achievement. Faculty need to be able to give feedback to students not only on disciplinary content and writing, but also on the quality of information search, retrieval, and analysis. Many faculty are not yet fully information literate themselves, and even fewer are equipped to provide effective feedback to students about this important outcome. Institutions will need to provide faculty development not just about the use of technology for themselves, but how to address information literacy as a learning outcome in each of their courses (as reflected in syllabi and evaluations of students).

For Accreditors

1. *Training team members to evaluate information literacy outcomes.* As long as information literacy is seen as a support service provided by the library, its review will be left to librarians serving on accrediting teams. But if information literacy were understood as a key outcome of all degree programs—graduate and undergraduate—then its review would (and should) become part of the scope of review of all team members reviewing academic areas. Accrediting agencies need to emphasize the importance of information literacy as a key area for review.

2. *Building institutional capacity to design and implement information literacy outcomes and sharing good practices.* Increasingly, accrediting agencies are sponsoring workshops to build institutional capacity for assessment of student learning. All agencies should work with institutions and statewide systems to share good practices in defining, applying, and assessing information literacy outcomes; connecting such outcomes to other aspects of the institution's mission and learning goals in such areas as writing, critical thinking, and diversity; and tie these outcomes to institutional assessment.

3. *Connecting information literacy achievement to the program review process.* A number of regional agencies are now calling for all institutions to engage in periodic program review, which are expected to incorporate assessment of student learning outcomes. The program review process becomes a natural way for each department (and general education) to assess the effectiveness of information literacy outcomes as part of the overall review process, and as accrediting teams review and evaluate the effectiveness of program review, information literacy outcomes can readily be added as an area of focus.

Key Questions for Both

How is information literacy defined? Is it treated primarily as a capacity issue or as a key learning outcome for all graduates across all disciplines?

How is information literacy assessed? Have standards of achievement been developed with higher expectations for graduates than first-year students? Is student work reviewed in relation to information literacy outcomes? Are faculty engaged in such reviews and supported to know how to give students feedback and assist them to improve their information literacy competencies?

How are information literacy outcomes incorporated into the institution's strategic plans, institutional assessment strategies, and course approval and program review processes? Are resources allocated to support the development of information literacy outcomes across the institution beyond support for capacity elements, such as student orientation?

Accrediting agencies have begun a significant shift to address information literacy from the standpoint of a support service of the library to a key learning outcome across the entire institution. Such a shift calls for addressing information literacy more specifically and comprehensively by both institutions and accreditors in the self-study and team review processes. This will involve significant development efforts for faculty and accrediting evaluators—to develop and assess levels of information literacy achievement for all graduates. Were accrediting agencies to give this kind of focus to information literacy, the result would be to shape the future of information literacy and build a far deeper understanding of its importance as a necessary and fundamental learning outcome for all degree programs.

At WASC such thinking regarding information literacy laid the philosophical foundation for the integration of library resources and services as well as information literacy into a revision of standards. The 2001 *WASC Handbook of Accreditation* weaves a thread of library use and students' acquisition of information literacy competencies throughout its "Standard 2: Achieving Education Objectives Through Core Functions," as well as in its "Standard 3: Developing and Applying Resources and Organizational Structures to Ensure Sustainability." (See Appendix A for excerpts from these standards' criteria for review and accompanying guidelines.)

While other regional accrediting agencies have not paid as much attention to the educational role of libraries as Middle States CHE and WASC, there is a national organization that has long promoted information literacy. The American Association of Higher Education (AAHE) was a founding member of the National Forum on Information Literacy (for more information on the Forum, see its Web site at http://www.infolit.org), and AAHE leadership has formally endorsed national standards for information literacy.

During its spring 2000 meeting, AAHE's Board of Directors voted
unanimously to endorse the Association of College & Research Libraries' "Information Literacy Competency Standards for Higher Education." Explained AAHE board member David Breneman, dean
of the Curry School of Education at the University of Virginia,
"With societal well-being so dependent on how its citizens find, review, and use information, institutions must help students become
information literate, in the fullest sense of the term, as set forth so
well in the ACRL standards."

This is only the second time that AAHE has endorsed a policy
position. (The Board approved the AAHE Statement on Diversity
in April 1999.)[22]

One of the reasons there is a growing awareness of the importance of
information literacy and, therefore, the role of library personnel and resources in student learning is that these concepts wear well in practice.
Once academic administrators discover the potential benefits of making
strategic use of campus libraries, they keep finding new ways to take advantage of their knowledge. In our earlier book we document Alan E.
Guskin's pioneering thoughts of twenty years ago regarding the library
serving as the center for computer use; this idea has since become com-
monplace in libraries. However, Guskin's concept for the role of the library in learning has continued to expand. In a 2003 *Change* article,
which he coauthored with Mary B. Marcy, his vision for the library in
creating a vital campus in a climate of restricted resources is as follows:

One area that should undergo significant internal restructuring—as
well as assignment to a more prominent role in educational delivery—is the library. Rather than operating as a separate unit that provides access to locally owned information resources, the academic
library is rapidly becoming part of an elaborate network of information provision and an essential portal for students and faculty to access global information resources.

The library of the future will need to become a true learning center for students and faculty, where available information-technology
resources are centrally and efficiently integrated to further student
learning and to facilitate faculty and staff transformation. A transformed library will constitute both the symbolic and concrete heart
of a learning-centered campus.[23]

A longtime promoter of information literacy beginning while he was
AAHE vice president, Pima Community College–West Campus president Louis S. Albert has frequently stated that "information literacy is

the cement that holds together all the best in today's learning concepts. Whether it is service learning, problem-based learning, or collaborative learning—each of these strategies has at its core the ability to access, evaluate, and effectively use information."[24]

FORGING A NEW PARTNERSHIP BETWEEN ACADEMIC LEADERS AND LIBRARIANS

Academic history has given us two major lessons about libraries. Over the years, a growing number of higher education leaders have shared a vision of an expanded and more integrated role for libraries, particularly in quality undergraduate education. Yet their visions have only occasionally effected a lasting change in the perceptions of libraries or in their roles. Few managed to translate their special understanding into concrete policies and programs.

We believe that the missing piece has been the partnership discussed in the preface. The best visions of academic leaders will not bear fruit until they join forces with librarians who share their visions and are able, with the leadership and support of their campus leaders, to translate visions into programs and services. Nor can the isolated vision of a librarian like Patricia Knapp, even when complemented by excellent administrative skills, effect significant change unless a president or academic vice president supports and guides the process of implementation.

While it would seem that the most natural partnership would be between the provost or academic vice president and the head of the library, history—including the more recent Adamany and Caret examples—seems to argue that the spark for major departures from business as usual for libraries is related to presidential visions for their campus libraries. But success cannot be achieved without buy-in from other campus leaders as well.

How can academic leaders and librarians jointly empower their libraries to act as effective allies in achieving institutional goals and objectives? How can they make the information society work for educational quality and institutional renewal? These are the issues explored in this book.

However, before we discuss in detail how libraries address the demands of instruction, research, and service and face the recurring challenges of reform, it is important to understand how the omnipresence of the Internet has changed the environment in which these issues and problems must be addressed.

NOTES

1. Gordon Davies, "Colleges Bring Better Lives . . . but Who Will Pay?" *The Chronicle of Higher Education* 15 (2 May 2003): B20.

2. Henry M. Wriston, *Academic Procession: Reflections of a College President* (New York: Columbia University Press, 1959), 132.

3. Ibid., 134.

4. Harvie Branscomb, *Teaching with Books: A Study of College Libraries* (Chicago: Association of American Colleges and the American Library Association, 1940), ix–x.

5. Carnegie Commission on Higher Education, *The Fourth Revolution: Instructional Technology in Higher Education, A Report and Recommendations* (New York: McGraw-Hill, 1972), 33–34.

6. Virgil M. Hancher, "The Library as a Teaching Instrument" (State University of Iowa, 1945, mimeographed).

7. Robert A. Plane, "What a College Administrator Expects of an Academic Library," in *A Colorado Response to the Information Society: The Changing Academic Library*, ed. Patricia Senn Breivik (Bethesda, Md.: ERIC, ED 269 017, 1983), 28–32.

8. Richard L. Van Horn, "Technology Serving a Grand Idea" (speech presented at the State Higher Education Executive Officers [SHEEO]/Western Interstate Commission for Higher Education [WICHE] Conference on Higher Education and the New Technologies: A Focus on State Policy, Denver, Colo., 25 September 1986).

9. William G. Bowen, *Princeton University Report of the President: The Princeton Library* (Princeton, N.J.: Princeton University, 1986), 7.

10. Ibid.

11. Patricia B. Knapp, *The Montieth College Library Experiment* (New York: Scarecrow Press, 1966).

12. See, for example, "The Prague Declaration: Towards an Information Literate Society" (http://www.infolit.org/International_Conference/index.htm). Retrieved 17 June 2005.

13. Robert M. O'Neil, "The University Administrator's View of the University Library," in *Priorities for Academic Libraries*, ed. Thomas J. Galvin and Beverly P. Lynch (San Francisco: Jossey-Bass, 1982), 5.

14. Robert M. Hayes, ed., *Universities, Information Technology, and Academic Libraries: The Next 20 Years*, Academic Libraries Frontiers Conference, Lake Arrowhead Conference Center, 13–17 December 1981 (Norwood, N.J.: Ablex Publishing Corporation, 1986), 135.

15. William A. Moffett, "What the Academic Librarian Wants from Administrators and Faculty," in *Priorities for Academic Libraries*, ed. Galvin and Lynch, 15.

16. Lorie Roth, "Information Competency: How Close Are We?" (panel presentation on Working Together for Student Success Conference at the California Community Colleges, San José, Calif., 29 March 1996), 1–3.

17. *ETS Collaborates with CSU to Assess 21st Century Skills.* Retrieved 4 April 2005 from http://www.calstate.edu/pa/news/2003/ETS.shtml.

18. Howard L. Simmons, "Information Literacy and Accreditation: A Middle States Association Perspective," in *Information Literacy: Developing Students as Independent Learners*, ed. D. W. Farmer and Terrence F. Mech (San Francisco: Jossey-Bass, 1992), 15.

19. Ibid., 18.

20. Middle States Commission on Higher Education, *Developing Research & Communication Skills: Guidelines for Information Literacy in the Curriculum* (Philadelphia: Middle States Commission on Higher Education, 2003).

21. Ralph A. Wolff, "Using the Accreditation Process to Transform the Mission of the Library," in *Information Technology and the Remaking of the University Library*, ed. Beverly P. Lynch (San Francisco: Jossey-Bass, 1995), 90.

22. Patricia Senn Breivik, "Information Literacy and the Engaged Campus," *AAHE Bulletin* 53, no. 3 (2000): 5.

23. Alan E. Guskin and Mary B. Marcy, "Dealing with the Future Now," *Change* 35, no. 4 (2003): 10.

24. Louis S. Albert, e-mail correspondence to Patricia Breivik, 24 May 2004.

CHAPTER 2

The Information Society and Higher Education

The Internet. It came. We saw. It revolutionized our lives. By August of 2001, Peter R. Young, the chief of the Cataloging Distribution Service at the Library of Congress, estimated there were 29 million Internet users generating $6 trillion in e-commerce and 35 billion e-mails daily.[1] Young cautioned that only 16 percent of resources are indexed by any single popular search engine and that 83 percent of the sites indexed contain commercial content versus the 6 percent that are educational or scientific.[2] This contrasts sharply with people's high confidence in Internet-obtained information. A December 2002 report sponsored by the Pew Internet & American Life Project concludes that the Internet has become the primary means for obtaining information, and even non-users have high expectations of what can be found on the Internet. Self-reported success in finding needed information is documented as in Figure 1.[3]

A 2002 UCLA report found that "52.8% of [Internet] users believed that most or all of the information online is reliable and accurate."[4]

Data compiled in 1999 and later also paints a fairly rosy picture about the national buildout of the infrastructure to support access to the Internet. However, a 2002 report prepared for the Computer Science and Telecommunications Board of the National Research Council raises three warning flags that should be of concern to all educators:

- Although the national scene is positive, there remains concern for access by certain groups (e.g., the poor, minorities, elderly).

Figure 1
Success in Finding Information Online
How often are you able to find the information you want?

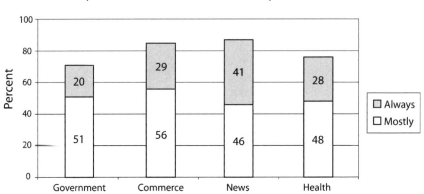

Source: Pew Internet Project September 2002 Survey. Percentages are for Internet users who have sought information in each category.

- Access does not ensure benefits to users (i.e., the issue is not connectivity to the advanced telecommunications services within classrooms, but rather how effectively technologies are used in the curriculum).
- "Increasingly, Americans are not differentiated by who's online and who's not, but by what they do online and how skillfully and intensively they do it, which is profoundly affected by the level of education."[5]

This report further documents a shift in the issues being studied. "The most recent analyses have begun to focus on the importance of content, literacy and ease of use as ways of motivating at-risk and voluntary non-users."[6]

Focusing on campus use of the Internet, we find both pluses and minuses. Clearly, higher education will never be the same as in pre-Internet years, so it behooves us to accentuate the positive and put in proper safeguards for the particular challenges that the Internet presents for the teaching/learning process.

First, looking at what we have gained, it would be hard to overestimate the benefits of the Internet in facilitating global communications among scholars and for ease of access to a rapidly growing universe of knowledge. There is every indication that the nature of research is evolving as scholars aggregate their scholarly efforts by bringing together from all the disciplines the relevant ideas and the people who understand them in order to solve problems that cannot be solved by any individual or even any single discipline.[7]

EDUCATIONAL CHALLENGES OF THE INTERNET

Inherent in these blessings are some annoying consequences. There is simply too much information coming across our desks, and precious research time is lost just keeping up with e-mail. In addition, far less thought and precision go into electronic communications being sent to us than when letters and reports came in print form. Online writers are often sloppy in both their thinking and the style of their writing, thus putting more of a burden on the receivers to mine out the jewels of thought now lost in unedited verbiage. But of course, there is no going back, nor would we want to return to pre-Internet days. It leaves each of us needing to determine how best to manage our significantly increased communications flows.

The greatest challenge for faculty is the impact of the Internet on how students approach their learning. Both faculty and students are increasingly using electronic resources outside of the library. Faculty know how to judge the inherent quality of the information, and their research schedules allow them to wait for print materials to be delivered where appropriate. Students do not have such skills of discernment and usually have little time in which to complete their research.

> Focus group and survey research conducted at Carnegie Mellon [University] indicates that undergraduate students typically turn to popular Web search engines when they need to find information. These search engines index only the "surface Web," where less than 7 percent of the information is appropriate for educational or scholarly purposes. No single Web search engine indexes more than 16 percent of the surface Web, yet we have no evidence that students use more than one search engine when they look for information. According to BrightPlanet, the "deep Web" is 500 times larger and growing faster than the surface Web. The deep Web provides information in all disciplines, for all constituencies; that is, 1,000–2,000 times better in quality than the surface Web. Approximately 95 percent of deep Web content is publicly accessible without fees or subscriptions, but deep Web content, like scholarly commercial resources licensed by the library, is not indexed and therefore not accessible using popular Web search engines. The growing concern among academic librarians interviewed by the author in the DLF

usage and usability survey is that many undergraduate students may be searching only 0.03 percent of the Web to complete their assignments, ignoring entirely the books, journals, databases, full-text digital resources and other scholarly materials provided by the library. The consensus appears to be that undergraduates are using library collections and services less than in the past because access to the surface Web is easy and convenient. . . . Even if undergraduate students turn to the scholarly electronic resources licensed by libraries, their search skills are poor. They seldom if ever use advanced search features, do not understand that result sets are not necessarily organized by relevance to their query, and look only at the first couple of Web pages of ten to twenty items retrieved.[8]

Studies document that the majority of students "believe that the Web is a time saver when looking for information, and has a modest influence on their grades."[9] In studies, Internet use has been seen to increase the number of bibliographic citations in papers through the addition of traditionally non-scholarly materials. Experience has shown that—even apart from the question of the quality of information obtained from non-scholarly materials—there is also the inability of many students to understand the proper use of downloaded information. This has led to a significant surge in cases of plagiarism and the birth of companies to help professors discern such occurrences. (See chapter 6 for more information on the role of librarians in addressing campus plagiarism problems.) To combat this, some faculty require students to submit their papers electronically to ease the verification of Internet citations and/or of plagiarism.

In many ways the problem is the same as in pre-Internet days. There continues to be a gap between the quality of materials that faculty expect students to use and what students do, in fact, use in their research.[10] The difference lies in the tools being used to access the research information and the difference between the attributes of traditional library catalogs and indexes and what is found through a Web portal.

The library itself has long been a metaphor for order and rationality. The process of searching for information within a library is done within highly structured systems and information is exposed and knowledge gained as a result of successfully navigating these preexisting structures. Because this is a complicated process, the librarian helps guide and navigate a system where every piece of content has a preordained place.

Contrast this world with the anarchy of the Web. The Web is free-associating, unrestricted and disorderly. Searching is secondary to finding and the process by which things are found is unimportant. "Collections" are temporary and subjective where a blog entry may be as valuable to the individual as an "unpublished" paper as are six pages of a book made available by Amazon. The individual searches alone without expert help and, not knowing what is undiscovered, is satisfied.[11]

The lack of students' ability to evaluate the quality of the information they are accessing is not unique to undergraduate studies. In 2003, one San José State University engineering faculty member summed up the problem in an SOS e-mail to the library:

> I spoke with the chairman of my department yesterday about organizing some kind of session at the library for our graduate students, so that they could get some training in resources and methods for conducting a literature review. I am appalled at how clueless our graduate students are when it comes to bibliographic research. Certainly, they all are fairly familiar with using the web, but to them, conducting a literature review is just doing a cursory search using Google. Most students are not even aware of journals in their field, let alone online journals that the library may have.[12]

Faculty need to accept the fact that students are largely motivated by the ease of access and time-saving aspects of Internet use, rather than in doing good research, and faculty need to assume responsibility for structuring learning assignments that require quality research efforts. Librarians can be effective partners with faculty in accomplishing this.

Increasingly, an awareness is emerging that the requirement for effective functioning in the information society goes far beyond computer literacy or, as is now more commonly used today, information and communications technology (ICT) literacy. Looking to the use of technology as an end in itself is just not enough. This awareness is evident at both the K–12 and higher education levels. Examples of this growing awareness are seen today in efforts such as President Bush's "No Child Left Behind" program, which has resulted in a prescribed set of twenty-first-century skills that include clear articulation of the need for learning skills (including critical-thinking as well as information and communication skills) along with more technical ICT skills.[13]

At the time of this writing, Educational Testing Service (ETS) was in the process of developing and piloting a test for ICT skills on a number of college and university campuses across the country. For this test, information literacy skills permeate the concept of ICT as opposed to aligning information literacy skills alongside ICT skills. ETS's purpose in this initiative is articulated in its report, *Succeeding in the 21st Century: What Higher Education Must Do to Address the Gap in Information and Communication Technology Proficiencies*, and aims primarily to provide a measurement for colleges and universities to use in assessing their students' mastery of ICT skills.

> This document is written for all those in higher education who are concerned with preparing students for success in today's world—success as individuals, as members of society, as workers, as lifelong learners. Given the remarkable extent to which technology has transformed our lives, bringing a vast new world of information resources into our homes, classrooms, libraries, and offices, it seems clear that among the most essential ingredients of success today is the ability to learn, communicate, evaluate, and manage all forms of information. . . .
>
> In recent years, much attention has been given to the so-called "digital divide" between those who have access to various technologies and those who do not. Yet far less attention has been given to what we might call the "proficiency divide"—the gap between those who have the blend of cognitive and technical capabilities required to negotiate information demands in the academy, or the workplace, or society, and those who lack them. . . .
>
> In response to this need, seven leading college and university systems in the United States joined with Educational Testing Service (ETS) in 2003 to form the National Higher Education Information and Communications Technology (ICT) Initiative. This effort is focused on developing a highly innovative, simulation-based assessment to measure the breadth and depth of ICT proficiency among those who are either seeking to continue their higher education or transitioning into the workplace.[14]

But even in a world transformed by technology, we must acknowledge that only a small fraction of existing information is available through computers, and computer-stored information is only as good as the sources from which the information is taken. While initially it was thoughtful librarians who recognized that computer literacy was only a small subset of information literacy, this issue, as evidenced above, is now one being championed by educators and business leaders alike.

Information literacy is a survival skill in the information age. Instead of drowning in the abundance of information that floods their lives, information-literate individuals know how to find, evaluate, and use information effectively to solve a particular problem or make a decision, whether the information they select comes from a computer, a book, a government agency, a video, or any of a number of other possible resources. Students have long relied on the knowledge of teachers and the information skills of librarians. In fact, when the volume of information was modest, they could often manage without becoming information literate themselves. What the information explosion has done is turn an old problem—functional illiteracy—into a new crisis. To address this crisis, we need a new learning philosophy based on a fuller understanding of the information explosion and a redefinition of literacy that includes information skills, and there must be a subsequent change in the educational role of libraries and the priorities we set for them.

THE INFORMATION EXPLOSION AND THE REDEFINITION OF LITERACY

Greater Expectations, the 2002 national panel report of the Association of American Colleges and Universities (AACU), lists the information explosion as a significant external pressure on higher education. Its impact is described as threefold:

- huge and rapidly increasing quantity of information widely available;
- looser review and control of information quality;
- shift from remembering facts to finding and evaluating information.[15]

Computerized databases, online journals, and electronic books contain but a small fraction of the totality of information, and the information explosion has affected and continues to affect all information formats. Some concrete examples may help to clarify the enormous information base with which academic libraries must contend, since academic libraries must support the total learning and research needs of their campuses either directly or through cooperative arrangements with other libraries. The importance of the academic information base to business and industry should also not be overlooked, for in many locations, academic libraries are either a major or the only information research resource for nearby agencies and firms.

In the United States alone, publication in new and traditional formats has increased sharply. New book titles increased from 51,058 in 1985 to 141,703 in 2001.[16] Periodicals increased from 11,090 in 1985 to 13,846 in 2002.[17] These numbers are only a small part of the picture. They do not take into account materials published in other countries, which many academic programs require, or other sources of information. For example, in 2003 the U.S. government published 14,045 tangible (i.e., physical formats such as print and microform) titles and 24,251 electronic titles,[18] and each year millions of scientific writings in the form of articles and reports add to the avalanche of information confronting academicians and business people alike.

While the U.S. Government Printing Office is moving toward having all of its publications available electronically and while there is a major shift to accessing journals electronically on campuses (see chapter 8 for more details), book publishing is not shrinking; indeed, book sales in 2002 totaled $26 billion, up 5.5 percent from 2001.[19] The lesson of history is that new technologies tend not to replace older ones but to supplement them. This is particularly true with information technologies. Movies did not replace books. Television broadcasting replaced neither; nor have videotapes and DVDs replaced television or movies. Ideally, the variety of formats enriches the learning and research environment and is helpful to students, who are increasingly the product of a television-dominated society.

There are some shifts in preferred use of information formats. Online journals are clear winners over print versions for most faculty and especially for students. The experience on many campuses is that even when there is a qualitative advantage in print versions (e.g., art journals), students still prefer the ease of access that online versions bring. On the other hand, e-books have not as yet experienced broad-based enthusiasm on the part of users—not even reference materials that initially seemed to offer the clearest advantage in an electronic edition over print.

These electronic resources have brought both a wealth of new possibilities and a new generation of problems for librarians and other information managers. Most problems are new aspects of an old problem—the low level of information literacy. Information literacy skills must now be expanded to include the ability to know when and how to effectively take advantage of the resources made available by the new technology. But getting students weaned from using popular search engines on the Internet to accessing scholarly databases will continue to challenge classroom faculty and librarians alike. Indeed, only a good partnering between the subject specialists and the information specialists will overcome students' creative ways to avoid taking the harder road. Only then will students reap the full benefit of today's information-rich environment. Students will be able to select among formats using criteria such as effectiveness, efficiency, and aesthetic value, or to match their preferred learning styles. One of the goals of higher education should be to graduate information consumers capable of such discernment in all disciplines.

NEW THREATS TO LEARNING

The benefits of the Internet age carry with them a number of serious issues concerning quality of information, access and commercialization of information, development and preservation of knowledge, and student learning. From the very outset of computer usage, people's tendency has been to put more faith in information simply because it appears on a computer screen; nor is there evidence that education has better prepared students to be discerning information consumers.[20] Back in 1986, author Theodore Roszak warned us of what he called the "cult of information" in his book by that title.

> Since information technology has been with us, its discriminating users have recognized the principle of GIGO: garbage in—garbage out. The computer can do no better than the quality of the information selected by a human intelligence to be entered into it. But this principle needs to be extended to another level. The mathematical rigor of the computer may mislead some into interpreting GIGO as what Ashley Montague once construed it to mean: garbage in—gospel out. We need another principle that makes us aware of the fallibilities which may be embedded in the programs that lie waiting inside the machine to receive the information. Even when the data are well selected, they may be ambushed by intellectual "garbage" of another order hiding in the depths of the program.[21]

Ten years later, the enormous toll that too much information makes had become evident. David Shenk, author and media critic, summarizes this toll as follows:

> As we have accrued more and more of it, information has emerged not only as a currency, but also as a pollutant.
> - In 1971 the average American was targeted by at least 560 daily advertising messages. Twenty years later, that number had risen sixfold, to 3,000 messages per day.
> - In the office, an average of 60 percent of each person's time is now spent processing documents.
> - Paper consumption per capita in the United States tripled from 1940 to 1980 (from 200 to 600 pounds), and tripled again from 1980 to 1990 (to 1,800 pounds).
> - In the 1980s, third-class mail (used to send publications) grew thirteen times faster than population growth.

- Two-thirds of business managers surveyed report tension with colleagues, loss of job satisfaction, and strained personal relationships as a result of information overload.
- More than 1,000 telemarketing companies employ 4 million Americans, and generate $650 billion in annual sales.

Let us call this unexpected, unwelcome part of our atmosphere "data smog," an expression for the noxious muck and druck of the information age. Data smog gets in the way; it crowds out quiet moments, and obstructs much-needed contemplation. It spoils conversation, literature, and even entertainment. It thwarts skepticism, rendering us less sophisticated as consumers and citizens. It stresses us out.[22]

(It does not take a Ph.D. to become a skeptical user of the Internet. *Good Housekeeping* started to give "seals of approval" to Web sites as far back as 2000.[23])

Another sticky problem concerns difficulty of access caused by the commercialization of information. There are inherent dangers to a democratic society in private or governmental control of information resources, and this situation is exacerbated by the newer information technologies. This is true of most computer-stored databases.

New communication technologies have made it possible to generate, process, assemble, store and disseminate enormous quantities of information. Huge private investments in the facilities to perform these tasks make it possible and profitable to handle information as a salable good. These newly offered opportunities for profit making are responsible for the quickening efforts to undermine and discredit the belief that information is a social good, a vital resource that benefits the total community when made freely available for general public use.[24]

This trend has gained momentum with the U.S. government's move away from free government publications toward commercialization of its information products.[25]

The end result of commercialization will be an increasing gap between the "haves" and "have-nots." One of the hopes for the information age has been that the growing information supply would provide solutions for ills such as illiteracy, international tensions, and educational restrictions. Instead, the heavy commercial focus of information technology seems likely to exacerbate old inequities in new ways. Early warnings surfaced repeatedly in the 1985–1986 regional seminars held by the American Association of State Colleges and Universities' National Commission on the Role and Future of State Colleges and Universities. Terrel H. Bell, who chaired the commission, noted the "danger of a new elite developing in our country: the information elite."[26] Warnings have also been issued about developments on health-science campuses concerning the prospect of information "haves" and "have-nots" within academic and health care communities, which would threaten the free and open availability and exchange of information integral to these communities.[27]

Another major issue raised by the selling of information concerns the instability of online information systems for research and knowledge generation. Commercial companies are unlikely to share the historical commitment of libraries to the long-term survival of information. "Researchers have long been able to advance knowledge because of the stability of information preserved in the printed word. They will be denied this legacy with paperless information systems because data banks, stored in computers under the control of the commercial sector, can easily disappear or be significantly changed."[28] A vast number of books, of course, are commercially produced, and this poses no threat to scholarship. It is the nature of the new technology that has made the commercialization of information such a serious problem.

> Publishers in the print-based environment do not keep books or other documents available forever. When the demand falls off, they are allowed to go out of print. There is no reason to assume that commercial vendors of computer-based, electronic information systems will behave differently from their counterparts in the print-based media. If retention of information in a computer-based system can no longer be sustained in economic terms, it may be purged from the system. The problem is that these similar, perfectly rational decisions on the part of the print publisher and the electronic information vendor have radically different implications for the stock of knowledge. Out-of-print books, to the extent that copies have been acquired, cataloged, and retained in libraries, continue to be available to scholars and anyone else who wishes to consult them. In an electronic environment, information no longer retained in a computer memory ceases to exist.[29]

To address these concerns, a number of initiatives have been undertaken largely by academic libraries and library-related organizations. For example, consortia of libraries have sometimes found it possible to negotiate contracts with vendors that guarantee the transfer of journal files if the publisher is no longer going to maintain them. Even more promising is the creation of JSTOR, a nonprofit organization originally funded by The Andrew W. Mellon Foundation. JSTOR digitizes scholarly journals, often beginning with their first issue, and provides access to this electronic archive. But this problem is far from solved, and for purposes of research and societal advancement, it is essential that information be preserved and be available to scholars. New knowledge can lead to re-examining old lines of inquiry that have been abandoned or rejected as invalid, and it is impossible to distinguish between information that is truly ephemeral and information that may later prove valuable for re-search. Much information is eventually used for purposes completely unanticipated when it was created—for example, it may be used to es-tablish the history of a society or a social movement.[30]

Other concerns remain, albeit seldom considered. For example, "data-bases are extremely vulnerable to improper additions, deletions, and re-visions. Security measures notwithstanding, they are inherently revisable, and thus conducive to plagiarism, forgery, fraud, censorship, and propa-ganda attempts."[31] And the impermanence of online sources has an even broader significance. In the case of a catastrophic disaster, "it would be almost impossible to draw on our accumulated knowledge for the recon-struction of society if the knowledge was only in magnetic form. The printed word would be needed."[32]

While popular magazines publish exciting articles about a compact disk containing all the holdings of the Library of Congress and the "golden age" of a paperless society in which everyone will access online infor-mation from home, office, or wherever they are, more thoughtful ana-lysts look at both the benefits and pitfalls of new information formats, as well as many people's continuing practice to print out for reading any document beyond the casual e-mails that flood our computers each day. We in higher education need to provide a meaningful framework for the various components of the expanding information base; we need to en-sure open access to information; and we need to teach people how to choose wisely among the variety of information resources. Nowhere are these issues being systematically addressed. Yet they are central issues for the survival of a free society in an information age, and, therefore, they raise questions that academic leadership cannot afford to ignore.

THE IMPORTANCE OF LIBRARIES IN THE INFORMATION SOCIETY

Libraries, as the access point to most information on campuses, in-cluding books, films, electronic journals, online databases, and a host of other formats, must play a key role in preparing people for the demands of today's information society. Historically, libraries have provided a meaningful structure for relating information in ways that facilitate the development of knowledge. Yet libraries remained all but invisible in the literature on the information society that began emerging in the 1980s. In arguing the case for the public library as the missing link of the information age, Theodore Roszak cites two causes for the low visibility of libraries. One is the well-financed marketing efforts of the computer industry aimed at both home and office. The second is the contrast between the aggressive male image projected by the computer industry and the more feminine, service-oriented image of libraries.[33]

Of all the education reform reports of the 1980s, only the 1986 Carnegie Foundation Report, *College*,[34] gave substantive consideration to the role of libraries in addressing the challenges facing higher education. Perhaps, as Roszak suggests, academic administrators find computers "sexier" than libraries. Whatever the reason, the omission of libraries in discussing the information society makes the development of an effective strategy to address current educational challenges unlikely.

Despite this continuing situation at the national and state levels, considerable progress has been made in both the K–12 and higher education sectors over the past fifteen years in articulating the need for information literacy. The concept first appeared as an issue in higher education in a 1987 symposium sponsored by Columbia University and the University of Colorado. This event resulted in a publication entitled *Libraries and the Search for Academic Excellence* and represented an initial attempt by leaders in higher education and librarianship to look beneath surface impressions to consider a greater institutional role for libraries. The issue is now a global one, as evidenced in September 2003 by a broad-based group of information literacy experts from twenty-three different countries who participated in a conference in Prague.[35]

To date, however, there is little consistency from campus to campus or from program to program as to how pervasive or effective current information literacy programs are. The question remains, how is higher education effectively preparing current and future generations of students to live and work in the information society? Within the Internet environment, can higher education grasp the implications of this age of information and use the new technology to enhance its operations and learning? If being able to use computer technology is not an appropriate—much less an adequate—response to the challenges of the information society, what is?

A NEW CONCEPT OF LITERACY

Underlying the challenges of the information society is the need to foster the development of information-literate people. To meet this challenge, higher education must first attain, then go beyond competency levels. It must graduate skeptical information consumers. So essential is the ability to gather information independently and appropriately that we need to expand the definition of literacy to include information management.[36] Currently, most people would define as literate a person who can read and write. However, historical examination of the concept of literacy reveals that a useful definition depends upon the information needs of the society.

The evolving definition of literacy has developed along three paths that mirror the expanding information needs of society. Qualitative standards have increased to encompass higher-order cognitive processes. The social and individual purposes that literacy serves have broadened. The scope of literacy has also expanded from the religious and scholarly elites to include the whole population.

Methods of determining literacy in the United States have become increasingly more rigorous. Before census data became available, a person's signature was used as an indication of literacy. No widespread testing measures were in effect. This changed in the mid-nineteenth century. Beginning with the 1840 census, literacy data was based on a respondent's view of his or her own ability to read and write. By 1940, the census used the years of schooling completed as an indication of literacy. Anyone who had completed four years of elementary school was considered literate. School-based criteria for literacy persist, although recently more attention has been paid to testing and competency-based criteria. These, too, are essentially unreliable, for "slight changes in the content and wording of test items can cause marked fluctuations in passage rates."[37] The search for more empirically based, accurate methods to test literacy has continued as society's need and ability to access information have increased.

While scholars experimented with new methods to test literacy, the written test gradually supplanted the oral examination, reflecting the pervasive shift from reading aloud to reading silently, from public to private performance, from upgraded community school to the complex, bureaucratized institution becoming familiar in the urban United States. As test-generated data proved unreliable, some literacy specialists began to focus on the concept of functional literacy, defined as "that demonstrated competence in communication skills which enables the individual to function, appropriate to his age, independently in society and with a potential for movement in that society."[38]

Most recently, the "what," or content and defining characteristics of literacy, is being viewed by scholars as a continuous spectrum. "Expert opinion has abandoned the dichotomous framework of literate or illiterate in favor of the conception of literacy as a continuum: At one end lies some ability to reproduce letter combinations with voice or hand, at the other end lies language using behaviors such as logical thinking, higher order cognitive skills, and reasoning."[39] In addition, there now seems to be a consensus that literacy is "highly context specific and context dependent."[40]

The definition of literacy has continued to evolve as society's need to acquire information evolves. Most scholars of literacy recognize the importance of its social, cultural, political, and economic context. Far beyond the ability to "reproduce letter combinations," literacy represents "value to the community, self and socioeconomic worth, mobility, access to information and knowledge, rationality, morality, and orderliness."[41] In the midst of the information explosion, the ability to access, retrieve, and evaluate information should constitute a significant part of today's definition of literacy. In an era when today's "truths" become tomorrow's outdated concepts, individuals who are unable to gather pertinent information are almost as helpless as those who are unable to read or write. The college-educated person can no longer rely on previous knowledge, textbooks, and faculty to provide the information necessary to make informed judgments; no single person or group of individuals is capable of assimilating all the available information or of keeping abreast of new information as it is generated. The ability to independently and appropriately gather information—not the ability to program a computer—will be a key element in an updated concept of literacy.

One of the earliest calls for the redefinition of literacy to include information-gathering came in a 1977 speech by Lee G. Burchinal, director for the Division of Science Information of the National Science Foundation.

> Regardless of how successful we have been with conventional literacy, we need to look ahead to achieving a new kind of national literacy—information literacy. To be information literate requires a new set of skills. These include how to efficiently and effectively locate and use information needed for decision-making. Such skills have wide applicability for occupational as well as personal activities.[42]

Now, more than twenty-five years later, a growing number of academic institutions can show significant campus-wide progress in addressing this need. Moreover, complementary national information literacy standards have been developed at both the K–12 and higher education levels, with the latter being endorsed by the American Association for Higher Edu-

cation (AAHE). (This was only the second time that AAHE had endorsed a policy position.) In addition, two of the regional accrediting
agencies have played leadership roles in promoting information literacy
as a means to enhance undergraduate learning and to prepare people for
lifelong learning in an information society. (More information about the
roles of the Middle States Commission on Higher Education and Western Association of Schools and Colleges is provided in chapter 1.)

Although information literacy may be called by various names, such
as information competence or information fluency, and although varying
definitions may be employed, information literacy has emerged both in
the United States and internationally as the term of choice, and the definition from the 1989 American Library Association Presidential Committee on Information Literacy report is the one most often used:

> To be information literate, a person must be able to recognize when
> information is needed and have the ability to locate, evaluate, and
> use effectively the needed information.[43]

This is the definition we shall use for this book.

Knowledge is power, and access to information is the first step to
knowledge. Few people ever stop to consider what this means for them
personally or professionally. It is time for higher education to not only
consider these issues, but to develop a consistent educational philosophy
to guide both research and reform.

PHILOSOPHY OF LEARNING FOR THE
INFORMATION AGE

The underlying problem confronting education in the information age
has been summarized in a popular aphorism: "General practitioners are
learning less and less about more and more until they will eventually
know nothing about everything, while specialists are learning more and
more about less and less until eventually they will know everything about
nothing." This paradoxical effect of the exponentially expanding information base is widely acknowledged. Yet no articulated educational philosophy currently addresses the fundamental realities of the problem
effectively and comprehensively.

Both educators and business leaders have identified elements that
should be incorporated in a philosophy that emphasizes integrated learning as a route to better and broader problem-solving.

- Anthony Comper, president of the Bank of Montreal, advised the 1999
  graduating class at the University of Toronto: "Whatever else you bring

to the 21st century workplace, however great your technical skills and however attractive your attitude and however deep your commitment to excellence, the bottom line is that to be successful, you need to acquire a high level of information literacy. What we in the knowledge industries need are people who know how to absorb and analyze and integrate and create and effectively convey information—and who know how to use information to bring real value to everything they undertake."[44]

- The president of the Toshiba Corporation stated: "In the private sector, to cope with big challenges in the information age, organizations are rushing to reform business processes based on information technologies and networking. This also needs drastic change of working style of people and improvement of individual's business ability, i.e., more information-centric, and more information literate. To get the job done quickly, effectively and creatively, people need to communicate and collaborate with each other through the networks, often beyond the boundaries of time, location and organizations."[45]

- Richard Van Horn, while president of the University of Houston, advocated that the kind of learning that takes place in the library should be replicated across the curriculum. This will help students gain experience within an unstructured universe such as they will encounter after graduation.[46]

- Peter Decker, a former member of the Colorado Commission on Higher Education, spoke against "the non-integrated, fragmented curriculum" that leads students to believe that "the sciences, the humanities and the arts are, each to themselves, discrete and wholly integrated bodies of knowledge."[47]

- Ernest L. Boyer, while president of the Carnegie Foundation for the Advancement of Teaching, repeatedly called for learning that has students move beyond competence in a very narrow field toward the integration of liberal learning within their majors, "so that through their specialties, students will start to ask fundamental questions."[48]

- The Aspen Institute for Humanistic Studies urges that higher education "call for new interrelations of knowledge that can be applied to major problems of our society," and stresses the need to "unite appropriate disciplines so that they identify more comprehensive problems and provide better tools together with the possibility for broader solutions."[49]

Many state legislative calls for student assessment are intended to ensure that graduates will have the skills they need to function effectively in their personal and professional lives. If properly designed, assessment programs will go beyond the measurement of content mastery in a single discipline and the testing of basic communication and mathematical skills. They will also challenge our institutions to measure how effectively their curricula have integrated learning to prepare students for the complex problems of today's information society.

Ernest L. Boyer has suggested outcome measurements that focus on integrating learning beyond individual classes. In his 1986 speech to the American Council on Education, Boyer called for testing students' capacity "to integrate knowledge, to analyze what they have learned and to apply knowledge creatively to contemporary problems."[50] His specific recommendations included a senior thesis requirement that focuses on some aspect of a student's major but places it within larger historical, social, and ethical contexts; seminars in which student theses would be orally presented and critiqued; and/or senior colloquia in which theses would be presented in a public forum and discussed with faculty and students. AACU's *Greater Expectations* echoes similar priorities, calling for a focus on learning over teaching and the creation thereby of lifelong "intentional learners," who among other empowering skills excel at "interpreting, evaluating, and using information discerningly from a variety of sources."[51]

We support the call for integrated learning and preparation for lifelong learning and active citizenship. We see this as the proper focus for quality undergraduate education in an information society. Our philosophy is based on three fundamental truths about information and problem-solving in the information society. First, the half-life of information is shrinking. We therefore believe learning strategies rather than memorization of facts should be emphasized during college years. Second, effective problem-solving requires an adequate and accurate information base. Learning in college should therefore be structured around information resources that will continue to be available after graduation. Third, the information base is constantly expanding in all formats. Students must therefore develop the skills to select among available formats in accessing and evaluating information resources.

In part, our philosophy echoes the Carnegie Foundation Report, *College*. We agree that the gap must be closed between the classroom and the library. We agree that the ultimate measurement of quality undergraduate education in an information society demands that students become self-directed, independent learners. And we have taken the report's vision of libraries and placed it at the center of our philosophy.

Libraries are places where the knowledge of all disciplines is related within a meaningful framework. Libraries provide a model for the information environment in which graduates will need to work and live. Libraries offer a natural environment for problem-solving within the unlimited universe of information. Libraries contain the framework for synthesizing specialized knowledge into broader societal contexts. And finally, libraries and librarians can help students master critical information literacy skills.

Until library-based learning is integrated into the curriculum and until the focus on our campuses shifts from faculty teaching to student learning, we believe little real change will occur in education. Unless students assume responsibility for their own learning and master information literacy skills, they will not become proficient at solving large or small problems in our complex world. They will not be prepared for lifelong learning and active citizenship.

A written statement of educational philosophy should set the stage for academic planning. For over twenty years, campus projects designed to encourage students to develop a sophisticated understanding of the library and to develop their information skills have met with minimal success. The commitment of classroom faculty has been weak, and we believe this is partially because they do not understand how such projects fit into a coherent and farsighted plan for reform.[52] The leadership and vision of the president, articulated in a campus statement of educational philosophy for quality learning, can provide the motivation for discussion and curricular change. Without strong leadership by the president and without a shared campus vision of the library as the pivotal actor in educational reform, it is unlikely that the next twenty years will see any significant progress toward graduating students who are genuinely at home in the information society in which we all live.

NOTES

1. Peter Young, "Electronic Services and Library Performance Measurement: A Definitional Challenge" (presentation at the 4th Northumbria International Conference on Performance Measurement in Libraries and Information Services, Carnegie Mellon University, Pittsburgh, Penn., 13 August 2001), 15. Retrieved 1 March 2004 from http://www.arl.org/stats/north/powerpoints/young Northumbria2001.ppt.

2. Ibid., 44.

3. John B. Horrigan and Lee Rainie, *Counting on the Internet* (Washington, D.C.: Pew Internet & American Life Project), 3. Retrieved 23 March 2004 from http://www.pewtrusts.com/pdf/vf_pew_internet_expectations.pdf.

4. Jeffrey Cole, *The UCLA Internet Report: Surveying the Digital Future, Year Three* (Los Angeles: UCLA Center for Communication Policy, 2003), 38. Retrieved 9 September 2004 from http://www.digitalcenter.org/pdf/InternetReport YearThree.pdf.

5. Amy Friedlander, *More Than Connected: Americans' Access to High Technology, A Review of the Recent Literature from the Perspective of Time* (prepared for

the Computer Science and Telecommunications Board of the National Research Council at the request of the National Science Foundation, 2002), 10.

6. Ibid., 8.

7. Duncan J. Watts, "Unraveling the Mysteries of the Connected Age," *The Chronicle of Higher Education* 49 (14 February 2003): B7–B9.

8. Denise A. Troll, "How and Why Libraries Are Changing: What We Know and What We Need to Know," *Portal: Libraries and the Academy* 2, no. 1 (2002): 115.

9. Philip M. Davis and Suzanne A. Cohen, "The Effect of the Web on Undergraduate Citation Behavior 1996–1999," *Journal of the American Society for Information Science and Technology* 52, no. 4 (2001): 309; and Philip M. Davis, "The Effect of the Web on Undergraduate Citation Behavior: A 2000 Update," *College & Research Libraries* 63, no. 1 (2002): 53–60.

10. Deborah J. Grimes and Carl H. Boening, "Worries with the Web: A Look at Student Use of Web Resources," *College & Research Libraries* 62, no. 1 (2001): 11–23.

11. *OCLC Environmental Scan: Pattern Recognition* (Dublin, Ohio: Online Computer Library Center, Inc., 2004), ix. Retrieved 4 April 2005 from http://www.oclc.org/membership/escan/downloads/introduction.pdf.

12. Burford J. Furman, e-mail correspondence to Patricia Breivik, 7 January 2004.

13. *The Road to 21st Century Learning* (Washington, D.C.: Partnership for 21st Century Skills, n.d.). Retrieved 4 April 2005 from http://www.21stcenturyskills.org/downloads/P21_Policy_Paper.pdf.

14. *Succeeding in the 21st Century: What Higher Education Must Do to Address the Gap in Information and Communication Technology Proficiencies* (Washington, D.C.: ETS, 2003), 3–4.

15. *Greater Expectations: A New Vision for Learning as a Nation Goes to College* (Washington, D.C.: Association of American Colleges and Universities, 2002), 6.

16. U.S. Bureau of the Census, *Statistical Abstract of the U.S.*, 121st ed. (Washington, D.C.: Government Printing Office, 2001), 310.

17. Ibid., 612.

18. Judith C. Russell, "Re: GPO pub data," message posted to GOVDOC L@LISTS.PSU.EDU, 19 November 2003.

19. *Bowker Annual of Library and Book Trade Information,* 49th ed. (New York: R. R. Bowker, 2004), 150.

20. "Computerized Information Found More Convincing," *The Chronicle of Higher Education* 33 (8 October 1986): 16, 18.

21. Theodore Roszak, *The Cult of Information: The Folklore of Computers and the True Art of Thinking* (New York: Pantheon Books, 1986), 120.

22. David Shenk, *Data Smog: Surviving the Information Glut* (New York: HarperSanFrancisco, 1998), 31.

23. "The Web Site Certification," *Good Housekeeping* 231, no. 6 (2000): 10.

24. Herbert I. Schiller, *Who Knows: Information in the Age of the Fortune 500* (Norwood, N.J.: Ablex Publishing Corporation, 1981), 48.

25. *A Comprehensive Assessment of Public Information Dissemination* (Washington, D.C.: National Commission on Libraries and Information Science, 2001).

26. Terrel H. Bell, communication to Colorado University president, E. Gordon Gee, September 1986.

27. *Challenge to Action: Planning and Evaluating Guidelines for Academic Health Sciences Libraries* (Association of Academic Health Sciences Library Directors/Medical Library Association, Joint Task Force to Develop Guidelines for Academic Health Sciences Libraries, October 1985, mimeographed final draft).

28. Gordon B. Neavill, "Electronic Publishing, Libraries, and the Survival of Information," *Library Resources & Technical Services* 27 (January/March 1984): 76.

29. Ibid., 81–82.

30. Ibid., 82–83.

31. Peter Briscoe et al., "Ashurbanipal's Enduring Archetype: Thoughts on the Library's Role in the Future," *College & Research Libraries* 47 (March 1986): 124.

32. Tom Norton, "Secondary Publications Have a Future in Libraries," *Aslib Proceedings* 36 (July/August 1984): 319.

33. Roszak, *Cult of Information*, 173.

34. Ernest L. Boyer, *College: The Undergraduate Experience in America* (New York: Harper & Row, 1987).

35. For more information on this event, see the National Forum on Information Literacy's Web site: http://www.infolit.org/International_Conference/index.htm.

36. The rationale for the expansion of literacy to include information skills was developed in 1985 by Lori Arp and Martin Tessmer, faculty at the Auraria Library, University of Colorado at Denver.

37. Victoria Seitz, "Literacy and the School Child: Some Perspectives from an Educated Country," *Educational Evaluation and Policy Analysis* 3 (1981): 21.

38. Robert L. Hillerich, "Towards an Assessable Definition of Literacy," *English Journal* 65 (February 1976): 53.

39. Geraldine J. Clifford, "Buch und Lesen: Historical Perspectives on Literacy and Schooling," *Review of Educational Research* 54 (winter 1984): 479.

40. Ibid.

41. H. Graff, *Literacy and Social Development in the West: A Reader* (Cambridge: Cambridge University Press, 1981), 3.

42. Lee G. Burchinal, "The Communications Revolution, America's Third Century Challenge," in *The Future of Organizing Knowledge: Papers Presented at the Texas A&M University Libraries Centennial Academic Assembly, 24 September 1976* (College Station, Tex.: Texas A&M University Libraries, ED 168 470, 1977), 11.

43. American Library Association, *American Library Association Presidential Committee on Information Literacy* (Chicago: American Library Association, 1989), 1.

44. "Bank on 'Information Literacy,' Graduates Advised," *The Gazette* (Montreal, Quebec), 21 June 1999, F8.

45. Julie N. Oman, "Information Literacy in the Workplace," *Information Outlook* (June 2001): 35.

46. Richard L. Van Horn, "Technology Serving a Grand Idea" (speech presented at the SHEEO/WICHE Conference on Higher Education and the New Technologies: A Focus on State Policy, Denver, Colo., 25 September 1986).

47. Peter Decker, speech at Mesa College, Mesa, Colorado, 9 October 1986, 13.

48. Ernest L. Boyer, "Renewal of the Undergraduate College" (speech presented at the American Council on Education Conference, San Francisco, 7 October 1986).

49. Samuel B. Gould, "Far More Than Formal Schooling," in *What Is an Educated Person? The Decades Ahead*, ed. Martin Kaplan (New York: Praeger, 1980), 184–89.

50. Boyer, "Renewal of the Undergraduate College."

51. *Greater Expectations: A New Vision for Learning as a Nation Goes to College* (Washington, D.C.: Association of American Colleges and Universities, 2002), 22.

52. Richard M. Dougherty, "Stemming the Tide of Mediocrity: The Academic Library Response," in *Libraries and the Learning Society: Papers in Response to a Nation at Risk* (Chicago: American Library Association, 1984), 3–21.

CHAPTER

Reforming Instruction

Throughout all reform cycles in education, the imperatives have remained largely the same. People need to be prepared for lifelong learning and active citizenship. In order to achieve this goal, higher education needs a new model of learning—learning that is active and integrated, not passive and fragmented. On an intellectual level, faculty and academic leaders appreciate the fact that lectures, textbooks, materials put on electronic reserve, and tests requiring students to regurgitate data from these sources do not make for an active learning experience, much less a quality one. Far too often, students fail to retain the information presented to them, let alone to analyze or synthesize it in the generation of knowledge.

Nor has the expanding use of educational technology served to correct this situation. In many cases, earning course credits has become easier for students because of distance education efforts that bring learning opportunities to their doorstep, but many of these courses do not require any more active engagement with real world information than do campus-based lecture halls. For example, some professors conscientiously provide online links to articles to facilitate enrichment reading by students. Yet—like the classic library-based reserve service—this does not ensure that students acquire the ability to locate and evaluate information for issues and problems outside the protected environment of the campus. More thoughtful educators, such as Vincent Tinto, Distinguished Professor of Higher Education at Syracuse University, reinforce the importance of ensuring that future leaders are able to evaluate information globally. In his 2003 Pullias Lecture on the Future of Higher Education, he concludes:

> There is little doubt that we are rapidly moving toward a future in which conversations between diverse peoples and belief systems will be commonplace. We will have (to some extent we already have) immediate access to information of all sorts from all corners and crevices of the world, and from a wide range of belief systems. The possibilities for learning will be immense. But so will the dangers. As the experience of the ERIC database demonstrates, we run the risk of being overwhelmed with so much information of such variable quality that meaningful shared discourse will be constrained, not advanced. All our citizens, but especially those who are likely to occupy positions of influence, must acquire the intellectual capacity to sift and discern, to weigh and consider, re-consider and even re-re-consider what meaning to draw from the forthcoming deluge of voices.[1]

To any thoughtful educator, it must be clear that now and in the future, teaching facts will be a poor substitute for teaching people how to learn—that is, helping students develop the abilities to locate, evaluate, and effectively use information for any given need. Change is slow in coming in this regard on many campuses, but the research for this book has revealed amazing progress in the practice, assessment, and documentation over the past fifteen years of what is generally referred to as information literacy. This is true on campuses in both the United States and in a number of other countries as well.

Increasingly, library personnel and resources are being engaged more effectively to create more active learning environments. While still jealous about the use of class time, faculty and other academic leaders, in increasing numbers, are articulating a vision or philosophy of learning to encourage integrating resource-based and classroom learning. Leaders from accrediting agencies, system offices, and campuses are providing frameworks in which print and electronic resources and library personnel can be effectively employed for active learning in such a way that prepares students for lifelong learning and engaged citizenship.

Our earlier book examined the shortcomings of the traditional reserve system, lectures, and textbooks and may be consulted if needed. Given the progress made over recent years in developing more student-centered alternatives, it now seems more appropriate to focus on the emerging positive patterns for learning in an information age. This is not to say that there are not still professors wedded to old approaches to teaching. Many follow a model in their teaching that is based on their own experiences as students. Paul A. Lacey, professor of English and former provost at Earlham College, clarifies this faculty perspective.

> What has been our experience as professors, after all? We have been accustomed to having the toughest courses we took and the toughest we teach introduce the longest list of books on reserve. Our professors gave us fine annotated bibliographies and we may do the same for our students. Often it has been our experience that the most challenging graduate seminars we took specified both the paper topics and the works we were to consult for all but the final paper; and frequently the final paper was an outgrowth of one of the shorter papers we did under instruction. That is to say, our best graduate courses in our discipline, like the best undergraduate courses we expected to teach, gave exclusive attention to mastering the content of major works in our field. Except in the rarest cases we were taught to regard the library solely as the place where all those things should be waiting for us.
>
> I think of my very good experiences with reference services in college and graduate school, but I recall that I, and everyone else I knew, tended to go to the reference desk as a last resort and that I asked questions with no notion that I might learn a generalizable method of research which could help me become more expert in research and conceive of more interesting questions to pursue, either on my own or with the help of a reference librarian. And, I would add, I do not believe I ever thought of a librarian as a teacher until I began to work at Earlham. . . . Each piece of study I did through college and graduate school, if it had a research dimension to it, was essentially another hit or miss, hunt and peck activity. . . .
>
> I did not know much if anything about how to branch out efficiently into a new area. My independence as a student and as a thinker was consequently very limited, and I didn't even recognize the fact. I thought of the library as a vast reserve collection where I could find what had been assigned or suggested.
>
> I suggest that my experience is not untypical of both undergraduate and graduate use of the library even now. If I am right in this, it would follow that many of us who are now teaching in colleges and universities are only slightly at home in libraries.[2]

If Lacey is right, faculty who are "only slightly at home in libraries" do not pursue an active, resource-based approach to teaching because they have never been exposed to a learning environment such as Earlham's and, thus, do not even conceive of what we called library-based learning in our earlier work, that is, learning that is based on real-world resources, including online databases. Given the incredible development of the Internet, however, the term seems too building focused. We now prefer the term more frequently found in K–12 literature, "resource-based learning." Faculty unaware of their own limitations as researchers are unlikely to realize how the reserves-lecture-textbook approach is limiting their own students from becoming independent learners—the need for which is only exacerbated by today's electronic resources and expanding information base.

In order to graduate independent learners, academic leaders are increasingly encouraging faculty to move beyond the old approach to become facilitators of learning, assisting students to make use of the wide range of information resources available in and through campus libraries and online. But many faculty will not become facilitators until they adopt a new approach to their own research process, as will be discussed in the following chapter. The challenge is for institutions to ensure an integrated approach that fosters active learning by students and offers incentives and opportunities through faculty development programs for faculty to become more active facilitators of learning.

**Commentary: "The Nexus of Learning:
Libraries Contribute to What We're All About"**

Barbara L. Cambridge
Senior Program Officer
National Council of Teachers of English

Libraries have a unique contribution to make to scholarship that makes a difference. That seemingly obvious statement has traditionally held true in higher education as researchers have posed questions, designed research projects to address the questions, studied the pertinent literature, and carried out their projects, building new knowledge across disciplines and professions. But the statement takes on new meaning as the valuing of scholarship in teaching and learning increases: more and more faculty and administrators recognize that important intellectual questions about teaching and learning warrant designed inquiry for the benefit of students, colleges and universities, and society. Colleges and universities have more and more reasons to focus on improving student learning as they serve diverse student bodies in a society that seeks more informed workers and citizens.

In their book *The Scholarship of Teaching and Learning: Building the Pedagogical Commons*, Carnegie Foundation scholars Mary Huber and Pat Hutchings call for a "pedagogical commons," which they define as "an emergent conceptual space for exchange and community among faculty, students, administrators, and all others committed to learning as an essential component of life in contemporary democratic society." Adding to conceptual space the adjectives "physical" and "virtual," the library becomes the nexus of scholarly work to both create knowledge and accomplish campus priorities.

I'd like to focus on two ways that the library is this nexus for a campus. I choose these two because all campus administrators need faculty and staff members to take as their responsibility engaging students in the students' own learning and learning from students what students have an exclusive ability to offer. These responsibilities have everything to do with how higher education can be successful in educating students and meeting societal expectations.

First, the library can take the role of integrator. Acknowledging the research that confirms that engagement directly relates to learning, colleges and universities are collecting and using information about student engagement. To help with this effort to use data in educational decision-making, the American Association for Higher Education and the National Survey for Student Engagement (NSSE) conducted national roundtables about effective educational practices, including one at the annual conference of the Association of College & Research Libraries (ACRL). At this roundtable, librarians generated innovative ideas about ways that they could help their campuses interpret and apply survey results for institutional planning and improvement.

For example, the library was seen as neutral space in which all campus constituents could discuss data, especially results less robust than the campus had expected or hoped for. Not identified with administration or with a particular discipline or department, the library offers a place for all parties to come together. One librarian stated, "Librarians are not seen as vested or tied to any interest group; therefore, we can help to create discussions around the data that no other group on campus can develop." As data are interpreted and analyzed, questions about engagement and learning can be posited and studied in a scholarly way that builds credibility for changes in curriculum, pedagogy, and educational environment. NSSE and other important data can also remain available in the library for future scholarly analysis and use.

Another integrative role for the library involves accountability. Librarians in the roundtable highlighted ways in which they can help address expectations of regional, disciplinary, and professional accrediting bodies through improving student learning experiences regarding multiple topics, including information literacy and critical thinking. A case in point is that the ACRL standards for information literacy are mapped onto NSSE benchmarks, providing a framework for analysis and change. The need for evidence of student learning for accreditors and for state funding agencies necessitates collaborative problem-solving across a campus: the library can be an accountability commons for generating designed inquiries and interpreting and representing outcomes.

In a second major contribution to learning, libraries can be a campus nexus for connecting digital natives and digital immigrants. Marc Prensky explains that young college students are native speakers of the digital language of computers and of the Internet, while those of us who may be fascinated with technological possibilities in teaching and learning come to them with an accent: we are digital immigrants. Students weaned on computers actually think differently and do their own scholarly work differently. They prefer quick access to information, graphics before text, random access as in hypertext, and frequent feedback and reward. Both process and content are different now. In addition to what Prensky labels the

Legacy content of reading, writing, mathematics, history, and science, we must now teach the Futures content that includes the "ethics, politics, sociology, and languages" that go along with "software, hardware, nanotechnology, and genomes." Students and faculty members must collaborate on this revolution of the process and content of learning because they each bring to the work their own abilities as natives and immigrants.

Fortunately, librarians have been in the center of this revolution. Ed Ayers, dean of the College and Graduate School of Arts and Sciences at the University of Virginia, contends that "librarians have been the real heroes of the digital revolution in higher education. They are the ones who have seen the farthest, done the most, accepted the hardest challenges, and demonstrated most clearly the benefits of digital information." Technology has changed the means for scholarly inquiry and even its representation. Ayers reports on his experiment with creating an online article that could be read in multiple ways depending on the reader's learning process and goals. With the help of the digital natives who produce information and read information hypertextually, librarians can aid scholars in finding and using information, generating new information, and representing it in virtual ways that make it rapidly accessible in this information age.

The pedagogical and accountability commons of the library does facilitate scholars in generating and using evidence that enhances student engagement and learning, and the library continues as a center for the collaboration of digital natives and immigrants. Yet, for a digital immigrant, the library remains a physical and emotional center in a different way. Two personal anecdotes will illustrate what I mean.

Many years ago as a doctoral student in a linguistics course, I decided to test the authenticity of the dialect of a mid-nineteenth-century Hoosier poet by comparing written documents from his period in history with the dialect in his poetry. Having requested from the librarian in the Lilly Library at Indiana University original letters from Civil War soldiers to their families in southern Indiana, I was presented with a pair of white gloves and a ribboned box. My wearing gloves would help preserve the paper epistles, which had not been opened in over a century. As I touched these personal expressions of longing for home and accounts of the angst of war, I was drawn into my scholarly project in a way that would not have been possible had I been reading the letters online. Physical and emotional elements of my researching were palpable.

Many years later, my younger son spent part of his junior year in college at the University of East Anglia in England. An acting major, he was cast as Caliban in *The Tempest*, a juicy role that I, as an English professor and as his mother, longed to see him play. When I learned that one performance would be shown on the Internet, I was elated and then deflated because my computer didn't have the capability to receive the broadcast. A librarian at Indiana University Purdue University Indianapolis where I was teaching took matters in hand. She set up five computers for my family members and me, provided us each with a print copy of the play to refer to, and joined us in watching the play live. She provided the physical conditions for a virtual experience full of emotion.

The library is at the center of what we in higher education are all about—generating and applying knowledge, fostering learning, and serving the needs of our communities and publics. As a physical, virtual, and even emotional nexus, the library serves an essential role in the twenty-first-century information society.

ELEMENTS OF A GOOD LEARNING EXPERIENCE

Before dealing in depth with the emerging role of academic libraries in enhancing student learning, it is worth reviewing the hallmarks of good learning experiences in order to better gauge the potential value of resource-based instruction in facilitating integrated learning and the development of lifelong learning skills. Such quality learning/teaching experiences, in fact, close "the gap between the classroom and the library" and realize the potential of resource-based instruction to provide the major characteristics of active, integrated learning listed below.[3]

That there is a need for thoughtful reflection on what good learning experiences incorporate is attested to by the number of current articles on this subject in higher education literature. For example, Peter Smith, who recently moved from the presidency of California State University–Monterey Bay to be the first American to become the assistant director-general for Education at the United Nations Educational, Scientific and Cultural Organization (UNESCO), addresses the sameness of learning opportunities in a 2004 article in *Change*. "Despite an enormous diversity of institutional types and our historic commitment to access, there is a numbing sameness across our campuses when it comes to the actual practice of teaching and learning. Different colleges recruit different students, serve different audiences, and teach different bodies of knowledge. But they do it all using the same basic academic model."[4] In looking for good alternatives to this sameness, there are some commonsense criteria that can be used.

First, a good learning experience imitates reality. Once students graduate, no one is going to stop work to lecture them every time they need to learn something new for their jobs. No one is going to hand them a textbook or reading list. No one is going to put books on reserve for them in the public library. However, if students gain an independent awareness of the literature of particular fields and learn how to access it, evaluate it, and use it effectively, they will be well prepared for the post-graduation, real-life situations they encounter. Resource-based instruction can prepare them to cope with the multimedia information that is so much a part of society today. It can prepare them to screen the information (and misinformation) with which the mass media bombards them. Faculty and librarians working together can help students learn how to deal with the realities of the world's vast, multitudinous store of information.

Second, a good learning experience is active. The lecture method, even if it allows time for questions and answers, falls far short of this goal.

Educators have said for years that students need opportunities to learn by discovery—to develop concepts from specific data by starting with an initial problem and thinking it through to a conclusion. Library or research skills clearly play a part in this process. Once students have acquired basic information management skills, they can begin to frame questions, find information related to those questions, and then sort and act upon the information they have gathered.

Third, a good learning experience is individualized. Young people reach college campuses with a wide range of academic abilities. Open-admissions policies, plus the large number of students who have learned English as a second language, have extended the range between well-prepared and poorly-prepared students. While differential placement is generally the rule in freshman English and mathematics courses, classes in other subject areas may contain both academically well-prepared students and students handicapped by poor secondary school preparation.

No one instructional approach can be effective for such a wide range of needs; no one textbook or single reading assignment can be effective with thirty students of widely divergent abilities. One way to individualize the learning process is to have students learn from information online and in libraries and other resources in the wider community. Students can deal directly with topics close to their areas of interest and choose materials appropriate to their individual reading levels. By concentrating on magazine articles rather than books, for example, a student with a reading deficiency can find time to go over the material repeatedly.

Fourth, a good learning experience will be responsive to a variety of student learning styles. Some students learn best by listening, some by seeing, some through practical application of knowledge, some work better in groups, and some prefer an individual approach. Once faculty feel more comfortable venturing beyond the traditional boundaries of the lecture, the textbook, and the reading or reserves lists, they can begin experimenting with approaches that utilize multimedia resources and broaden both their own teaching styles and the learning opportunities available to their students.

Fifth, a good learning experience accommodates constantly changing information. Because most information rapidly becomes obsolete, almost every school and college pay at least lip service to preparing people for lifelong learning. Education should help students acquire an appreciation for the rich variety of information sources in each discipline and to develop basic search strategies for locating and evaluating needed information. This type of learning will not stop when students receive their diplomas, for they will have the skills for accessing and monitoring the changing information bases in their fields. Recognizing this need in the populations they serve, public libraries continue to respond to nonschool learning needs by providing adult independent-learning programs, reader advisers, and in-depth reference services.

Sixth, students learn best when the environment is least threatening. Learning/teaching approaches in which students learn by discovery in working through problems relieve the pressure students feel when trying to guess what their teachers "really" want. Students may initially be fearful when taking greater responsibility for their own learning. Once weaned, however, from a closely controlled learning environment, students will no longer need to lose a good deal of learning time trying to figure out just what it is their teachers want them to accomplish. They will develop their own standards of accomplishment.

Only when classroom instructors and librarians cooperate in shifting the focus toward learning based on real-world information resources will these six elements of a good learning experience come together in undergraduate education. A shared campus vision of the implications of the information age and a corresponding statement of educational philosophy, as suggested in the previous chapter, are important steps toward promoting such cooperation. Crucial to the process is institutional leadership.

LEADERSHIP FOR MORE ACTIVE AND INTEGRATED LEARNING

In the time between our two books, two outstanding higher education leaders died: Ernest L. Boyer and Frank Newman. While neither spoke much on libraries, both participated in the first higher education summit on libraries and education reform held in 1987,[5] and both helped to direct thought to the role of libraries in learning.

Under the leadership of Boyer, the 1986 "Prologue and Major Recommendations of the Carnegie Foundation's Report on Colleges"[6] directly acknowledges the relationship between libraries and quality undergraduate education. The opening summary statement of the "Resources for Learning" section (see Appendix B) could serve as a campus challenge for presidents wishing to promote more active and integrated learning on their campuses. It states, "The quality of a college is measured by the resources for learning on the campus and the extent to which students become independent, self-directed learners."

In his summary of the summit mentioned above, Newman pointed out:

all learning does not go on in the classroom, because a faculty member stands up front. In fact, the best thing the faculty member can do is to empower the student to become a learner. It takes skill to empower a student to become a learner, to excite the student about wanting to learn, to draw on sources of information, knowledge and ideas. That is exactly what a good librarian does. In that sense they have a common function. That's not to say that the way they function is the same, because they are set in different points. But the ideal librarian, as far as students go, is someone who does all those things and engages them in a learning process.[7]

Since the 1987 conference, other educational leaders have gone on record along similar lines and some have been quoted in chapter 1. The question is what has actually changed since we last wrote, when we reported the following:

Library-based learning has, in fact, been slowly evolving on many campuses. Usually referred to as library or bibliographic instruction, most efforts to date have been initiated by librarians and have been largely directed at helping students improve their performance in particular courses. The problem with such library initiatives is their impermanence. Individual librarians working with individual classroom faculty or with a particular program may successfully integrate the library into particular courses only to have a change in personnel undo years of effort. Only when academic leaders institutionalize these efforts and provide the necessary leadership and faculty development opportunities will these advances become permanent.[8]

The answer is that a great deal has happened and is happening! We shall first look at several higher education systems initiatives that have taken a coordinated approach to information literacy and then an example of a campuswide initiative. This will be followed by an overview of the significant body of research and literature that now undergirds this movement and the trends that are evident within it.

SYSTEM- AND CAMPUS-DRIVEN INITIATIVES IN INFORMATION LITERACY

In the mid-nineties, two major university systems undertook what became sustained and significant information literacy efforts. They were the State University of New York (SUNY) and the California State University (CSU).

The SUNY effort was initiated within the SUNY Council of Library Directors, and its September 1997 report on the Information Literacy Initiative[9] was later quickly followed by an initiative to develop "modular, generic, web-based information literacy course(s) for use throughout the SUNY system."[10] This course was developed by Ulster Community College and was modified and used by several campuses; the SUNYConnect Information Literacy course is now available to any library in the world, provided they use an attribution copyright statement. More significantly, however, within two years, the SUNY Board of Trustees adopted a general education requirement for all undergraduate programs that included an Information Management Competency. The general education requirement was implemented in fall 2000, and there is an ongoing three-year assessment cycle in place. The annual SUNY Conference on Instructional Technologies has an information literacy track where best practices are shared and issues are discussed in a collegial forum with faculty, librarians, and instructional technology staff.[11]

Another very robust program has developed in the CSU system, where from the beginning there was an active partnership between librarians and academic leadership in the Chancellor's Office. The CSU initiative was sparked by Lorie Roth, who serves as assistant vice chancellor for Academic Programs in the CSU Chancellor's Office, and the history of that effort is well documented.[12] Beginning with systemwide conferences that brought together classroom faculty and librarians, this effort has set standards, addressed assessment challenges, encouraged faculty-librarian partnerships through a grant program, and sponsored workshops for classroom and library faculty, as well as faculty development officers. The small grant program has allowed information literacy initiatives to be tailored to specific academic program needs and opportunities and has often led to replication on sister campuses. (For a partial listing of these projects, see http://www.calstate.edu/LS/Outcomes.shtml.) In addition, the CSU system has commissioned a number of research projects to better understand "the practices students currently use to determine an information need, to search for information, and to organize, evaluate, synthesize and present information to an audience"[13] and to determine how best to promote students' information literacy abilities and effectiveness as scholars.

Nor have system- or statewide information literacy initiatives been the sole prerogative of universities. Community college information literacy efforts also got underway in the mid-1990s. While the recent horrific budget cuts in California have challenged the coordinated progress of its community colleges, their collaborative approach can serve as a model for other systems.[14] The community colleges also have an information literacy articulation agreement with the CSU system with regard to information literacy standards and assessment.

Another significant community college information literacy initiative occurred in the state of Washington when the Instruction Commission of the Washington Association of Community and Technical Colleges accepted a report on "Information Competency: An Initiative for Integrated Learning" in 1993. The report summary states:

> The college's goal is to instill in students the knowledge and skills essential for their individual development and their useful contribution to society. Achieving this requires that our students know how to find and use information. Learning how to learn depends upon a knowledge base, a recognition of the need for sufficient evidence before drawing conclusions and the understanding that application, analysis and synthesis of information underlie thoughtful judgment. . . . The establishment of Information Competency as an instructional priority means a commitment to educating the full person for today's world, and fulfills the community and technical college mission of comprehensive education for lifelong learning.[15]

Nine years later at the national level, the American Association of Community Colleges Board of Directors approved a position statement on library and learning resource center programs, which states that "learning resources programs that provide information literacy skills are essential to the development of the independent lifelong learner."[16] Of course, how individual campuses implement information literacy programs varies as much as their parent institutions vary.[17]

For private campuses and those not part of a system, campus leadership can promote the establishment of information literacy programs, but opportunities for leveraging resources for program development and assessment are not as rich. What is clear is that campus leadership from outside the library is key to the ease with which across-the-curriculum initiatives are established. (As discussed in chapter 1, in some regions, accrediting agencies are a source for such leadership.)

For example, at Florida International University, both library and faculty development personnel took seriously a statement made by FIU President Modesto A. Mardique in the campus strategic plan. He stated, "When ubiquitous computing arrives, we will be limited, not by the quantity of information but by its quality, and our ability to retrieve, manipulate, and analyze it."[18] After much work, the FIU Undergraduate Council developed a comprehensive proposal for an information literacy program that was subsequently accepted by the Faculty Senate and implemented in 1998.[19]

As academic leaders are developing an integrated vision and philosophy to guide a campuswide shift toward more active, lifelong learning, the role of resource-based learning can be explored within established instructional planning procedures. Whether the institution is focusing on identifying minimum competencies or value-added education, whether a faculty committee is considering a new core curriculum, or whether academic planning is localized within individual schools and tied to program reviews, presidents, academic vice presidents, and deans can encourage faculty to consider how information retrieval and evaluation skills are mastered within their areas of instructional responsibility. Resource-based instruction is the logical answer once such questions are seriously considered.

The librarian's perspective could be of considerable value in discussing how to achieve the educational goals and objectives of the campus. In the initial stages of planning, as campus groups explore the unique demands placed on higher education in the information age, it is best to consider the potential role of academic libraries or information literacy in meeting these demands. To facilitate this, academic leaders could encourage the placement of librarians and certain faculty, who have made more than traditional use of libraries in their teaching, on key curriculum planning and evaluation committees. They could encourage and support faculty visits to campuses with successful resource-based learning programs, or they could bring in consultants from such campuses to discuss options with faculty.

FACULTY AND THE LIBRARY

As mentioned earlier, planners seeking faculty support for the integration of library resources into the curriculum must understand that most faculty are not comfortable in library settings beyond their narrow areas of specialization. This reality was documented as early as 1930s in a study conducted by the Association of American Colleges.[20] Since then, not only has this situation not significantly improved, but it has gotten worse. The increasing amount and complexity of online resources have only served to exacerbate faculty's inability to keep up with broadly based research tools and resources. Only faculty development efforts can improve such situations. The relationship of faculty development to information literacy, student learning, and research productivity of faculty and students is discussed in chapter 4. Suffice it here to observe that faculty development efforts to address these concerns could encompass the following:

- Keeping faculty apprised of new information resources and services in their own fields of research;
- Familiarizing faculty with relevant resources and services beyond their areas of specialization;
- Familiarizing faculty and/or their assistants and secretaries with the time-saving tools and services of the library;
- Helping faculty understand the research capabilities and needs of their students;
- Working with faculty in developing learning experiences based on the use of books, magazines, newspapers, online and media resources; and
- Working with faculty in structuring experiences that will effectively promote the mastery of information literacy and other critical thinking skills.

The first three activities directly promote faculty comfort with and use of libraries and online resources. The last three activities, though directed at student learning, will promote the same ends, as faculty and librarians work and learn together while developing and offering resource-based learning experiences. When librarians work as members of a research team, faculty knowledge of available resources and services will also grow, as discussed in chapter 4.

Once an institutional climate that supports faculty development activities and a better use of libraries by faculty and students is created, there is a very rich and continually growing body of literature that can be mined for approaches and materials that have proven successful in other settings and that can be far more easily adapted to another campus than be created from the ground up. One excellent example of this is the TILT online tutorial program that was developed at the University of Texas at Austin library, which has made it available at no charge since 1999. Designed primarily for undergraduates, this interactive information literacy tutorial has been adapted by many other colleges and universities across the United States, as well as in other countries.[21] "The design is attractive, modular and based on active learning principles. . . . Tutorials such as these are available 24 hours a day, 7 days a week. They can be used by faculty as course units or consulted by students as independent study aids."[22]

INFORMATION LITERACY ACROSS THE CURRICULUM

In our earlier book, we included examples of how information literacy learning had been incorporated into courses across the disciplines. Because there are now so many examples from which to choose, it makes little sense to document the few that space would allow. Instead, we encourage faculty development personnel along with library and classroom faculty to undertake a thorough literature search as part of all planning efforts, whether addressing general education and/or discipline-specific curriculum approaches. A selected list of resources is available in Appendix C.

There is a growing body of related literature that focuses on all aspects of information literacy. In the area of assessment, for example, like other assessment efforts underway to respond responsibly to demands for outcomes assessment,[23] information literacy assessment models run the gamut from assessment of entry-level skills to assessment of individual course assignments to full program assessment and/or to exit or graduation assessment. One review of the literature on information literacy found that between 1973 and 2002, there were 5,009 items published and reviewed,[24] and each year, beginning in 1973, *Reference Services Review* presents a bibliography of information literacy publications with some analysis of trends.[25]

Two sources can provide a particularly good starting point for campuses wanting to develop successful information literacy programs. The first, *Developing Research & Communication Skills: Guidelines for Information Literacy in the Curriculum*, written and published by the Middle States Commission on Higher Education (MSCHE), is a handbook providing colleges and universities with suggestions for how they might develop and implement a mission-driven approach to integrating information literacy across the curriculum.[26] Second, the Association of Research and College Libraries maintains a Web portal that provides information on standards and guidelines, best practices, and assessment issues, among many other resources.[27]

Out of the evolving literature on information literacy has emerged consensus of the importance of careful planning that follows much in the pattern of how writing across the curriculum developed.[28] Moreover, four characteristics of successful programs are evident in the literature. First, there are some fundamental skills that all students should acquire before graduation and that should be integrated into general education requirements. Second, building on those generic skills, the specifics of what information literacy abilities students need to learn differ according to the literature of the particular disciplines and professions, and planning efforts must be appropriately tailored to each program accordingly. Third, for information literacy programs to be successful, assessment of student learning outcomes is essential. Fourth, none of the above succeeds without faculty buy-in. As already stressed, information literacy is fundamentally a learning issue, not a library issue.

Commentary: "Engaging Faculty in Information Literacy Instruction"

Oswald M. T. Ratteray
Associate Director, Middle States Commission on Higher Education

Faculty members always have been involved in information literacy instruction, even if they have never applied that label to what they routinely do. The issue facing higher education today is how best to engage faculty more deeply in invoking a deliberate and focused approach to the principles of information literacy as they seek to promote student learning.

From the very first day of a course, faculty begin to shape students' understanding of what they know, do not know, and still need to discover before the end of the course—and, we can hope, for the rest of their lives.

In a narrow sense, faculty are concerned with information literacy as it relates to specific study assignments, which may be either precisely or sometimes loosely considered "research," especially as it relates to assignments that require the use of a library. Thus, grades are assigned for a student's skills in framing the research question for the assignment and for acquiring, evaluating, and using the information they uncover. Faculty also have the last word on advising students about some of the mechanics of acquiring information, the metrics involved in evaluating it, how information should be used for the purposes of an assignment, and how all of these should be done ethically and legally.

In a larger sense, however, faculty members also are concerned about the application of these same skills to the totality of the learning goals expressed in the syllabus for a course—in other words, the aggregate of all lectures and out-of-class study assignments. In this macro sense, the information-literate student is the "educated" student who can cope successfully with a range of post-training environments, even transferring discipline-specific strategies to information challenges in other arenas.

The faculty member has many campus allies in the task of information literacy instruction, including other faculty members involved in the academic program in which the student is enrolled, librarians, student services personnel, and even supervisors and coaches in co-curricular programs. Each ally has a unique role in collaboration, and all of them should be working toward an institution-wide goal of developing information-literate graduates. Coherence in academic programming and collaboration in instruction, therefore, become a matter of utmost importance.

An important concept that faculty—and librarians, as their first line of support—may wish to convey to students is that the principles of information literacy can serve as a metacognitive device that enables the student to better manage the learning process. That is to say, information literacy enables students to recognize the stage of their understanding: the point at which they determine what they know and do not know; their need to plan the steps they should take, in either a linear or recursive manner, to proceed through the process of acquiring, evaluating, and using that information; and their obligation to do all of these ethically, legally, and within specific policies of the college or university.

Librarians in particular can provide specialized knowledge about information resources, within and across disciplines. They are current with the shifting technological sands that affect how best to gain access to those resources. They often are the primary coach for a student's initial strategies for evaluating the sources, and they can help lay a foundation for the faculty member's role in guiding the student's evaluation of the information content and using it for a specific purpose.

Once the faculty member begins the process of stimulating a student's thirst for knowledge, both academic and co-curricular advisors can reinforce the strategies students use to manage their time and study habits. They can help students negotiate the social, political, and other aspects of college or off-campus life that can have a major impact on their readiness to learn. They also can help students reconcile their personal needs and wants with the institution's mission and services. Co-curricular advisors in particular can communicate to students the significance and utility of deliberately applying the principles of information literacy to activities outside their academic courses. They can help students make connections among all the institution's formal and informal offerings and remain on track during the formal learning process that the faculty members have designed.

Finally, it is in the best interest of the institution as a whole if administrators can help maintain a campus environment that supports inquiry and provide the incentives that encourage both faculty-librarian collaboration and deeper faculty engagement in applying information literacy principles directly in their teaching.

These types of interaction, however, cannot be accomplished effectively with an arm's length approach, one in which all parties remain in their respective campus enclaves and instruct the student to shuttle back and forth between the various resources. In an ideal situation, faculty members, librarians, and administrators should see themselves as partners. They first would collaborate on some of the elements of instruction that are likely to best accomplish the faculty member's proposed course of instruction. Each then could contribute to a student's learning process at different points, and each could contribute to the overall course, program, and institutional objectives.

For the purposes of program review and institution-wide planning, it would be useful if all of these contributions were summarized on a single matrix. Not only would everyone be able to see more clearly how they contribute to the overall institutional objectives, but a matrix could shed light on where the institution may need to concentrate additional efforts. It certainly could facilitate an accreditation process that required an institution to demonstrate that it is producing information-literate graduates.

It is also worth underscoring that often a strong foundation for integrating information literacy into the curriculum already exists within the research efforts faculty require and/or desire of their students. Then it is simply a matter of more deliberately articulating information literacy concepts and desired outcomes and fine-tuning how class assignments are given to students. (See, for example, the University of Louisville's document, "Promoting Information Literacy through Classroom Assignments"[29] in Appendix D.) Certainly, where faculty have embraced problem-based learning, information literacy is a natural ingredient.[30] So a good place to start in planning information literacy efforts is by acknowledging and emulating the best that already exists on your campus.

Academic leadership—both within and outside the library—needs to articulate a vision for its graduates that include lifelong learning abilities for today's information society. Then, with the existence of national, widely-accepted standards for information literacy, the challenge for each academic institution is to ensure that information literacy learning opportunities are designed and implemented in such a way that standards are systematically introduced, reinforced, and mastered across the curriculum.

ACQUIRING INFORMATION LITERACY FOR LIFELONG LEARNING

Once the institutional climate is positive and faculty have had the opportunity to integrate information literacy learning outcomes into their courses, real progress should be possible in producing information-literate graduates. Eventually, this should ensure that an increasing number of people are prepared for effectively working and living in today's information-rich society. In particular, we need graduates who are prepared as independent learners in a world characterized by the rapid obsolescence of information and technology with the resulting shifts in employment opportunities. This goal is not a new role for higher education, for the heart of liberal education has always been the goal of graduating independent lifelong learners; in successful information literacy programs, "the teacher and the instructional librarian are the guides and facilitators, but the student is in charge of the learning, making use of available resources to solve the problem"[31]—creating a perfect partnership for the development of independent lifelong learners. However, a new urgency now attends this need, and increasingly information literacy is being appreciated as a key to independent lifelong learning. While the goal is the same, the environment is significantly different: the digital culture versus the culture of print.

University of California Berkeley Professor Peter Lyman explores the question of the relationship between the values and practices of the digital culture that encompasses information and the culture of print in a 2001 issue of *Liberal Education*.

> The act of reading a digital document begins with information retrieval. . . . [s]earching is one of the distinctive characteristics of digital information because it allows the reader to find and provide order to a digital text. Yet such a seemingly technical process can be curiously random. The same search term given to different Web search engines results in different answers for many reasons: different algorithms, different cataloging procedures, advertising payments to place one Web site above another, and so forth. . . . While user search technique can be improved by mastering Boolean logic, technical training about searching alone is insufficient because the problem concerns judging the quality of answers.
>
> For, as any librarian will tell you, a search will be fruitless without a full understanding of the question you are asking; this is the purpose of the reference intake interview, the dialectic that librarians apply to print and digital sources. In choosing from among a list of search results, a reader is tacitly choosing from a list of inferences or possible answers. Technique alone might solve a problem, but it cannot answer a question. Yet, it is curious that liberal education often acts as if the reverse is true, that students can be expected to engage in research without formal instruction in basic techniques of information retrieval. While it might be true that the Web brings the library to the desktop, one of the implications of this is that the user must learn the reference skills of the librarian or the scholar.[32]

Clearly, people who are prepared for independent lifelong learning within a digital environment will have the edge in the changing job market, and companies with information-literate employees will be the winners. We shall deal with business demands for information-literate workers more fully at the beginning of chapter 6, but it is worth underscoring here that the need for such skills has been well documented in the business sector. For example,

> Building on the competency framework established by the [1991] SCANS Report, the U.S. Department of Labor has been supporting the Occupational Information Network (O*NET), an electronic database of occupational information that provides a common language and framework that can be accessed directly by the public as well as employers and educators. The heading of cross-functional skills—defined as those that facilitate performance of activities that occur across all job areas—lists the following skills:

- Problem identification
- Information gathering
- Information organization
- Synthesis/reorganization
- Idea generation
- Idea evaluation
- Implementation planning
- Solution appraisal[33]

How well these abilities are learned will depend on the importance placed on these skills by the president, academic vice president, deans, and faculty.

ACQUIRING INFORMATION LITERACY FOR ACTIVE CITIZENSHIP

Students also need to understand how the skills they are learning can be applied to both civic and home situations. If they finish their education thinking that they can find all the information they need through a fast Google search and that libraries are useful only for classroom assignments and recreational reading, they are not information literate. Indeed, transferability is the essence of information literacy.

Information literacy abilities are also fundamental to active citizenship. Harlan Cleveland, former dean of the University of Minnesota Hubert H. Humphrey Institute of Public Affairs, has written eloquently on how the information society affects education for citizenship. When large numbers of people are empowered by knowledge, it is more difficult to keep policy-making in the hands of a few. Cleveland calls for a "theory of general education clearly relevant to life and work in a context that is more and more based on the information resource—a rapidly changing scene in which uncertainty is the main planning factor."[34] Though he implies it in his writings, Cleveland never directly ties his concerns to the use of libraries or to the need for information literacy skills. Others, however, have made that connection.

As far back as the 1930s, the role of colleges in safeguarding their students from propaganda directed at the layperson through popular media has been discussed; and there is a strong international movement addressing the need for media literacy. Media literacy efforts, with its focus on discerning use of the mass media, complements the broader concept of information literacy, and the terms sometimes are used interchangeably.[35]

One scholar concluded that anything short of providing students with easy access to all points of view was likely to be counterproductive,[36] but today his concern with providing a broad base of materials for students' reading is incomplete without a consideration of how selected evidence presented through broadcast and other media can influence people's perspectives. Moreover, the single greatest danger today for the manipulation of people's thinking may not be the persuasive newscaster but rather people's tendency to place undue confidence in information that appears on computer screens.

Nor is that the only challenge to democratic decision-making. Research out of Emory University documents that only 15 percent of respondents to a study conducted by psychology professor Drew Westen "actually bothered to consider the evidence when forming their opinions."[37] Most people base their decision-making on existing biases. Clearly, such concerns need to be systematically addressed in today's curricula. To some it seems best addressed by seeing "information literacy as a liberal art," as presented in an article by that name. "If the information society is to be a free and humane one—especially if we share the Enlightenment goals of abolishing unnecessary inequality and creating a society of liberty—then let us take up the challenge. . . . Let us contribute to liberty through advancing citizens' knowledge, through democratizing education. Let us design comprehensive, multi-dimensional and thoughtful information literacy curriculum."[38]

One of the outcomes when students develop skills for accessing, evaluating, and using information in academic libraries is that they should then be prepared for active use of public libraries after graduation. The public library, which was seen as a means of education and a better life by many of the over 20 million immigrants of the late 1800s and early 1900s, is still the strongest and most far-reaching community resource for lifelong learning—despite public libraries in many locations receiving far from adequate resources to meet existing user needs. Kathleen Blake Yancey, R. Roy Pearce Professor of Professional Communication at Clemson University, underscores the importance of public libraries as sites for lifelong learning in a 2005 *Change* article:

> In the United States, libraries, like schools, have served as "information equalizers." Historically, if you were a person of color, a person without means, or a person new to the country, you went to the library to learn to read, to become socialized into a local version of American life, and to acquire the skills and knowledge required to become a citizen. . . . Those of us who are committed to education, and especially to lifelong learning, should take another look at libraries. They have recently re-created themselves for the 21st cen-

tury in ways that might be suggestive for an even more time-honored institution, the college or university.

While continuing their historic service of providing books for free, in recent years libraries have expanded their functions to include diverse services:

1. providing different kinds of materials in many ways;
2. helping patrons learn to write and to use communication technologies;
3. helping patrons learn to read "visually";
4. providing alternative learning sites for specific populations;
5. linking "free" library services with retail services, so that the free services are extended; and
6. providing a site for community fairs, celebrations, and citizenship.[39]

To ensure that their graduates can take full advantage of public and other accessible libraries, colleges and universities need to take their students' knowledge of and attitudes toward lifelong use of libraries seriously. In 1822, James Madison warned that "a popular government, without popular information, or the means of acquiring it, is but a Prologue to a Farce or a Tragedy; or, perhaps both."[40]

NOTES

1. Vincent Tinto, "Taking Student Learning Seriously: Rethinking the University of the Future," in *Charting the Course: Earl V. Pullias Lecture Series on the Future of Higher Education* (Los Angeles: University of Southern California Rossier School of Education, fall 2003), 35. Retrieved 8 April 2005 from http://www.usc.edu/dept/chepa/pullias/2003/pdf/2003PulliasBooklet.pdf.

2. Paul A. Lacey, "The Role of the Librarian in Faculty Development: A Professor's Point of View," in *Library Instruction and Faculty Development: Growth Opportunities in the Academic Community*, ed. Nyal Z. Williams and Jack T. Tsukamoto (Ann Arbor, Mich.: Pierian Press, 1980), 20–21.

3. Information in this section is taken in part from "Resource-based Learning in an Information Society," in *Managing Nonclassroom Learning Resources*, ed. Patricia Senn Breivik (San Francisco: Jossey-Bass, 1986), 47–55; and Breivik, *Planning the Library Instruction Program* (Chicago: American Library Association, 1982), 2–5.

4. Peter Smith, "Curricular Transformation: Why We Need It, How to Support It," *Change* 36 (January/February 2004): 28–35.

5. Patricia Senn Breivik and Robert Wedgeworth, eds., *Libraries and the Search for Academic Excellence* (Metuchen, N.J.: Scarecrow Press, 1988).

6. Ernest Boyer, "Prologue and Major Recommendations of the Carnegie Foundation's Report on Colleges," *The Chronicle of Higher Education* 33 (5 November 1986): 21.

7. Frank Newman, "Academic Libraries and the American Resurgence," in *Libraries and the Search for Academic Excellence*, ed. Breivik and Wedgeworth, 180.

8. Breivik and E. Gordon Gee, *Information Literacy: Revolution in the Library*, American Council on Education Oryx Press Series on Higher Education (Westport, Conn.: Greenwood Publishing Group, 1989), 40–41.

9. See http://www.sunyconnect.suny.edu/ili/final.htm, accessed 7 February 2005.

10. See http://www.sunyconnect.suny.edu/ili/scld.htm, accessed 7 February 2005.

11. Mary Ruth Glogowski, e-mail correspondence to Patricia Breivik, 4 April 2005.

12. Lorie Roth, "Educating the Cut and Paste Generation," *Library Journal* 124 (1 November 1999): 42–44.

13. Linda J. Pulliam, *Information Competence Data Analysis: Using All Sources of Data Collected in Phase II*, prepared for the Office of the Chancellor, California State University, Systemwide Library Initiatives, 30 August 2002. Retrieved 8 April 2005 from http://www.calstate.edu/LS/Data_Analysis.pdf.

14. *Information Competency: Challenges and Strategies for Development*, Academic Senate for California Community Colleges, adopted fall 2002. Retrieved 1 April 2005 from http://www.academicsenate.cc.ca.us/Publications/Papers/Info Competency2002.htm.

15. *Information Competency: An Initiative for Integrated Learning*, Library/ Media Directors Council (LMDC), Washington State Community and Technical Colleges, accepted by the LMDC, September 1993. Retrieved 18 February 2005 from http://www.cis.ctc.edu/pub/groups/lmdc/infocomp.doc.

16. American Association of Community Colleges, *AACC Position Statement on Library and Learning Resource Center Programs*, 2002. Retrieved 18 February 2005 from http://www.aacc.nche.edu/Template.cfm?Section=Position_Statements &template=/ContentManagement/ContentDisplay.cfm&ContentID=9634&inte restCategoryID=224&Name=Position%20Statement&ComingFrom=InterestDisplay.

17. Katherine Branch and Debra Gilchrist, "Library Instruction and Information Literacy in Community and Technical Colleges," *RQ* 35 (summer 1996): 476–82. Retrieved 10 February 2005 from Expanded Academic ASAP Plus database.

18. Patricia Iannuzzi, "Faculty Development and Information Literacy: Establishing Campus Partnerships," *Reference Services Review* 26 (fall/winter 1998): 101.

19. Florida International University Undergraduate Council, *Information Literacy at Florida International University: A Proposal for Faculty Senate from Undergraduate Council*. Retrieved 18 November 2002 from http://www.fiu.edu/~ library/ili/iliprop.html.

20. Harvie Branscomb, *Teaching with Books: A Study of College Libraries* (Chicago: Association of American Colleges and the American Library Association, 1940), 8.

21. For information about TILT, see http://tilt.lib.utsystem.edu/resources/index.html.

22. Joseph M. Brewer et al., "Libraries Dealing with the Future Now," ARL Bimonthly Report 234, June 2004. Retrieved 24 June 2004 from http://www.arl.org/newsltr/234/dealing.html.

23. See, for example, Richard J. Shavelson and Leta Huang, "Responding Responsibly to the Frenzy to Assess Learning in Higher Education," *Change* (February 2003): 11–18.

24. Hannelore B. Rader, "Information Literacy 1973 2002: A Selected Literature Review," *Library Trends* 51 (fall 2002): 242–48.

25. This bibliography appears in the fourth issue of *Reference Services Review* each year.

26. See http://www.msche.org for ordering information.

27. See http://www.ala.org/ala/acrl/acrlissues/acrlinfolit/informationliteracy.htm.

28. James K. Elmborg, "Information Literacy and Writing across the Curriculum: Sharing the Vision," *Reference Services Review* 31 (February 2003): 68–80.

29. Information Literacy Program, University of Louisville, *Promoting Information Literacy Through Class Assignments: How Faculty Can Help*. Retrieved 24 February 2004 from http://www.louisville.edu/infoliteracy/promotinginformationliteracy.htm.

30. Alexius Smith Macklin, "Integrating Information Literacy Using Problem-based Learning," *Reference Services Review* 29 (2001): 306–13.

31. Roxanne Mendrinos, *Building Information Literacy Using High Technology: A Guide for Schools and Libraries* (Englewood, Colo.: Libraries Unlimited, 1994), 12.

32. Peter Lyman, "Information Literacy," *Liberal Education* 87 (winter 2001): 28–37.

33. Breivik, "Information Literacy Background Paper," in *Information Literacy: Advancing Opportunities for Learning in the Digital Age* (Washington, D.C.: The Aspen Institute, 1999), 31.

34. Harlan Cleveland, "Education for Citizenship in the Information Society," *EDUCOM Bulletin* 20 (fall 1985): 11–17.

35. See, for example, Renee Hobbs and Richard Frost, "Measuring the Acquisition of Media-Literacy Skills," *Reading Research Quarterly* 38 (July/August/September 2003): 331–54.

36. Douglas Waples, "Propaganda and Leisure Reading," *Journal of Higher Education* 1 (February 1930): 73–77.

37. Leonard Pitts, Jr., "We Believe What We Want, Regardless of the Facts," *San José Mercury News*, 2 January 2005, 5(P).

38. Jeremy J. Shapiro and Shelley K. Hughes, "Information Literacy as a Liberal Art: Enlightenment Proposals for a New Curriculum," *Educom Review* 31

(March/April 1996). Retrieved 29 January 2002 from http://www.educause.edu/pub/er/review/reviewArticles/31231.html.

39. Kathleen Blake Yancey, "The 'People's University': Our (New) Public Libraries as Sites of Lifelong Learning," *Change* (March/April 2005): 14.

40. Gaillard Hunt, ed., *The Writings of James Madison*, vol. 9 (New York: G.P. Putnam's Sons, 1910), 103.

CHAPTER 4

Improving Research Productivity

C ritics of the poor quality of undergraduate instruction frequently blame higher education for overemphasizing research at the expense of teaching. Yet among presidents of universities and four-year campuses, relatively few would claim to be completely satisfied with either the overall level of research on their campuses or the research productivity of most faculty. Often, a small minority of faculty conduct the preponderance of campus research, and the number of productive researchers would likely drop further without the impetus of tenure requirements.

The unsatisfactory level of campus research has implications far beyond the bounds of any one institution. The United States continues to struggle to maintain its leadership position in research in the face of increasingly effective competition from other nations.[1] Moreover, there have long been concerns about the rate of technological development—the translation of research into technological advances and innovation—which affects U.S. industry and the U.S. position in the world economy.[2]

How can academic leaders help reverse this trend and enhance both the quality of research and the productivity of campus faculty? If research and teaching are viewed as conflicting demands, it might seem that a more active role in improving undergraduate instruction, as discussed in the previous chapter, would further erode research productivity. Indeed, many faculty may resist the faculty development efforts we suggest because they see this as a further drain on time for research. Yet the partnership programs between library and classroom faculty, such as those we suggest in chapters 3 and 6, will benefit both teaching and research. Excellence in either pursuit requires active and effective use of information resources and services.

INFLUENCES ON PRODUCTIVITY

The quality of campus research is, of course, strongly affected by the degree of support a campus gives its researchers. Along with antiquated laboratories and scarce dollars for faculty travel and secretarial support, inadequate or cumbersome access to scholarly materials limits research productivity. Far too often these research support needs must compete with each other for limited dollars, because no overall plan for systematically building the campus research infrastructure exists. Consequently, libraries often find their capital needs competing poorly against pressures for new or updated laboratories, even though libraries seldom get additional space more frequently than every twenty to thirty years. Libraries have no counterparts like the local professional groups, alumni organizations, and accrediting agencies that provide strong support for enhanced laboratories, nor is the direct relationship of libraries to quality programs and faculty productivity well understood. The situation must change if libraries are to play the central role in supporting research, which they are capable of doing.

But the changes taking place today in the means of access to scholarly materials provide the potential for much stronger support for faculty and student research and more research by librarians themselves. Whereas the lack of access to needed information was the major problem in pre-Internet days, today *too* much information and the need for time and tools to efficiently "fish" for the needed scholarly material are of prime concern to scholars. The overabundance of materials produced within the last quarter of the twentieth century has seriously clogged the scholarly communications system,[3] and the situation continues to worsen. At the same time, a growing number of distance education faculty and students plus independent learners and scholars need access to academic libraries, further straining resources.[4]

The problems caused by these changes are reflected in a survey of over 7,000 faculty members conducted in the fall of 2003, which found that "the exuberance about electronic resources, evident several years ago, has been replaced by a growing dissatisfaction with scholarly materials that are available online."[5] Other conclusions from this survey reported by *The Chronicle of Higher Education* further documented this dissatisfaction.

Eighty-one percent of the faculty members agreed that unavailability of journal articles was a "substantial problem" for them, up from 68 percent in a similar survey conducted in 2000.

In addition, 65 percent of those surveyed last year strongly agreed that "the process of locating information in academic journal literature is tedious and often hit or miss, and the act of physically searching through hard-copy collections is much too time-consuming and onerous." Fifty-nine percent had agreed with that statement three years earlier.[6]

One service has emerged to address such concerns on campuses where faculty research interests have been profiled and where adequate library resources exist to provide awareness-raising services. These selective dissemination of information (SDI) services can operate at various levels of sophistication. At the simplest level, title pages of selected journals can be sent to faculty, and/or lists of newly received publications in discipline areas can be compiled and sent to departmental faculty on a regular basis.

At their best, however, SDI services screen all materials arriving in the library in all formats, match them against individual faculty research interests, and notify faculty regularly of newly arrived materials that match their interests. In business settings, administrators who appreciate the importance of using managers' and researchers' time efficiently have established SDI services. On most campuses, however, the best that faculty can currently expect is informal notification about items of possible interest through personal contact with a librarian.

In their traditional roles, librarians have done and continue to do a great deal to make the expanded resources of the information age accessible to researchers. Yet their efforts are meaningless if researchers do not use the tools librarians currently offer and are developing. In particular, faculty who are only "slightly at home" in libraries are simply unskilled in using the rapidly changing resources of their libraries, much less introducing their students to them. Moreover, insofar as faculty lack the skills to cope with the wealth of data available and fail to use library Web sites, search engines, and document delivery services designed specifically to help them, the research productivity of the United States has more difficulty keeping pace with other countries.

Academic leaders can address this problem by encouraging a more active linkage between library and classroom faculty. An ongoing partnership in which the information expertise of the librarian complements the subject expertise of the classroom faculty member could offer tremendous time savings on research projects. Academic leaders can set an example for faculty by making good use of library personnel and resources in their own decision-making, as suggested in chapter 6.

EXPANDING LIBRARIANS' ROLES IN THE RESEARCH PROCESS

The most underutilized research resource in most academic libraries is their professional staff, and this is one area that can make a significant contribution to improving research support. Historically, the library's primary research function has been to gather and organize information to provide a meaningful structure for faculty researchers who synthesize information in building knowledge. Librarians have performed this function well in the past and have been aggressive in responding to the opportunities offered by the newer information technologies.

For example, librarians have made possible both the growing accessibility to holdings from home and office provided by online catalogs and document delivery services and have significantly increased the efficiency and ease of bibliographic access and citation confirmation. By linking different types of information sources and providing easy-to-use tools to search across multiple databases, librarians have supported researchers' ability to handle the overabundance of information available. As interdisciplinary studies continue to expand and as faculty build global perspectives into existing courses, this linking function of academic libraries will become even more important to researchers. For academic librarians, the challenge of the past has been linking information among various subject areas. The challenge of the future will be to incorporate digitized information in a way that "preserves the linkages to the existing knowledge base, encourages and stimulates the productive use of new technologies, and provides coordinated gateway access to the universe of knowledge in a manner convenient and invisible to the end user."[7]

Researchers working across disciplines will rely on these linkages: "Each experienced future user of electronic data bases can have his own personal view of the data base. But even experienced users are likely to need help with unfamiliar topics."[8]

In 1999, it was reported that interdisciplinary programs for undergraduates had nearly doubled over a ten-year period.[9] Within this context, both faculty and students will be extending their research efforts into the literature of less familiar disciplines. Many education leaders applaud the increasing focus on interdisciplinary research and teaching. For example, Vartan Gregorian, president of the Carnegie Corporation of New York, put it this way: "The challenge for higher education, then, is not the choice between pure research and practical application but, rather, the integration and synthesis of compartmentalized knowledge. On our campuses, we must create an intellectual climate that encourages faculty members and students to make connections among seemingly disparate disciplines, discoveries, events, and trends—and to build bridges among them that benefit the understanding of us all."[10]

If this occurs, it will, in turn, challenge the librarians' role as solely supporters of faculty research. "While collections may, in fact, contain the necessary content for such studies, traditional models for research and bibliographic instruction are not always sufficient to help students find the resources they need to complete assignments and research projects that increasingly require cross-disciplinary searching."[11] Research conducted by librarians can provide information important for improving information management, reference services, and better support for faculty research within interdisciplinary fields. For example, a detailed analysis of citations by Library of Congress Classifications for resources related to tourism proved helpful in identifying types of material for purchase that otherwise may be overlooked and in getting a detailed sense of how interdisciplinary scholars do their intellectual work, thus allowing librarians to better understand and anticipate the future information needs of these scholars.[12]

ADVANTAGES OF FACULTY-LIBRARIAN PARTNERSHIPS

Because of their education and the daily need to keep up with technological changes in how information is stored, accessed, and processed, librarians offer a significant benefit to faculty researchers. Faculty skills in these newer areas may not be current with their own institution's and the library's online resources. Some of the information needed for research comes from laboratory experimentation and other forms of primary data collection, but much of it must come from existing information resources, and it is in this area that librarians and teaching faculty sometimes disagree about concepts of library use and research.[13] While librarians approach information through indexing systems, faculty tend to emphasize browsing and serendipitous discovery—an approach that is currently being challenged in the need to provide structured means for searching the vast information available online, because a search inquiry often results in thousands of citations that may be of little value to the scholar. Librarians' education makes them research strategists par excellence in locating and evaluating information for particular purposes. Moreover, the materials they supply the researcher contain bibliographies and references that can lead to further informed research. Working in a close partnership can stimulate librarians and researchers to recognize that their approaches to research are complementary, not mutually exclusive.

Incorporating librarians into the research process should yield a number of concrete advantages for all researchers, faculty, and students. Classroom faculty, for example, lack exposure to the wide range of available information that librarians must work with daily. Librarians who keep abreast of evolving information resources, tools, and services can help researchers take advantage of these valuable services. A closer relationship should facilitate better use of more traditional forms of information. For example, faculty are likely to largely overlook the usefulness of government publications in humanities research.[14]

Despite the continuous good track records of librarians in gathering and organizing information into a meaningful structure for research, what has always been missing is a vision of what a librarian's primary function in research could be. Generally, librarians are not seen as active agents in the research process despite their knowledge of the rapidly changing information base and their obvious mastery of the indexing controls of scholarly materials. Librarians play a limited role in the research of classroom faculty, and most do little or any research themselves.

Teaming with Librarians in Research

The benefits of cooperation between librarians and researchers—and the stumbling blocks in achieving it—have been documented as far back as 1985 in a book entitled *Information Specialist as Team Player in the Research Process*.[15] The author Julie Neway analyzes differing information habits of researchers from major discipline areas and describes a sizable number of projects in the United States and abroad in which information services were tailored to meet the needs of researchers in the social sciences, humanities, sciences, medicine, and business. Understanding differences in the types of information, research strategies, and communication patterns of researchers was found to be essential to the successful integration of librarians (information specialists) into research groups. Examples of both successful and unsuccessful programs and projects afford fruitful models for academic leaders interested in boosting faculty research productivity. Neway concludes that the "potential benefits of the information specialist as an active team member in the research process have only begun to be explored."[16] Her book is a useful guide to this exploration. The incentive to make such cooperative endeavors a priority is clear.

> When information specialists become part of the research team, they are able to provide the right information at the right time to the right person in the right manner. The computer search intermediary is one example of an effective buffer between the needs of the user and the ever-growing mass of information. The future role of the information specialist lies in continuing to find solutions to the current information overload. Information needs to be repackaged. The information specialist can act as a facilitator and negotiator by keeping the human element alive in the knowledge transfer process.[17]

Presidents and academic vice presidents who wish to increase research productivity on their campuses through more active involvement of librarians usually have some nearby models to draw on. In a growing number of research centers and hospitals, for example, librarians function as valuable members of research teams. As will be discussed in chapter 6, other even more ambitious models can be found in the business sector.

For example, one model of active librarian involvement in research is the clinical medical librarian (CML). CMLs participate in rounds or patient information conferences to identify information needs, then perform manual or online searches to find the needed materials. The benefits include "enhancement of patient care; physician, health care team, and medical student education; greater awareness of library services and resources; time saving for physician and health care team; exposure to a wider variety of journals; and information sharing among colleagues. The library gained increased visibility, which promoted library services."[18] In addition, social and behavioral scientists have found that "librarians, as those most knowledgeable about archival data, can undertake unobtrusive research with creativity and rigor."[19] This can be particularly helpful in confirming results obtained from research with human respondents.

All of these examples of librarians being aggressively involved in research activities are as possible in the academic as in the business environment. Implementing such models on campus, however, will require academic leadership both in promoting a new research role for librarians and in reallocating resources to allow greater participation by librarians in research. Time will show the degree to which campus research productivity can be increased by such changes, but there is no reason to believe that benefits should be any less than those found in the business sector.

Teaming to Support Undergraduate Research

Librarians partnering with faculty to support undergraduate research is also becoming more important as the complexities of information resources that challenge even faculty prove more intimidating to students. One study came to these conclusions about student research procedures.

> Students use research strategies that they perceive will reap the greatest benefits with the least cost in terms of time or social effort. The fact that students want to avoid interactions that they believe may be painful should not be surprising. Educators, however, should be aware of these perceptions and how they influence students' undergraduate experience. Perhaps students are inadvertently circumventing the very experience they are intended to gain. If factors such as the speed of the research process, a limited knowledge of reference tools, and fear of failure are determining students' approaches to writing research papers, they may be missing the point of the assignments. By using sources primarily because they are familiar and/or easy to use, students may bypass an avenue of research that will not only be more relevant, but also more productive.[20]

For campuses with freshman-level research courses, early introduction to information literacy skills is essential. For example, the University of Hawaii campus at Manoa has a Rainbow Advantage Program (RAP), which each spring showcases the outcomes of students' yearlong studies of the nature of scholarship and the research process as demonstrated in a service-learning project. "RAP students enrolled in the program's foundation courses during the fall semester and learned about scholarly processes and information literacy. They also were involved in service learning that placed them in community agencies as volunteers. During the spring semester, students formed research teams to design and execute their projects on behalf of the agencies for which they did their service learning."[21] Efforts such as this to develop students' information research skills at the beginning of their college experience lay the foundation for a more successful undergraduate performance all the way through senior theses or projects.

David W. Chapman, dean of the College of Arts and Sciences at Samford University, sees student research as a way of celebrating what we value most in academe and sees undergraduate research as quite different from graduate and faculty research. "Undergraduate research takes place not in the designer's showroom of new ideas, but in the bargain basement of existing materials and methods."[22] For this type of research, information literacy skills are essential.

LIBRARIANS AS RESEARCHERS

Just as research productivity can be enhanced by increasing librarians' support of faculty research efforts, productivity can also be enhanced by encouraging the contributions of librarians as independent researchers. Indeed, it can be argued that the potential of library-based research in support of campus priorities is only beginning to emerge, as evidenced in part by the fact that the Association of College & Research Libraries only held its first conference with refereed papers in 1978. These biannual conferences continue to encourage quality research endeavors, and by 1992, the Association of College & Research Libraries College Library Section had adopted a national research agenda. An analysis of the peer-reviewed research published in *College & Research Libraries* (C&RL) and *The Journal of Academic Librarianship* (JAL) between 1990 and 1999 found that the researchers did not address some of the areas defined in the research agenda, but that "articles on the research areas of collections and services, staffing, and the Internet occupy the major portion of the peer-reviewed sections of the C&RL and JAL."[23]

Academic librarians, whether or not they hold faculty status, have so far seldom been heavy researchers on their own initiative. They usually begin work after completing a master's degree and so have little research training. Librarians often hold twelve-month appointments, and the nature of their work creates heavier time demands than the average faculty time commitments of classroom teaching and student advising. On campuses that award librarians tenure, there are growing expectations for librarians' performance to include research and publications; however, the level of expectation tends to be lower than for classroom faculty for the reasons cited above. Because the library profession as a whole has not emphasized independent research, librarians generally expect to facilitate the research of others rather than undertake their own research agenda. Should they have ambitions as researchers, they typically lack institutional incentives and support in pursuing their research interests.

Operations and Service-Based Research

Although collectively, academic librarians do not have a noteworthy record as researchers, this situation is changing; increasingly, librarians are becoming actively involved in research despite the disincentives cited above. Historically, their efforts have usually focused on identifying disciplinary variations in faculty styles of research, translating variations in disciplinary research patterns into information literacy offerings, and organizing collections and services to reflect research needs and preferences.[24] Much of this research has focused on bibliometrics, which measures the use of publications according to methods that yield comparable results and produce outcomes useful for fine-tuning library acquisitions and services.

For example, while the emergence of bibliometrics is addressing some of these issues, efforts to date have been too few and too isolated to provide the guidance necessary to effectively match limited resources to evolving instructional and research demands. Based upon extensive experience as a collection officer in research university libraries, Charles B. Osburn did a scholarly analysis of changing patterns in academic research since World War II and their implications for collection management, which was published in 1979. He emphasized in his closing remarks that it is "imperative that selection decisions be based on the best information possible and on a solid understanding of research and scholarship so that the quality of resources available is the highest possible."[25] Such an effort would consist of a major, ongoing research agenda in and of itself; nonetheless, its importance increases as financial resources continue to shrink in relation to the size of the knowledge universe.

One recent research project involved a longitudinal citation study of foreign language use by humanities scholars. Outcomes of the research yielded practical guidance for information management. "Consistent levels of foreign-language citation from humanities scholars indicate a need for U.S. research libraries to continue to purchase foreign-language materials and to recruit catalogers and collection development specialists with foreign-language knowledge."[26] Another area requiring ongoing monitoring of researchers' needs is where technology-driven changes are occurring, and significant research has been undertaken to understand changing scholarly expectations.[27]

Few of these applied research projects can be adequately researched without involving librarians. This research agenda, which addresses issues directly related to the quality of research and instruction, awaits the attention of librarians with the time and administrative support to undertake research programs. The results should eventually provide a sound basis for library planning for both collection development and services. Reliable research should also provide a far more sensible basis for determining library allocations than a rule-of-thumb percentage of the institutional budget.

Another applied research area that can be used to enhance library services is to study the library resource and service needs of targeted populations. These studies lend themselves well to collaborative efforts between faculty in a particular discipline or student service personnel and librarians. What, for example, are the particular needs of distance education students[28] or education students in field placements distant from campus?[29] Or a study might focus on information-seeking patterns within local government done in collaboration with city or county agencies to undergird a possible community outreach effort,[30] or a study done of the information needs of local small businesses as a prelude to initiating an economic development effort. (See chapter 6 for examples of library-based services to businesses.)

Expanding Research Questions

There are many other issues that require research. Starting in the 1930s, faculty at the University of Chicago Graduate Library School addressed questions that have taken on new urgency with the growing concern for adult literacy and higher literacy skills. What, for example, are the social effects of reading?[31] As the newer media eclipse reading for many people, what will be the new place of the printed word?[32] Since then, the list of questions has grown. How do the characteristics of documents (format, length, language, age) affect their usefulness?[33] How does the use of information vary by discipline? How are changes in the scholarship of the various disciplines affecting library holdings and services?[34] While much study is still needed regarding these questions, today's technology and information explosion realities have greatly expanded the areas needing research. These concerns are often highlighted in *The Chronicle of Higher Education* under topics ranging from the need to understand "the networked world"[35] to the need to "begin comprehensive investigations of the current and long-term impacts of the Internet."[36] Certainly, librarians would be good partners in such interdisciplinary research projects.

Another major area for research concerns the costs of lack of information and of not having an information-literate workforce. A 2001 study by a leading information industry research and advisory firm, which analyzed 6,300 knowledge workers in 20 different industries, reported the following.

> Employees spend an average of 8 hours a week, or 16% of their work-week, looking for and using external information content. The salary cost alone to American business is $107 billion a year. "There's a significant opportunity to companies to enable their employees to be more efficient and effective at putting the external information to work for them," said [Outsell's vice president, Mary] Corcoran. "Most knowledge workers rate themselves as very adept or skilled using on-line or Web-based information products, yet they've received little or no formal instruction on information skills."[37]

Better understanding of how effectively campus personnel are using information resources might also be illuminating given how much time they spend processing information. In 1998, an international survey documented scholars spending "approximately 43% of their office hours [based on a 45-hour work week] on working on the Net, and 57% on paper-based and face-to-face activities."[38]

Just what is the cost of low information literacy skills among faculty? This seems an appropriate question to ask since a 2002 extensive study of faculty and students found that almost 90 percent of researchers start online first, although they trust more in print resources.

> The study also looked at library-use patterns. Undergraduates said they spent a third of their study time in the library and half of their study time at home. In a finding that surprised the researchers, faculty members said they spent only 10 percent of their work time in the library; 85 percent of the time, they worked in their office or at home.
>
> Thirty-five percent of the respondents said they use the library "significantly less" than they did two years ago. The figure was higher, at 43 percent, among faculty members.[39]

Information Literacy Research

Although there are many research opportunities that are particularly well suited for librarians, by far the greatest increase in their research activity centers around information literacy issues. Indeed, the volume of this output has been so large as to elicit further research on the amount and focus of this new field. One major study identifies nine clusters of topics in information literacy research:

- Development and evaluation of information literacy programs,
- Student information seeking and behavior in context,
- Information literacy as a generic skill or graduation attribute,
- Transfer of skills from formal education to the workplace,
- Need for information technology skills,
- Development of effective information literacy programs,
- Information use and behavior in workplace context,
- Use of information and communication technology, and
- Information access for social action.[40]

While most of the literature on information literacy is based within United States higher education institutions, the amount of research in other countries is also growing. Australia has produced an impressive amount of information literacy research and clearly has been the leader in research into the manifestation of information literacy abilities in the workplace. The first major research publication on this topic was authored by an Australian, Dr. Christine Bruce, entitled *The Seven Faces of Information Literacy*.[41] Published in 1997, the study analyzed the different information literacy abilities required by people working in higher education. Since then, the research methodology has been replicated for other professions such as auditors, engineers, health care professionals, and lawyers.[42] Such research provides valuable insights into how information literacy programs should be customized within the various disciplines.

Bruce's *Seven Faces* was an outgrowth of her dissertation, and information literacy is now the focus of a growing number of doctoral dissertations in the United States. Topics have ranged from seventh-grade students' search behavior to an assessment of information literacy skills among graduating teacher education majors. Nor have all been by librarians. Dr. Lana Jackman, who approached the topic from her background in student services at Lesley University in Boston, wrote a dissertation focusing on information literacy as an issue of equity for minority students.[43]

CREATING NEW KNOWLEDGE PRODUCTS

This chapter would not be complete without noting one more area of scholarly collaboration among discipline-based faculty and librarians, an area that is both research-based and that facilitates the research of countless other scholars. Such partnerships are being undertaken to provide structure and ease of access to information on a particular subject for communities of scholars. These can range from two-person undertakings to large multi-institutional efforts. The following list is a very small sample of such endeavors.

- "Santa Clara University's Diversity Web Site Project. In this collaborative initiative, two faculty members and a librarian collaborated to create a Web site of local ethnic resources to provide information and teaching resources to a variety of constituencies, including the core curriculum, the Freshman Residential Community, the Ethnic Studies Program, and community users. The neighboring city of San José is 24 percent Hispanic, 23 percent Asian, and 4 percent African American. The Diversity Project provides universal access—through the Internet—to the cultural richness of the Silicon Valley, while supporting the multicultural emphasis in the curriculum of Santa Clara University."[44]

- "Case Studies in Science: A Workshop and National Clearinghouse. This ambitious collaborative project from the State University of New York at Buffalo has been designed to help undergraduate science faculty teach with active learning techniques, especially case studies. It features a grant-funded, five-day workshop on case study methodology and a Web site created as a national clearinghouse for case studies in science."[45]

- The SLAC and DESY Partnership. This partnership, which has existed for almost three decades, was "begun by the Stanford Linear Accelerator Center (SLAC) and the Deutsches Elektronen-Synchrotron (DESY) libraries—and later joined by universities in Great Britain, Japan, and the former Soviet Republic—to collect, organize, and provide access to particle physics research information. . . . The partnership's first goal was quite traditional, to identify, organize, and provide access to the prepublication literature of the fields of particle and accelerator physics. . . . This list eventually became a full-fledged bibliographic database."[46]

- Annual Review of Particle Physics Research. This partnership between a SLAC faculty member and a librarian has grown into "a full-fledged review of the past year's research findings and an overview of trends in the field. The annual top-cited list, and all-time top-cited compilation, along with the faculty member's review, are all published on the SLAC library's Web site and advertised by the library on its Web pages and on appropriate electronic lists."[47]

- The Tree of Life. "The Tree of Life is an ambitious, collaborative Web project to building [sic] an encyclopedic resource on the phylogeny and biodiversity of all species. Organized in a cross-referenced taxonomy, the content is peer-reviewed and continually expanded and updated by scholars from around the world. Over 350 biologists have already created 2,600 pages of content that are managed through a system produced by programmers and metadata librarians. It seems relevant to note that a librarian served as Co-Principal Investigator on this project."[48]
- GROW. "The Geotechnical, Rock and Water Resources Library (GROW) introduces students of all ages to civil engineering through the development, collection, and dissemination of reviewed and ranked interactive learning resources continually enhanced by new technological innovations. GROW was created by a team of civil engineers, librarians, and computing professionals."[49]

These projects indicate the breadth of possibilities for joint library and scholarly efforts to achieve goals that both solve specific problems in a community and bring benefits beyond the original intent of the project.

WHAT ACADEMIC LEADERS CAN DO

We hope the case has been made for the importance of librarians moving beyond gathering and organizing information into a meaningful structure for research. Yes, librarians' expertise is still needed to streamline campus research efforts by efficiently and effectively filtering the abundance of existing information to select only relevant and useful material for advancing the specific research project.[50] But beyond this traditional role, moving librarians into research partnerships with faculty and into independent research of their own will require that academic administrators include appropriate provision for librarians in official campus policies and procedures concerning research. For example, campus incentives such as faculty research awards should be open to librarians as well, and librarians should be eligible for membership on campus research committees. Flexible schedules could provide blocks of time away from the reference desk and other service-demand activities. Mini-research sabbaticals of a week or more could allow librarians to pursue agreed-upon research efforts, and librarians could be given sabbaticals or administrative leave according to institutional guidelines for faculty. Ten-month contracts would be a good option for librarians who evidence a particular commitment to and ability for research. Faculty development activities are important in helping librarians enhance their research capabilities, to learn how best to incorporate writing projects into demanding service schedules, and to boost their motivation. For the most part, librarians and classroom faculty have similar ways of coping with pressures to publish. It would seem, therefore, that any successful effort to support one group might well prove beneficial to the other. Finally, research should be a factor in considering faculty status for librarians.

Presidents, provosts, and academic vice presidents could also encourage dialogue among librarians and faculty interested in the issues cited above by informal suggestions to deans and faculty. On campuses where such research is already in progress, administrators can highlight these cooperative endeavors at research forums and on other appropriate occasions. They can encourage the library dean to foster interest in research, and they can work with the dean in facilitating any organizational changes this will require. If faculty are skeptical about accepting librarians as part of research teams, academic leaders could use faculty development programs to educate researchers about the potential benefits of such partnerships. Incentives could also encourage faculty to at least try this approach. For example, junior faculty research grants qualifications could include provision of extra credit for building a partnership with a librarian.

Clearly, if library staffs are already stretched thin, not much research will be possible through internal shifts within the library. However, where good plans for increasing librarians' research activities have been developed, a reasonably modest infusion of funds could finance a significant jump in campus research productivity. The cost of hiring clerical staff to relieve librarians of routine tasks is a relatively small investment to enhance research productivity, and it will make possible a more effective use of librarians' talents. It is a far better investment than increasing secretarial support for researchers, for it will increase both the quantity *and* quality of faculty research.

Working in close cooperation with their library deans, academic leaders need to develop an integrated plan for bringing classroom and library faculty together into partnerships that will benefit both parties and enhance campuswide research. Ideally, the administrative staff of the library, starting with the dean, should provide role models by pursuing their own research interests; library administrators need to analyze the workload of librarians committed to research to determine which responsibilities could be transferred to clerical staff, freeing time for their research. In these ways, academic leaders could support the opportunity for American higher education to be at the forefront of the global research community.

NOTES

1. Frank Newman, *Higher Education and the American Resurgence* (Princeton, N.J.: Princeton University Press, 1985), 112.

2. Ibid., 121.

3. Association of Research Libraries, *The Changing System of Scholarly Communication* (Washington, D.C.: ARL, 1986), 2.

4. Leila M. Hover, "The Independent Learner and the Academic Library: Access and Impact," in *New Horizons for Academic Libraries*, ed. Robert D. Stueart and Richard D. Johnson (New York: K. G. Saur, 1979), 545–49.

5. Vincent Kiernan, "Professors Are Unhappy with Limitations of Online Resources, Survey Finds," *The Chronicle of Higher Education* 50 (30 April 2004): A34.

6. Ibid.

7. Caroline Coughlin and Pamela Snelson, "Searching for Research in ACRL Conference Papers," *The Journal of Academic Librarianship* 9 (March 1983): 21–26.

8. W. Bede Mitchell and L. Stanislava Swieszkowski, "Publication Requirements and Tenure Approval Rates: An Issue for Academic Librarians," *College & Research Libraries* 46 (May 1985): 249–55.

9. Carolyn Kleiner, "Why the Walls Are Quickly Tumbling Down," *U.S. News & World Report* 127 (30 August 1999): 68–70.

10. Vartan Gregorian, "Colleges Must Reconstruct the Unity of Knowledge," *The Chronicle of Higher Education* 50 (4 June 2004): B14.

11. Lisa McNamara and Rachel Matre, "Interdisciplinary Research: The Role of the Reference Librarian," *Texas Library Journal* 78 (spring 2002): 71.

12. Juris Dilevko and Keren Dali, "Improving Collection Development and Reference Services for Interdisciplinary Fields through Analysis of Citation Patterns: An Example Using Tourism Studies," *College & Research Libraries* 65 (May 2004): 216.

13. Stephen K. Stoan, "Research and Library Skills: An Analysis and Interpretation," *College & Research Libraries* 45 (March 1984): 99–109.

14. Barbara J. Ford and Yuri Nakata, "Government Publications in Humanistic Research and Scholarship," in *New Horizons for Academic Libraries*, ed. Robert D. Stueart and Richard D. Johnson (New York: K. G. Saur, 1979), 445–49.

15. Julie M. Neway, *Information Specialist as Team Player in the Research Process* (Westport, Conn.: Greenwood Press, 1985).

16. Ibid., 162.

17. Ibid., 158.

18. Kay Cimpl, "Clinical Medical Librarianship: A Review of the Literature," *Bulletin of the Medical Library Association* 73 (January 1985): 24–26.

19. "Footnotes," *The Chronicle of Higher Education* 32 (April 9, 1986): 6.

20. Barbara Valentine, "Undergraduate Research Behavior: Using Focus Groups to Generate Theory," *The Journal of Academic Librarianship* 19 (November 1993): 304.

21. Margit Watts, e-mail correspondence to Patricia Breivik, 13 July 2004.

22. David W. Chapman, "Undergraduate Research: Showcasing Young Scholars," *The Chronicle of Higher Education* 50 (12 September 2003): B5.

23. Xue-Ming Bao, "An Analysis of the Research Areas of the Articles Published in C&RL and JAL between 1990 and 1999," *College & Research Libraries* 61(November 2000): 536–44. Retrieved 1 April 2005 from WilsonWeb database.

24. Herbert C. Morton and Sharon J. Rogers, "Fostering Research," in *Libraries and the Search for Academic Excellence*, ed. Patricia Senn Breivik and Robert Wedgeworth (Metuchen, N.J.: Scarecrow Press, 1988), 93–104.

25. Charles B. Osburn, *Academic Research and Library Resources* (Westport, Conn.: Greenwood Press, 1979), 148.

26. Charlene Kellsey and Jennifer E. Knievel, "Global English in the Humanities? A Longitudinal Citation Study of Foreign-Language Use by Humanities Scholars," *College & Research Libraries* 65 (May 2004): 194.

27. Amy Friedlander, *Dimensions and Use of the Scholarly Information Environment* (Washington, D.C.: Digital Library Federation and Council on Library and Information Resources, 2002). Retrieved 1 March 2004 from http://www.clir.org/pubs/reports/pub110/contents.html.

28. Evadne McLean and Stephen H. Dew, "Assessing the Library Needs and Preferences of Off-Campus Students," *Journal of Library Administration* 41, no.1/2 (2004): 265–302.

29. Martha Henderson, "Collaborative Activities with Faculty: Grant Writing, Action Research, and Scholarly Activities," in *A Guide to the Management of Curriculum Materials Center for the 21st Century: The Promise and the Challenge*, ed. Jo Ann Carr (Chicago: Association of College and Research Libraries, 2001), 129–36.

30. Cheol H. Oh, "Information Searching in Governmental Bureaucracies: An Integrated Model," *American Review of Public Administration* 26 (March 1996): 41–70.

31. Douglas Waples, Bernard Berelson, and Franklyn R. Bradshaw, *What Reading Does to People: A Summary of the Evidence on the Social Effects of Reading and a Statement of Problems for Research* (Chicago: University of Chicago Press, 1940).

32. Waples, Berelson, and Bradshaw, "What Reading Does to People," in *Research in the Three R's*, ed. C.W. Hunnecutt and William J. Iverson (New York: Harper & Brothers, 1958), 10–17.

33. Council on Library Resources, *Twenty-Ninth Annual Report* (Washington, D.C.: Council on Library Resources, 1985), 10.

34. Sue Stone, "Humanities Scholars: Information Needs and Uses," *Journal of Documentation* 38 (December 1982): 292–313.

35. Duncan J. Watts, "Unraveling the Mysteries of the Connected Age," *The Chronicle of Higher Education* 49 (14 February 2003): B7–B9.

36. Jeffrey Cole, "Now Is the Time to Start Studying the Internet Age," *The Chronicle of Higher Education* 50 (2 April 2004): B18.

37. "Outsell, Inc., Releases Findings Analyzing Content Habits, Preferences and Budgets of More Than 6,300 Information End Users," press release, 3 May 2001. Retrieved 29 March 2005 from http://www.outsellinc.com/outsell/press%20room/pr_release/pr20010503_01.htm.

38. T. M. Ciolek, *The Scholarly Uses of the Internet: 1998 Online Survey.* Retrieved 29 March 2005 from http://www.ciolek.com/PAPERS/InternetSurvey-98.html.

39. Scott Carlson, "Students and Faculty Members Turn First to Online Library Materials, Study Finds," *The Chronicle of Higher Education* 49 (18 October 2002): A37.

40. Sylvia Edwards, Christine Bruce, and Lynn McAllister, *Information Literacy Research: The Consolidation of a Theme.* Draft provided by Christine Bruce in e-mail correspondence to Patricia Breivik, 8 September 2004.

41. Christine Bruce, *The Seven Faces of Information Literacy* (Adelaide: Auslib Press, 1997).

42. Bonnie Wai-yi Cheuk, "Modelling the Information Seeking and Use Process in the Workplace: Employing Sense-Making Approach," *Information Research* 4 (October 1998). Retrieved on 29 March 2005 from http://informationr.net/ir/4-2/isic/cheuk.html; and Gloria J. Leckie, Karen E. Pettigrew, and Christian Sylvain, "Modeling the Information Seeking of Professionals: A General Model Derived from Research on Engineers, Health Care Professionals, and Lawyers," *Library Quarterly* 66 (1996): 161–93.

43. Lana Webb Jackman, "Information Literacy: An Issue of Equity for New Majority Student," (Ph.D. diss., Lesley University, 1999).

44. Dick Raspa and Dane Ward, *The Collaborative Imperative: Librarians and Faculty Working Together in the Information Universe* (Chicago: Association of College and Research Libraries, 2000), 104. http://www.scu.edu/diversity/scvgroup.html.

45. Ibid., 99. http://ublib.buffalo.edu/libraries/projects/cases/case.html.

46. Patricia A. Kreitz, "Librarians as Knowledge Builders: Strategic Partnering for Service and Advocacy," *C&RL News* 65 (January 2004). Retrieved 10 March 2004 from http://www.ala.org. http://www.slac.stanford.edu/spires/hep/.

47. Ibid. http://www.slac.stanford.edu/library/topcites/.

48. Joseph M. Brewer et al., "Libraries Dealing with the Future Now," ARL Bimonthly Report 234, June 2004. Retrieved 24 June 2004 from http://www.arl.org/newsltr/234/dealing.html. http://tolweb.org/tree/.

49. Ibid. http://www.grow.arizona.edu/.

50. Evelyn H. Daniel, "Educating the Academic Librarian for a New Role as Information Resources Manager," *The Journal of Academic Librarianship* 11 (January 1986): 362.

CHAPTER 5

Enhancing Service to the Community

Service has long been accepted as the third major purpose of higher education institutions, though it usually trails far behind instruction and research. The reasons for a public academic institution to build active ties with its local community—particularly the local business community—form an interconnected chain. Identifying and providing needed services can strengthen the local economy and/or the civic or cultural environment. Better understanding and appreciation, particularly of the campus role in supporting economic development, can increase political support, which in turn improves the chances of adequate funding at the state level.

Even private universities have learned the mutual benefits of being a good neighbor. For example, David Adamany, while president of Wayne State University, spoke to the important link between the research efforts of private universities and their urban surroundings.

> The traditional research mission of universities is so closely allied to the service role of universities in urban settings that the door is now flung wide for a much more prominent urban role for those traditional universities that are *in*, but not *of*, our urban areas. It is the research connection, not the student body, that empowers the Penns, the Harvards, the Columbias, and their kin to play a role in urban life that they would formerly not have considered or been well fitted to.[1]

ROLE OF LIBRARIES IN COMMUNITY SERVICE

There is a longstanding tradition on some campuses, such as those at land grant universities, for libraries to play an intrinsic part of campus outreach efforts.

> Since its inception, outreach has been one of the primary components of the mission of the land grant university. In keeping with this, an essential role of the reference librarian at the land grant university is in the area of outreach to diverse constituencies. Because the state land grant university is the people's university, that is, it functions to make education and its products accessible to everyone, the constituencies served by the land grant university library include all citizens of the state. Although students and faculty are the primary clientele of the land grant university, and even though extension agents exist to serve many of the information needs of state citizens, all citizens are entitled to services from the library, and hence, librarians, at the land grant university because it is a state public service institution.[2]

Beyond land grant missions and libraries' support for urban research, service considerations should also address the problem documented in chapter 3—poor information literacy—for it is also a challenge in this service function of higher education. Many business people have little awareness of how to access information beyond using a popular search engine, and they know even less about how to evaluate and use information effectively. Few people in the business sector—even those with college degrees—are truly information literate. While many of them may have used an academic library during their schooling, their experiences did not prepare them to efficiently use local libraries or online resources for practical business needs. This lack of preparedness is another grassroots manifestation of the national problems caused by the information explosion. The solution must come from within academe and, in particular, from libraries.

Just as corporations have been encouraged to share their resources with higher education institutions, academia is challenged to make a commitment to share its resources with the corporate world.[3] Since innovation, economic vitality, and trade all depend on the generation and use of relevant, accurate information, among the most valuable resources that academic institutions have to offer the corporate world are their libraries and the expertise of their librarians. Having the library open to the public is not enough, for the "problem generally is not lack of information, but inefficient communication, accessibility, organization and feedback."[4] Providing for the effective use of libraries within the business community requires an understanding of users' needs, an educational/ public relations effort, and cooperation with other information resources in the area.

In view of the fact that the number of campus-sponsored service-learning programs has grown significantly over the last decade, this chapter will give some consideration to the role of libraries in these community-based activities. For the most part, however, it will focus on the contributions that academic libraries are making or could make in promoting economic development. This chapter will describe a number of successful library-based efforts to serve the business community and thereby enhance both community/campus relations and, in some cases, state or regional economic development. The initiative to provide needed services may come from the library itself, but the most comprehensive and ambitious efforts will, of course, require presidential leadership as part of a campuswide effort.

UNDERSTANDING AND ADDRESSING BUSINESS NEEDS

The need of business and industry to access information for problem-solving and decision-making is well established. Increasingly, these needs are being articulated not only in terms of general university support but also in terms of access to and the ability to effectively use academic research collections.

The Underlying Need for Information Literacy

The place of the United States in international affairs depends upon timely access to information, and the greatest source of needed information resides in our country's research libraries. This is true for the whole continuum of business firms, but perhaps the greatest need is found in small businesses, that are the backbone of economic development both locally and nationally. Victor Rosenberg, a professor in the School of Information at the University of Michigan, summarizes the situation.

> Information Literacy, as variously defined, has the same characteristic distribution as conventional literacy. While there are those who are exceptionally information literate, knowing the appropriate sources of information in almost any field, there are those who are at the bottom of the scale and might be termed the information il-

literate. Between the extremes are the vast majority of people who have some access to information and some knowledge of how to use the information in their work. The question becomes how much information literacy is necessary to function in the modern economy and how do we measure that literacy?

The need for increased information literacy is magnified for the employees of small businesses because small or medium sized businesses typically do not have the resources to compartmentalize the information gathering and use functions, nor do they have the resources to construct the infrastructure necessary to access and use the information. So the need for information literacy in small and medium sized enterprises (SMEs) is arguably higher for most employees than in larger corporations and organizations.[5]

Rosenberg points out that "often small businesses would like to plan, but do not have the luxury of resources that can be used for long-term strategic planning. The best avenue is to use available information to gain strategic advantage, and this should be the focus of the curricula of most business schools."[6] Unfortunately, many schools of business do not as yet ensure that their graduates master information literacy abilities; and, of course, many small business owners and employees do not have business degrees. Academic libraries could address this need either independently or by working with small business centers or with business schools.

Understanding the Needs of Business for Library Services

To serve the business community successfully, librarians will need new marketing skills plus a clear understanding of the information requirements of each business's clientele.[7] One of the first things to understand is that the business consumer is unsentimental. "Information has value in direct proportion to the control it provides him over what he is and what he can become."[8]

Another important key in responding to any business information need is convenience. Even when business people appreciate the value of information, time is money; and the more conveniently information can be provided, the more likely it is to be used. For example, a service that could meet the convenience criterion is to answer business reference questions over the phone and/or by e-mail. Some campuses—often in collaboration with other libraries—now offer 24/7 reference services for campus personnel. With adequate support, these services could be made available to respond to the information needs of the business community and thereby offer a valuable and highly visible form of service by the campus library.

One model we suggested in our earlier book is to actually conduct the research for the companies on some kind of retainer or fee basis and/or provide document delivery. It would have been logical to have expected that the growth of the Internet would have negated the market for such services; but in fact, campuses have found a good niche that continues to be successful. Success may, however, be best measured not by the income achieved but by enhanced campus visibility and relationships with alumni, nearby businesses, local government agencies, and other key groups and individuals. In addition, such services frequently relieve stress on the reference department and provide some flexible funding.[9] Some see such services "as a bridge between academia and the business world . . . so that the university isn't just going out and fundraising but can point to this as one of the services that are offered to the community."[10]

Fee-Based Services

A 2000 survey by the Association of Research Libraries regarding fee-based services determined that the most heavily used services were "photocopying and delivery of journal articles, reports, and book chapters followed by loaning of books and other materials."[11] The survey analysis concluded:

> Fee-based services are exploring a variety of unique library services with varying degrees of success. With continued experimentation, fee-based services can effectively serve as a way of meeting existing demand for library services from external users, generating income for the library, and establishing new library service models for all users. In the process, these services will help reinvent and shape the library of the future. Collectively, fee-based services now reach a significant number of users who would otherwise be underserved or not served at all.[12]

Two good examples of long-established fee-based services are located at the University of Colorado Technical Research Center (CTRC), established in 1976, and the Technical Information Service (TIS) at Purdue University, established in 1987. The CTRC advertises itself as providing "the data and the documents that companies need to make informed business decisions. CTRC offers expertise in researching industry and market trends, competitive intelligence, emerging technologies, and patent and trademark searches."[13] Today, it "continues to be a successful, full-service, self-funding unit," but it has seen a significant shift in customer demands from literature searching (pre-Internet days) to now a 70 percent document delivery and 30 percent custom research operations.[14] Purdue's TIS also provides both document delivery and research services for scientific, technical, and management information needs, with clients from around the world.[15]

Smaller academic libraries are also offering fee-based services. It took the University of Nevada at Las Vegas a while to find its niche, but it now has two successful services. It provides trademark and service mark searches, and, through its IGT Gaming Resource Center, provides information to the gaming industry, including regularly offering seminars in gaming regulation and casino management.[16]

COLLABORATIONS THAT WORK

Today, one of the most exciting models of libraries directly supporting business development is in Singapore. The National Library Board (NLB) of Singapore has as its mission "to expand the learning capacity of the nation so as to enhance our national competitiveness and to promote a gracious society,"[17] and it provides an interesting example of what some academic libraries could do independently or in conjunction with other units (e.g., the business college) on campus.

> The NLB of Singapore has received national and international recognition for developing and operating innovative and creative business initiatives. . . . Two of its innovative business initiatives tap librarian skills of research and content management. "Ask Stupid Questions" is a consultancy where NLB librarians are hired to conduct retreats and workshops for organizations, corporations and others. The idea is to "brain dance" and "stretch targets" far beyond simple business or work plans, then suppose the real leaps of organization and technology it would take to reach the target. The NLB librarians follow up with research and prepare relevant briefs to help the clients reach their stretch targets. Clients and librarians credit the professional preparation of the briefs for the success of this program. Another innovative program is called Aspiration Pathfinder where librarians and partners from education, technology, arts and other fields conduct 3-day programs that take a client group into completely new territory: businessmen on an archeological dig, en-

gineers to the theatre, etc. The librarians, again, provide relevant and professional information packages that are designed like travel guidebooks. And again, it is the librarian prepared briefs that make these "tours" attractive and valued. Both programs are self-supporting, earn recognition for innovation and are a cause of pride and enthusiasm for the more than 20 librarians and the institution.[18]

Another interesting service collaboration operates at University College Dublin, where its Developmental Studies Library (DSL) "holds an extensive collection of books, reports, and journals on development issues. In existence since 1986, it holds almost 5,000 books and subscribes to more than 170 journal titles. This excellent research centre was initially established by UCD and the Department of Foreign Affairs. It promotes quality research and acts as a national focus for development information. Today the DSL is supported by the National Committee for Development Education and by Ireland Aid."[19]

Within the United States, the Johns Hopkins library stands out as being the most entrepreneurial of academic libraries. Few libraries could duplicate what it has done, but it should serve as an inspiration for campuses that are willing to think beyond service commitments to their primary clientele to creatively and ambitiously engage in fee-based services. From the beginning, the focus was on generating revenue for the libraries, and the initial undertaking was to design, implement, and manage virtual library services for the virtual university.[20] The resultant Entrepreneurial Library Program (ELP) (http://www.library.jhu.edu/departments/elp/) became the basis for other fee-based services—the first being for alumni.

> Thus began a new partnership between the libraries and the Development Office that is already paying big dividends for both. Together our offices developed a questionnaire to be sent to a large sampling of alumni, testing interest in general and specific electronic resources—as well as willingness to pay. The overwhelmingly enthusiastic response was more surprising to the Alumni Office than to the libraries, but it was sufficient to induce the Alumni Office to pay ELP all of its costs for developing and implementing the alumni online library and to agree to a 50-50 share of any profits. I am happy to report that, less than a year after our first conversation about the project, our beta site for 5,000 alumni went live on Monday. Through "Hopkins Knowledgenet" *all* alumni will have free access to a huge array of electronic resources—books, newspapers, and jour-

nals, including all the journals published through Project Muse. Additionally, for a fee of only $125 annually, alumni can have access to every electronic resource we have available for faculty and enrolled students as well as reference assistance (via email or phone) from ELP librarians.[21]

One almost immediate benefit of this service to alumni was an increase in contributions designated for the libraries. In addition, these ELP-based experiences have led to the establishment of two other fee-based services.

One is providing contract information services to the corporate sector, primarily in the Baltimore-Washington region that is full of small entrepreneurial companies particularly in the info-tech and bio-tech fields—such as the Consumer Health Research Report Service. For these companies, ELP is in effect becoming their out-of-house special library, offering customized information profiling for clients, competitive intelligence, and other information. The second is Hopkins Personal Librarian, a name ELP has trademarked, which offers in-depth research to individuals (not Hopkins students!) on an ad hoc basis or as part of one of our other virtual library services. The experience gained by ELP has also been indispensable to us in planning library services for the Hopkins faculty who are engaged in face-to-face teaching but in geographically dispersed areas.[22]

While such fee-for-service models are worth considering by campuses committed to partnering with their communities to promote economic development, the increasing body of literature on knowledge management (see chapter 6) suggests that information literacy workforce training opportunities might well be the more timely and appropriate approach to take in promoting economic development.

INFORMATION LITERACY IN LIBRARY OUTREACH SERVICES

A useful approach to addressing the lack of information literacy abilities in employees of business and government is for librarians to work with members of the targeted organizations to determine specific information needs and then to develop seminars, workshops, or programs on improving the business community's access to information. The librarian might open by commenting on the implications of the information age and presenting statistics on information resources of interest to the group being addressed. This could be followed by a short presentation on how better access to information can help the organization be more productive. The bulk of the presentation should consist of case studies of actual problems. For each problem, the librarian should explain to the group what useful information they can find in the library, in addition to what is available from the Internet in their offices. The contracts for many online databases allow public use within the library but are not available offsite except at high costs; and, where appropriate, this needs to be explained.

Practical Applications by University Libraries

Responding to indications of local needs, some university libraries are providing training support to government and business personnel. For example, the first outreach efforts to local government by Purdy/Kresge librarians at Wayne State University were "a series of six half day seminars for members of the Detroit City Council Research and Analysis Department":

> These seminars introduced the participants to the information resources available in Purdy/Kresge and other [campus] libraries. Participants also learned effective techniques for locating economic, social, legal and business information using print and electronic library tools, and for accessing government documents and statistical data over the Internet. . . . Responses from the participants were enthusiastic and especially gratifying for the instructors involved as they almost universally requested even more information on the subjects and more time to practice what had been learned. Kathie Dones-Carson, Director of the Research and Analysis Department, commented that her staff "came back very enthusiastic about the training sessions, especially the Internet. They are reinvigorated."[23]

Such training can also take place as targeted opportunities within the campus curriculum. Librarians at the Transportation Library (TL) at Northwestern University in Evanston, Illinois, provide information literacy training and reference services to police officer students at the School of Police Staff and Command (SPSC) Traffic Institute. In the adult learner situation, this was their approach:

> One of the major underlying philosophies in the SPSC program is to foster in the participants the idea that skills that they acquire are not only useful for writing their research paper but of paramount importance when they return to work. The Transportation Library has

a very special relationship with the law enforcement community and encourages the students to continue using the library and its services even after they graduate. By the same token, the library continues to provide reference and document delivery services, by phone, email and onsite, on request. Students are told to recommend TL and its services to their colleagues—even to those who did not attend the program. So the librarians have two complementary goals in serving the students in the program—the immediate goal of assisting them in gathering materials for their research paper and the long-term goal of exposing the law enforcement officers to the wealth of library and information tools for future research projects.[24]

The University of Akron Libraries (UAL) has also creatively responded to the information needs of its students and graduates. Its outreach program partners with nearby nonprofit organizations to enhance library resources and services in the urban region. In Akron, they established a Corporate Services Center (CSC), and their efforts included the following:

> To pool collections when possible and create a union catalogue of holdings in the UAL online catalogue; to build and enhance science and engineering holdings by combining purchasing power through functioning as a unique consortium of academic and corporate libraries; to become recognized as a center for science and technology, and related engineering disciplines; to look for cooperative ways to provide materials resources to researchers, either through access tools or document delivery of materials; and finally . . . to establish a "library for one's working life" for those from the area who go to the school in the area and work as researchers on behalf of industries in the area.[25]

Of particular concern was how to establish "educational support services as well as research and self-education opportunities for those students (particularly graduate students) who go on to work in the various profit-centered companies."[26]

> The idea of the CSC was to bridge the gap, that is, make the transition from school to work transparent by finding ways to provide the same levels of research support that students enjoyed in the workplace. For students, the benefits are obvious. They can depend on familiar databases, search engines, pertinent books and journals that they already know, and the reliance on bibliographic search

skills of trained librarians. For the corporations, the gains should be in the quality of research done in the laboratories and on the fundamental business building blocks that applied research can generate for them. For the university, among other things, there would be the recognition of the connection between a sound education from this particular institution and the quality of life of its graduates. The likelihood of students returning to UA, sending their children there, or recommending to others that they do so could be high—an obvious boon to any university, and to UA in particular. In short, there are positive advantages to everyone to pursue such a goal.[27]

Practical Applications by Community College Libraries

Nor should it be thought that such services can only be offered by university libraries. In North Carolina, the Carteret Community College (CCC) has played an active part in attracting business to Morehead City.

> CCC is one of the first community colleges to have a Small Business Center (SBC), and the first where the library and the SBC actively cooperate to provide business information.
>
> When the Department of Community Colleges created the SBCs, it stipulated that each center must provide business information services. The library director at CCC saw this as an opportunity to develop a program which has become a model duplicated by other community colleges in North Carolina. He suggested to the SBC director that the library provide electronic business information services and that the SBC use its funding to provide small business programming.[28]

The ability of CCC to provide needed information was credited by Bally Engineering Structures, Inc., president and chief executive officer Tom Pietrocini as one of the key factors in relocating its headquarters to Morehead City.[29]

The resources and services of one academic library have placed it in the center of moviemaking and tourism. Fleming A. Thomas, director of libraries for Northwestern State University of Louisiana, explains it this way:

> Next to New Orleans, the small city of Natchitoches is probably the most tourist-conscious city in Louisiana due to its historical background. It was founded in 1714, which makes it older than New Orleans and the oldest city in the entire Louisiana Purchase; around 1990 it became clear that tourism, which now contributes approxi-

mately $60,000,000 to the economy of Natchitoches, was going to become one of our primary industries.

In this context a role for the Cammie G. Henry Research Center, a department of Watson Library, to support the tourist ambience of Natchitoches in several ways became clear and focused as the following three examples illustrate.

In 1988, the film *Steel Magnolias* was produced and filmed here in Natchitoches (the author, Robert Harling, is a native of Natchitoches). Personnel of the Research Center provided all of the background information about Natchitoches, especially photographic information. The resulting publicity from the nationwide showing of the film was enormous, and to this day tourists travel to Natchitoches looking for scenes shown in the film.

Second, the . . . [re]discovered American author, Kate Chopin, lived much of her life about twenty miles to the south of Watson Library in the small village of Cloutierville. The Cammie Henry Research Center probably has the best collection of primary material about Chopin anywhere, and scholars from all over the country come to Natchitoches to research Kate Chopin's life.

Third, the Cane River Creole National Historical Park was created in 1994, in an effort to preserve the six antebellum plantation homes along the Cane River as part of our national heritage, and to make certain these invaluable records of our past do not deteriorate further. Most of the information about the plantations is available only in the Cammie Henry Research Center, and it is used extensively and almost daily by Park personnel. Needless to say, the plantations are perhaps the most significant year-round tourist attractions, and this has led to employment opportunities for parish residents, particularly painters, carpenters, and landscape gardeners skilled in preserving the historical integrity of the landscape and architecture.

The library's success in these efforts benefited the University, as well. The Center now has something of a national reputation as the source of historical information for all of Northwest Louisiana. As a result of this reputation, the University has just recently been granted authorization to offer a graduate degree in Cultural Resources. This degree will invariably involve considerable utilization of the Center's resources and personnel to help support programming that will bring this heritage to a more general audience. Plans are underway for seeking grant support from both state and national agencies for this purpose.[30]

Many campus special collections are rich in local history. How those resources could best be used in service to the community depends on how seriously campus leadership considers the potential service role of its library.

Library Services to the Community through Campus Programs

In addition to offering businesses and local government services directly, library resources and services can be incorporated into business assistance centers and other campus efforts related to community development. For example, at CSU Northridge, the Center for Management and Organizational Development (CMOD), which is a nonprofit consulting practice in the College of Business Administration and Economics, asked a campus librarian to develop information literacy presentations for a Los Angeles County workforce training and development program. The LA County Academy, which serves people who work in all of LA County's departments, focuses "on the key skills needed by managers to meet the increasing demands of a continuously changing environment."

After an overview of key information retrieval tools and services, students learn about the various services available, compare their ease of use and the quantity and quality of their results, and have a clearer knowledge of how to perform increasingly complex searches.

Links to searching resources and informative Web sites are presented to the participants for use at work after the program ends. Upon completion of this session, students are better able to find information using a combination of search sites and resources; know a variety of sites on the Internet that can be used to find references to information on specific topics; are able to better evaluate which of these resources best meets their needs; and can compose simple and advanced search queries from a combination of keywords and symbols that can expand or narrow a search. Reviewed resources include recommendations made by librarians, the program faculty, and LA County.

This class has marked the first introduction to online research for many of these adult learners who serve so many in the community. In a sample survey of students, 92 percent stated that they had never had instruction about using the Internet or online research techniques, while 67 percent stated that they spent 15 to 19 hours a week online at work. The survey results also show that 75 percent of the students were more likely to use the Internet to find an answer to a work-related research question than consulting resources available through their institutional intranet, advice from a colleague, or consulting a librarian.[31]

The work that such centers undertake with a particular community is usually of a set duration, but one of the lasting benefits of such projects can be an increased awareness by the public of academic resources available to the community including the information resources of the library.

Sensitive Issues in Fundraising

Empowering local firms and agencies to do their own research and development also means keeping the business community's research needs in mind in collection-development policies. If the U.S. economy is to prosper, this service function of our higher educational institutions will need to be promoted and supported by college and university presidents. Yet to be successful, meeting community needs cannot be achieved at the expense of campus instruction and research needs. To prevent this, additional resources will almost always be required either from the campus or from the business community itself. Such two-way support efforts between the business community and the library will require the active involvement of the president and those campus units concerned with building town/gown relationships.

If the ability to generate funding is a significant consideration in deciding to initiate or build library/business community relations, careful planning will be needed to ensure that dependence on corporate funds does good rather than harm. Because such funding is not dependable, it should not be used where funding interruptions would cause difficulties (e.g., journal buying).

The appropriateness of the role of librarians must also be carefully delineated. A modified version of Harvard University's framework for reviewing possibly problematic situations can provide a good basis for evaluating library/business partnerships. It divides activities into three categories.

1. Activities that are clearly permissible. These include consulting or service arrangements that do not detract unduly from primary library objectives.
2. Extramural activities that should be discussed with the director or associate director. For example, a librarian may direct students to a service area from which the librarian expects to derive financial gain.
3. Sensitive activities that could present serious problems. These might include: (a) the acquisition of a substantial body of research material

that does not directly support university interests for the benefit of out-side parties; (b) arrangements in which commingling of funds makes it difficult to maintain policies ensuring open access to information.[32]

ACADEMIC LIBRARIES AND CIVIC ENGAGEMENT

Over the last decade, the role of academic libraries in support of civic, community, and cultural events has received greater attention than in previous years. While such a role is shared with public libraries, acad-eme's move toward civic engagement and service-learning has been well reflected in campus libraries.

> A learning society, lifelong learning, learning for life, the knowledge-based economy: the emergence of learning as an important political agenda has challenged libraries, museums and related organizations to show that they can make a difference, that they add value, that they are central to educational and civic missions. This is a common international theme, played out in different social and political con-texts. Interestingly, this theme emerges at the same time as a more general questioning about the value of public goods and the open availability of resources.[33]

There has been great diversity in how academic libraries have addressed this challenge. We have already discussed support for the knowledge-based economy; and, of course, where campus libraries welcome people from the community to use its services and resources, both the business and the civic communities could benefit. Maximizing such benefits requires a certain amount of public relations effort, which, based on a survey of thirteen library directors, is not as common as libraries' in-volvement with outreach services.

> The fact that every academic library in the study provides extensive service to community members is encouraging. The level of service to this group is much higher than expected and reflects the strong ties that all of the institutions have with the community. Service to the community is a very important public relations tool whether rec-ognized as such or not. The libraries are accepted as part of the larger community and act as a bridge between the community and the col-lege or university campus. Library staff, however, rarely target com-munity members for public relations. Understandably, academic library directors may be wary of over-publicizing their libraries and creating more demand for materials and services than can be met by existing resources and staff.[34]

Campus leadership would do well to carefully consider the balance between the value of library outreach efforts and the investments needed to mount such programs.

Commentary: "The Metropolitan University Library"

Robert L. Caret
President, Towson University

Our American colleges and universities were founded with no less a goal than to produce an eminently educated citizenry who would be future leaders for the benefit and betterment of society. That founding tenet evolved from the European model of revered universities like Oxford and Padua, which were based on classical Christian consciousness—leading to the concept of the "moral" university.

Though it reflects a major leap through time and space, today's metropolitan university continues to embrace that goal, but does so in a much more complex educational and societal environment that has developed over almost ten centuries. We continue to believe that a broad-based education is critical to an educated individual. Our graduates certainly still need to be proficient readers, writers, and communicators, but they must have as well the critical thinking skills that will allow them to thrive in the explosive world of information in which we now live. Further, today's graduates also need to have garnered specific career skills that allow them to begin work immediately and grow apace within their chosen careers. While the base for this education comes from our Western European tradition, it has been expanded to provide both international and multicultural perspectives. And while we continue to build on the social democratic values of providing an education that leads to civic engagement and belief in the common good, we must foster as well the development of a value system that we can more globally share and believe in. Thus, the success of our society is tied inextricably to the success of our educational institutions. We urgently need citizens, workers, family, and community members who understand the need to take a broad societal perspective in addressing many imminent challenges. We cannot focus only on the *me*; we must focus on the *us* because the social democratic ideal of our educational system is critical to the success of a democratic society. Providing that education to all who have ability is a tenet unique to the American system of education. Access to education, education of high quality, and education that is affordable are crucial goals as we strive to shape an educational system that will support a brave new world.

As an engendering force of this, the library has always been the hub, the nucleus of the educational enterprise. It is our primary educational resource and serves as the arena in which teaching and learning intersect and thrive. Through its professional staff, it provides expertise to help find information, answer questions, and serve as a community focus—not only for the campus but for the broader communities in which it resides. Our libraries have been referred to "as the heart of the university," and we have protected and nurtured them to reflect that role. In many ways, they are *the* catalyst that allows us to take our educational goals and transform them into individual and societal outcomes.

Given all this, it behooves us to recognize both the import of using our libraries as effective partners in achieving our missions, as well as the multiple roles they play both on our campuses and in the communities around us. There are numerous examples throughout the country of libraries and/or specialized libraries that serve as community resources for such things as community health, law, public policy, business, and government, to name a few. We also find specialized libraries with a cultural and language perspective that serve the needs of our recent immigrants. Whether these libraries are small or large, multifaceted or singly focused, they are resources for all of our communities, the entire region we serve, and provide the input that allows us to achieve our goals. The network of libraries available to us, including the information they provide in a plethora of formats, is an apt metaphor for the information age itself.

In the age of virtual information, when information is available to us through many avenues with great ease, the skills of the educated citizen become even more critical. Data becomes information, information becomes knowledge, and eventually, with some luck, as it is assimilated and processed through the minds of educated people, wisdom develops. The ability to work in a world rife with information, to gather, process, assimilate, and disseminate it, discern what is valid and what is not, and transform it into salient thought—those are the exalted outcomes that education must provide.

Currently, we are being deluged with more and more data, more and more information. The mass of information we find on the Web alone is a treasure trove, but there is so much of it we often feel like we are drowning. Couple that reality with the increased production of journals, periodicals, books, monographs, and other forms of traditional media, and there is a significant challenge before us. It helps to temper that awesome responsibility by remembering that information and data are simply that—information and data.

To help us learn to sort and balance and grasp all the bright prospects, the metropolitan university, along with other regional institutions, must serve its geographic region, its immediate locale, as an enduring partner. And since the universities that define themselves as such believe their role must be focused primarily on the regions in which they reside and the citizens they serve, their teaching, service, research, and expertise must be shared, in an "extended" sense, with their surrounding communities. Most metropolitan universities recognize that the library must serve as the nucleus of this new and broader mission, that the library will continue to be at the core—the heart of the metropolitan university enterprise. It provides the base for achieving institutional goals, societal goals, and our overall educational goals. And though today's library may look different, feel different, and do business in very different ways from libraries of the past, it still reflects the goals and characteristics of the library of the 1600s and beyond. Today's virtual library, awakening us to the world of virtual information, is a vital asset to our communities, our institutions, and our students. We must ensure its vitality and see to it that it develops in tandem with the evolving mission of our institutions of the future.

Successful School Outreach Programs

School outreach efforts are discussed in chapter 6, but the following are brief descriptions of other community outreach programs in which academic libraries have been active.

- The College of St. Catherine library director, faculty, and students from several programs worked with the St. Paul Public Library to create a family literacy program targeted at immigrant mothers and children. "This exciting partnership has given students, college staff, and public library staff a chance to create and learn from each other's worlds. [They] had the joy of nurturing and growing a program for families together, in a very team-like way."[35]

- Many academic libraries become focal points for community discussions. For example, libraries were encouraged by University of Washington Assistant Professor David Silver to bring communities together on September 11, 2004, to "foster discussions about freedom and democracy"; and the July 23, 2004, issue of *The Chronicle of Higher Education* reported on the quite different approaches several academic libraries were taking to hosting such events.[36]

- Rare book and local history collections in academic libraries lend themselves readily to exhibits and programming opportunities that can appeal to both campus and community people. Book talks can also successfully bring town and gown together and enrich the cultural environment. Other campus or community events can be enhanced by complementary events and/or exhibits in the library. For example, a holiday like the birthday of Dr. Martin Luther King, Jr., could easily lend itself to both displays and programming. Such events could involve students from one or more classes, as well as inviting both the general public and school communities to participate.

- Workshops on how to do research can be helpful to civic groups. "Colleges and universities and external training groups, which include professional societies, consultants and researchers, and a variety of industry organizations are sources for training in information literacy."[37]

Some academic libraries get involved with ongoing projects that capitalize on their organizing abilities in order to enrich both campus and community information resources and services. For example, "the Raymond H. Fogler Library at the University of Maine was selected to create an online database of public resources which would link the entire University System in a way which is highly visible, easily accessible to the public, responsive, and expandable without detracting from individual public service initiatives of the separate campuses."[38] The database was to include "non-bibliographic information, comprised of records of individuals, programs and services, and facilities."[39]

DALNET, the Information Hub

Few areas of the country have been more challenged than the region around Detroit, so perhaps it is not surprising that one of the most robust of library collaborative efforts emerged there. For over ten years prior to becoming a nonprofit organization in 1985, libraries at Wayne State University, University of Detroit Mercy, and other two- and four-year campuses worked with public and special libraries to gain efficiencies in operations and to better serve their various users. Planning in the mid-1990s projected a larger vision for their efforts to encompass serving as an information hub that would more aggressively address the information needs of the region.

The Detroit Area Library Network (DALNET) was designed to serve as a southeast Michigan information hub that would link libraries and other institutions in a seven-county area. The intent was to meet lifelong educational, cultural, research, professional and recreational needs.[40] DALNET has shown remarkable flexibility in staying true to that vision despite the challenges of collaboration in a continuously changing environment. That story is captured in the case study provided by Margaret Auer, dean of university libraries at the University of Detroit Mercy and a longtime DALNET leader.

"DALNET: A Case Study"

Margaret Auer
Dean of University Libraries
University of Detroit Mercy

The Detroit Area Library Network, DALNET, is a consortium of academic, public, and special libraries located in southeast Michigan. Founded as a nonprofit corporation in 1985, DALNET initially enabled its members to better serve the information needs of their users through cooperative efforts among libraries in the metropolitan Detroit area with its shared, advanced library automation applications.

From 1985 through mid-1998, DALNET had a single online catalog maintained by a central site host institution as part of its integrated library services. However, when DALNET converted to a new online product in 1998, the DALNET vision was expanded to become an information hub that would incorporate regional information along with traditional library holdings.

Following a planning retreat in late 2002, the environment changed when the two largest institutions in DALNET announced their intent to purchase and implement new computer system software that was different from one another and different from the remaining DALNET members. Internet access to three different online systems has posed only minor problems, while the loss of the significant economic support of the two largest DALNET institutions has put the organization not only into financial crisis, but confronted it with questions on how or whether the members would continue to work cooperatively when the main focus of the organization had always been serving the public through a shared system.

After months of financial review, staff downsizing, and discussions of options and host site location, the board members determined it would be advantageous to maintain a single catalogue for those members who shared the same software; the board is currently pursuing that goal. The two largest institutions, although on different software systems, also reiterated their continued support and membership in DALNET. With all this settled, DALNET only needed to slightly adjust its vision of itself to become a DALNET that is a decentralized but highly collaborative and a well-managed urban information network whose members, through partnership and shared effort, are committed to a role as a model regional information hub.

Even while the minds and efforts of many board members were preoccupied with the changing of systems, addressing the planning retreat results, and follow-up investigation, the development of the information hub concept went forward. The Hub Committee established ten goals to move the organization toward a realization of the "DALNET Information Hub." These goals included development of an array of image databases, a collection-development plan that includes a set of criteria for selecting hub projects, a process for funding digitization projects, a plan to secure a search engine and user interface that will allow users to search across the various hub databases in an integrated fashion, and others. Planning for the development of the hub and work on hub projects went on simultaneously. For example, the DALNET Health Calendar Project, an online events calendar where organizations that provide health-related events to citizens in the seven-county Detroit metropolitan area, went live during the planning process. This ongoing project continues to require a strong cooperative effort between DALNET and many social and health-related organizations and has become a major repository of health-related information for the community.

Another aspect of the information hub concept is the commitment to an evolving collection of electronic resources. Residents of the DALNET libraries' service areas reside in an area rich with special collections related to the cultural and economic history of the area. However, many of these collections are not publicly viewable due to fragility caused by age and/or light sensitivity or have not been identified with user-friendly access points. In trying to address this situation, DALNET established three state-of-the-art digitizing facilities at the three largest member libraries. Representatives from the three institutions jointly determined the equipment specifications in order to maximize the benefit of establishing the three digital laboratories and to ensure compatibility of hardware and software. The three host institutions agreed that the use of the equipment and software purchased would be shared with DALNET staff and other DALNET member libraries' staff for their digitization projects. In May 2001, the IHC (information hub committee) ranked the seven top DALNET digital projects on which its members should focus. Four of the projects have been completed, another project has the text images completed with the metadata currently being developed, but the remaining two have seen no activity. What is most encouraging is that six additional digitization projects, which were not part of the original ranking, have been put online by the members.

The Michigan Library Exchange (MiLE) is an innovative program of resource sharing in southeastern Michigan where two library cooperatives, the Suburban Library Cooperative and the OWLS Region of Cooperation, are partners with DALNET in serving over 51 percent of the population of Michigan. In this program, the participating groups have created the linkages necessary to allow for patron-initiated interlibrary loan that seamlessly integrates with the local library systems. With these linkages, a virtual catalog of libraries in six counties (serving 3.7 million patrons) was created. To enhance the information hub concept of serving the community, each of the partners joined an existing truck resource delivery service offered by The Library Network. When a statewide document delivery system was established in October 2004, the three partners moved to serving an even broader community.

DALNET is working in a new environment with different automated systems, fewer staff members to complete the required work, and member representatives stepping forward to pick up assignments previously handled by staff members. Another significant change has been the loss to the consortium of the expertise and contributions of members of the largest institutions and a different political environment where board members do not get to vote on every issue, only on issues in which their particular institution participates.

But in spite of these changes, the values and principles to which the DALNET membership subscribes have not changed. DALNET principles continue to place the highest priority on service, including end-user research, recreational reading needs, commitment to research sharing, and providing ease of access to information. DALNET strives to recognize partner diversity, maintain flexibility in implementation of initiatives, build strength based on common goals and needs, be creative, and provide leadership in information issues within Michigan.[41]

DALNET's vision—of being a regional information hub linking together local information from many sources and making them available to all—is a vision well worth replication. Wherever such a vision can be coupled with the endorsement and active support of high-level campus leadership, the outcomes could well surpass what has been accomplished in Detroit to the betterment of the campus and the community.

LIBRARIES AND SERVICE-LEARNING PROJECTS

Campus libraries and information literacy efforts should also be actively integrated into service-learning projects, and faculty should ensure that each project provides opportunities for students to learn the importance of undergirding their efforts with an adequate information base. For example, a service-learning course whose goal is to register and get people to vote might include information about the issues on the ballot and the candidates' positions on topics of concern.

Lack of thoughtful consideration of the information foundation for service-learning projects may result in some painful learning experiences. The Pima Community College West Campus president, Louis S. Albert, tells the story of a service-learning class that collected 500 pounds of used clothing to send to a rural community in Mexico. These students also raised cash to cover the cost of shipping the clothing. The success of the clothing drive was short-lived, however, when they discovered—after the fact—that Mexican law places severe limits on the shipment of used clothing into that country. The United States-based shipping company accepted the payment and shipped the clothing, but either did not know or failed to inform the students of the possibility that Mexican customs might impound the shipment. The clothing became untraceable, and the students never received compensation from the shipping company. In essence, all their hard work went "down the drain," because they had not thought it through or obtained the information they needed to ensure the success of their project.[42]

Commentary: "Information Literacy and Civic Learning: A Powerful Combination"

Louis S. Albert
President, Pima Community College West Campus

In 1999, Campus Compact, a consortium of nearly 1,000 college and university presidents, issued *The Presidents Declaration on the Civic Responsibility of Higher Education*, a document signed to date by more than 500 university and college presidents. The Declaration reads in part:

> We believe that the challenge of the next millennium is the renewal of our own democratic life and reassertion of social stewardship. In celebrating the birth of our democracy, we can think of no nobler task than committing ourselves to helping catalyze and lead a national movement to reinvigorate the public purposes and civic mission of higher education. We believe that now and through the next century, our institutions must be vital agents and architects of a flourishing democracy.

In 2004, Campus Compact followed up on the Declaration by initiating the Campaign for Civic Learning. The goal of the campaign is ambitious but long overdue—to make civic learning an expected outcome for every college graduate.

During the past decade, colleges and universities have taken important steps toward achieving this goal, especially with the extensive development of volunteer community service and course-based service-learning programs. Students in all sectors of higher education, in significant numbers, are volunteering in their communities, enrolling in courses that require community-based work, and participating in other forms of civic engagement such as lobbying and voting.

But if the civic learning movement is to find its way into the heart of the curriculum, it needs both external support (the purpose of the Campaign for Civic Learning) and new ways of organizing undergraduate education within the academy. The current emphasis on a curriculum that focuses narrowly on helping students develop workplace skills will need to be expanded into a curriculum that emphasizes both workplace skills and civic competency. Moreover, the success of such efforts are dependent upon students acquiring skills that allow them to work effectively in our information society after graduation when there is no prepackaged information available.

Many of the skill sets associated with civic learning—teamwork, problem-solving, critical thinking, and information competency—are indeed the same skill sets associated with general education outcomes expected of all college graduates, which are important for both civic and business purposes. Employers tell us that they prefer new hires that have those skills. It's a hard combination to dismiss: workers who think, citizens who can make a difference.

For such skills to be acquired and, thereby, this dual emphasis to be effective, new forms of collaboration will need to be established—between faculty from multiple disciplines, between faculty and student development professions, between faculty and staff as learning moves from the campus to the larger community. And if the new curriculum is to be successful, new and stronger collaborations will also be needed on the parts of faculty in the disciplines and academic librarians. It takes their combined efforts to facilitate students developing the analytical and problem-solving skills needed to be effective in finding solutions to community-based problems. These same librarians will also need to work directly with community partners in collectively finding solutions to the problems communities face.

Imagine how students' experiences can be enriched throughout their undergraduate years:

- Imagine a first-year learning community in which a cohort of thirty students co-enroll in four three- to four-credit courses and receive instruction from library faculty on how to gather pertinent information, evaluate, and analyze it prior to planning and implementing a community-based project in conjunction with selected community partner agencies. Studies show that students who participate in these first-year learning communities learn more, exhibit improved persistence and retention, and graduate earlier. Other studies show that the faculty who work together in learning communities—including library faculty—are learning from one another and perfecting their crafts. Their partnering is also an effective message to students regarding the importance of learning from each other and the importance of having more than one source for key information needs.

- Imagine those same students engaging in service-learning courses during their second and third years of college—both in their majors as well as in their general education courses—while simultaneously participating in co-curricular activities that emphasize civic responsibility and engagement. In these courses, the working relationships between discipline and library faculty and students become more focused and more complex. The community work deepens student academic learning, and their studies lend context and effectiveness to their work in the community.

- Finally, imagine these students, as seniors, enrolling in a capstone course that enables them to integrate what they have learned and asks them to design and implement a sophisticated community service project as a requirement for graduation. When these students cross the stage at graduation, they will have justifiable confidence that they can effectively address new issues and problems that will confront them in both their work and civic responsibilities. They will have this confidence because they will have mastered the skills needed to be independent, lifelong learners. Moreover, they will graduate with a sense of urgency about their role as informed and responsible members of the community in which they live and work.

As public expectations for civic learning outcomes expand, presidents and other senior campus officials will need to support the vital role information specialists play in responding to those expectations. Presidents and especially chief academic officers need to be sure that appropriate lines of collaboration are established between their libraries and other academic units, and that resources are provided to support those collaborations. Similarly, because so much of the success of these programs depends on the quality of the relationship between colleges and their community partners, access to college library services must include access by our community partners.

The results will speak for themselves—graduates who are skilled in their disciplines and professions and who have the knowledge and ability to shape a more vital and effective society!

In a Middle States Commission on Higher Education publication, *Developing Research & Communication Skills*, examples are given of student service-learning experiences that can both benefit the community and facilitate students in mastering information literacy skills in a real-world environment. The list includes the following:

- Third-year accountancy students at an urban university design and implement free assistance in filing income taxes for low-income community members.

- Students enrolled in a first-year learning community design and implement a holiday food drive that requires them to research health department regulations regarding food preparation and storage and also to investigate issues of personal and institutional liability related to the delivery of the food to poor families at off-campus locations.

- Biology majors work with local environmental agencies to design and implement environmental impact studies related to water quality.

- Service-learning students engaged in an honors seminar are assigned to work with homeless clients at a nearby shelter. Their first reflective essay assignment is to interview agency personnel and others in the process of writing an essay entitled "Anatomy of an Agency."

- Research, design, and write a "business plan" for a United Way Agency, including a description of the agency's services, profile of clients, projection of requests for services, as well as a profile of agencies that offer similar and supporting services.[43]

Vanderbilt faculty member Janet Eyler and her colleague Dwight Giles from the University of Massachusetts, Boston, won the Campus Compact's prestigious Thomas Ehrlich Faculty Award for Service Learning in 2003. In responding to the future of campus-community engagement, Giles states that the next step is to move to "a broader enterprise of being an engaged campus with a specific civic mission . . . the cutting edge is where teaching, scholarship and public service are connected and reciprocal."[44] Certainly, where and when campuses reach this level of engagement, it is logical that the campus library be integral to the enterprise.

SCHOLARLY INTEGRITY

In his 2003 book, *Universities in the Marketplace*, Derek Bok raises concerns about the effects of commercialization on higher education. He identifies the greatest danger as the loss of reputation for scholarly integrity.

> A democratic society needs information about important questions that people can rely upon as reasonably objective and impartial. Universities have long been one of the principal sources of expert knowledge and informed opinion on a wide array of subjects ranging from science, technology, and medicine to economic policy, Supreme Court rulings, and environmental trends. This function has grown steadily more important now that so many issues that concern the public—biological warfare, global warning, nutrition, and genetic engineering—have become too technical for ordinary citizens to understand. Once the public begins to lose confidence in the objectivity of professors, the consequences extend far beyond the academic community. At a time when cynicism is so prevalent and the need for reliable information is so important, any damage to the reputation of universities, and to the integrity and objectivity of their scholars, weakens not only the academy but the functioning of our democratic, self-governing society. That is quite a price to pay for the limited, often exaggerated gains, that commercialization brings to even the best-known institutions.[45]

We would argue that providing access to a rich and broad array of information resources—coupled with support in accessing and evaluating needed information—is necessary to scholarly integrity. Moreover, when made available to the public, such access can do much to strengthen a campus's reputation for scholarly integrity. Over time, this may be the greatest service libraries can offer to academe and to the communities we serve.

NOTES

1. David Adamany, "Sustaining University Values while Reinventing University Commitments to our Cities," *Teachers College Record* 95 (spring 1994): 326.

2. Mary Anne Hansen, "The Land Grant University Reference Librarian of the 21st Century," in *Expectations of Librarians in the 21st Century*, ed. Karl Bridges (Westport, Conn.: Greenwood Press, 2003), 2.

3. Robert Anderson, "Business—Higher Education Cooperation Key to Global Market Challenge" (speech made at American Council on Education Conference, October 1983), quoted in *Higher Education and National Affairs* 32 (14 October 1983): 3.

4. Business—Higher Education Forum, *America's Competitive Challenge: The Need for a National Response* (Washington, D.C.: Business—Higher Education Forum, ED 231 331, 1983), 27.

5. Victor Rosenberg, "Information Literacy and Small Business," July 2002 (white paper prepared for UNESCO, the U.S. National Commission on Libraries and Information Science, and the National Forum on Information Literacy, for use at the Information Literacy Meeting of Experts, Prague, The Czech Republic, October 2003), 2. Retrieved 15 October 2004 from http://www.infolit.org/International_Conference/papers/rosenberg-fullpaper.pdf.

6. Ibid., 9.

7. T. Philip Tompkins and Gary D. Byrd, "The Urban University Library: Effectiveness Models for 1989," in *New Horizons for Academic Libraries*, ed. Robert D. Stueart and Richard D. Johnson (New York: K. G. Saur, 1979), 578.

8. Paul G. Zurkowski, "The Information Service Environment: Relationships and Priorities," National Program on Library and Information Services, Related Paper No. 5 (Washington, D.C.: National Commission on Libraries and Information Science, ED 100 391, 1974), 6.

9. Suzanne M. Ward, Yem S. Fong, and Damon Camille, "Library Fee-Based Information Services: Financial Considerations," *The Bottom Line: Managing Library Finances* 15, no. 1 (2002): 5–17. Retrieved 8 April 2005 through Emerald database.

10. Wendy Smith, "Fee-Based Services: Are They Worth It?" *Library Journal* 115 (15 June 1993): 40–41.

11. Association of Research Libraries, *Fee-Based Services, SPEC Kit 259* (August 2000), 3. Retrieved 26 June 2003 from http://www.arl.org/spec/259sum.html.

12. Ibid., 6.

13. University of Colorado, *University of Colorado Technical Research Center*. Retrieved 8 April 2005 from http://ucblibraries.colorado.edu/ctrc/.

14. Ward, Fong, and Camille, "Library Fee-Based Information Services," 6.

15. See the TIS Web site at http://www.tis.purdue.edu/html/index.html.

16. Matthew Simon, "One University's Experience Starting Fee-Based Information Systems: Two Case Studies from UNLV," *The Bottom Line: Managing Library Finances* 10, no. 4 (1997). Retrieved 27 February 2003 through ProQuest database.

17. Bob Hageman, "Singapore Library Visit by Bob Hageman," 24–27 July 2003, document attached to e-mail correspondence to Richard F. Woods, librarian, San José State University, 25 September 2003; revisions made by Gene Tan, National Library Board of Singapore, in e-mail correspondence to Patricia Breivik, 5 November 2004.

18. Ibid.

19. "32,000 References on the Development Studies Database," *Library @ UCD: University College Dublin Library Newsletter* (spring 2002): 3. Retrieved 1 April 2005 from http://www.ucd.ie/library/news/pdf/libno4.pdf.

20. Winston Tabb, *Academic Libraries: New Directions, New Partners* (7th International Bielefeld Conference, 4 February 2004). Retrieved 5 April 2004 from http://conference.ub.uni-bielefeld.de/proceedings/tabb.pdf.

21. Ibid.

22. Ibid.

23. R. McGinnis, "Librarians Train Detroit City Council Research Staff," *Wayne State University Library System Newsletter* 39 (spring 1997): 5.

24. Hema Ramachandran, "Reference Services to Police Officer Students at the School of Police Staff and Command, Traffic Institute, Northwestern University," in *Reference Services for the Adult Learner: Challenging Issues for the Traditional and Technological Era*, ed. Kwasi Sarkodie-Mensah (New York: Haworth Press, 2000).

25. Roger Durbin, *Distance Education and the Researcher Employee* (17th AAOU annual conference on 12–14 November 2003), 4. Retrieved 16 November 2004 from http://www.stou.ac.th/aaou2003/Paper/Roger.pdf.

26. Ibid., 1.

27. Ibid., 5.

28. Edward T. Shearin, Jr., "The Library's Commodity for Economic Development," *North Carolina Libraries* 52 (summer 1994): 48.

29. Ibid.

30. Fleming A. Thomas, correspondence to Patricia Breivik, 6 December 2004.

31. Lynn D. Lampert, "Who's Afraid of Partnerships for Information Literacy Initiatives? Working Together to Empower Learners," *C&RL News* 64 (April 2003): 247.

32. Harvard framework quoted in Ellen McDonald, "University/Industry Partnerships: Premonitions for Academic Libraries," *The Journal of Academic Librarianship* 11 (May 1985): 86.

33. *2003 Environmental Scan: Pattern Recognition* (Dublin, Ohio: Online Computer Library Center, 2004), 58.

34. Nancy J. Marshall, "Public Relations in Academic Libraries: A Descriptive Analysis," *The Journal of Academic Librarianship* 27 (March 2001): 121.

35. Carol P. Johnson et al., "Collaboration Generates Synergy: Saint Paul Public Library, the College of St. Catherine, and the 'Family Place' Program," *Reference & User Services Quarterly* 41 (fall 2001): 21.

36. Scott Carlson, "On September 11, Libraries Hope to Foster Open Discussions," *The Chronicle of Higher Education* 50 (23 July 2004): A29.

37. Jerry Kanter, "Guidelines for Attaining Information Literacy," *Information Strategy* 12 (spring 1996): 6–11. Retrieved 28 July 2003 through WilsonWeb database.

38. Marilyn Lutz et al., "Using the Community Information Format to Create a Public Service Resource Network," in *Information Technology: IT's for Everyone! Proceedings of the LITA Third National Conference*, ed. Thomas W. Leonhardt (Chicago: American Library Association, 1992), 56.

39. Ibid.

40. "DALNET Receives $100,000 Grant from Ameritech," *Wayne State University Library System Newsletter* 46 (winter 1999): 1.

41. This summary of DALNET provided by Margaret E. Auer, dean of university libraries, University of Detroit Mercy, was taken from DALNET program proposals, project plans, planning retreat, minutes of meetings, and its brochure, "DALNET, the Detroit Area Library Network: One Region Sharing the World."

42. Louis A. Albert, e-mail correspondence to Patricia Breivik, 22 October 2004.

43. *Developing Research & Communication Skills: Guidelines for Information Literacy in the Curriculum* (Philadelphia: Middle States Commission on Higher Education, 2003), 37.

44. "To the Next Level: Ehrlich Award Winner Discusses the Future of the Service-Learning Movement," *Service Connections: The Newsletter of the Massachusetts Campus Compact* 8 (summer 2003): 1.

45. Derek Bok, *Universities in the Marketplace* (Princeton: Princeton University Press, 2003), 117–18.

CHAPTER 6

Supporting Administrative Priorities

The preceding chapters have discussed how libraries can serve as empowerment resources in fulfilling the traditional roles of higher education institutions. Beyond these areas of instruction, research, and service, there are other campus concerns for which creative use of library resources and services can prove beneficial. While there is some research confirming that the mere existence of "library volumes and serial subscriptions contribute significantly to [the] prestige of all academic programs including the social sciences, physical sciences and math, engineering, and humanities,"[1] this chapter will highlight how more active use of libraries can assist academic administrators in other areas, such as promoting more effective and productive operations, enhancing campus fundraising efforts, fostering campus/high school relations, recruiting and retaining students, contributing to faculty development, deterring plagiarism, and addressing globalization concerns.

MORE EFFECTIVE OPERATIONS WITH KNOWLEDGE MANAGEMENT

Universities have always been equated with knowledge and the creation of knowledge. Yet, to date, they have been slow to inculcate knowledge management (KM) approaches into how they operate. However, KM is receiving increasing attention in the corporate sector and can offer guidance to campuses, including how to use campus libraries as a key resource in KM efforts. In the business world, the corporate library and information services are seen as key resources in KM efforts as they "have been doing KM and have been our primary repository of explicit knowledge throughout history."[2] Adaptations from the business sector are appropriate since campus leaders desire the same outcomes that corporate executives agree on for "a standard measure of success for KM efforts—improved productivity at the individual and organizational level."[3]

The Conference Board, whose stated mission is to improve the business enterprise system and to enhance the contribution of business to society, has issued a number of reports on KM through which three key ingredients emerge: people, process, and technology. Emphasized is "the need for a holistic approach to knowledge management, one that balances and integrates the human, organizational, and technological components of a knowledge environment. The characteristics of knowledge that give it value—its complexity, its humanness, its sensitivity to context, and its living ability to absorb and adjust to new information—require this type of multidimensional effort."[4] Among the three ingredients, technology comes in last. "Technology alone cannot solve knowledge problems or create knowledge-sharing environments. Insisting that technology is secondary to human and organizational issues has been an important part of the knowledge management conversation."[5]

The importance of people empowerment over the technology aspect of KM is stated even more strongly by Julie Oman, information steward at the Dow Chemical Company. "Information overload. Information fatigue syndrome. Information. Information. Information. Pity the poor employee who deals with this bombardment on a daily basis! Knowledge management has been considered by many to be the solution to our information woes. But the focus on technology in most knowledge management programs has only contributed to the problem. The key is how people deal with the information."[6] The technology is necessary, it just is not sufficient by itself. Unilever, a multinational consumer goods company, found this to be true. "Over the past five years an increasing number of end-user information tools have been made available to Unilever scientists via their desktops. There was evidence, however, that these were underutilized and poorly understood. Clearly, training needed to be extended."[7]

In another example, the World Bank increasingly finds knowledge (intellectual capital) the most critical resource—even over money lending—it has to offer in promoting sustainable economic growth in developing countries.[8] Other KM leaders agree. Angela Abell, director of TFPL, a U.K. organization advising business on knowledge, information, records, and content management, states: "Developing an appropriate culture, designing knowledge processes, obtaining and structuring the content of knowledge bases, and designing physical and electronic infrastructures for knowledge sharing are all features of the KM approach. But, in the end, it is the ability of everyone in the organization to manage and use information that is the critical success factor."[9] Abell details the importance of information literacy skills within a KM organization, and the lack of them in most.

> The continuing concern with information overload, and the inability of most people to deal with it, are just one indication of the low level of understanding of information management within organizations. . . . Information literacy skills are needed throughout the organization and need to be part of the daily skill set. It is likely that, just as computer skills were spread throughout the workforce through primary, secondary and higher education, we will eventually see an information literate society. But that is a long term view and organizations need to create the capability now. To achieve this, information literacy skills must be actively and visibly valued by the organization and people must be given the time, space and encouragement to develop them. People need to see the relevance to their work and understand the objectives and benefits of a more information intensive way of working. It should add quality to their lives— not more burden. If core competencies can help them deal with information overload they will see an instant benefit.[10]

For campus administrators and staff, time savings gained by good information literacy skills, hence better information or knowledge management, can potentially be significant, based on data from the workplace. A Ford Motor Company executive stated in a Conference Board discussion that "we typically can only find half of the information we need to do our jobs and spend up to 30 percent of our time looking for the other half."[11] Another estimate made in a U.S. Department of the Navy article, which describes its information literacy efforts, is that an average worker "spends an estimated 150 hours per year looking for information."[12]

There is further agreement among other business leaders that the next step in continuous business improvement is information literacy.

> PricewaterhouseCoopers is a leader in the area of information services management. It has earned this position by aggressively reengineering its information services support model to maximize cost savings while increasing staff productivity. . . . The goals of PwC's information services support model are to: promote greater user self-sufficiency; build greater competencies around understanding where

to find information, search the Web, and evaluate the quality and validity of sources; provide best-in-class content; support a mobile workforce; and ultimately increase firm productivity.[13]

One Conference Board participant articulated the future of KM as being information literacy. "As we entered the new millennium one assessment of what comes after knowledge management offered the following: 'Enterprise wide information literacy needs the same attention as computer literacy received during the last decade. Ensuring that everyone in the organization has the ability to use the same base IT tools does not, on its own, enable knowledge mobilization.'"[14] Another foresees the next step after KM as being "learning management."[15]

Knowledge Management and Librarians

It would be ironic if the very campuses that adopt and promote student information literacy learning outcomes would fail to benefit from such skills in their own administrative operations. Yet, higher education literature shows little evidence of KM practices or of viewing libraries as valued resources in promoting individual or campus efficiency and productivity.

If the goals of knowledge management seem desirable to academic officers, they might consider an approach to using information in campus decision-making that would parallel procedures in the corporate setting. The academic library and librarians could serve as primary suppliers of information. An effective administrative procedure would dictate that information be supplied to the president's staff, not to the president directly; that it be provided in a condensed form for easy use by the president or his staff; and that it be delivered quickly for efficient decision-making.[16]

On most campuses, administrators collect information for decision-making by gathering statistical data, drawing upon the collective experiences of the management team, purchasing a current book on the topic, or touching base with other professionals either on the faculty or among the personal networks of the administrative team. Although all of these sources can be valuable, it is unlikely that they will produce either the most recent information or a reasonably comprehensive information package. In this scenario,

> [scholars turned administrators] retain the typical faculty relationship with the library, its resources, staff, and services: namely, a soli-

tary interaction between themselves and the materials that embody their area of research. Their view of libraries and librarians has not changed as their administrative responsibilities (which may even include the library) have evolved. What this will often mean, in practical terms, is that the administrator still knows and uses libraries in only one way—by paying a personal visit, consulting a few tried and trusted sources, browsing the stacks, and in general doing everything directly, for oneself, by oneself. After all, as a scholar, one is expected to know the library, and not to have to ask for assistance.[17]

Moreover, in contrast to their scholarly pursuits, administrators are "much more likely to require applied research, current policies and procedures from other institutions, and raw data brought together into a useful whole."[18] Few academic officers use their campus libraries as a significant source of information for their decision-making. Few administrators seriously consider how librarians might serve their administrative needs.

Campus librarians can play three important roles in assisting academic decision-making. They can collect and organize relevant information (information management), instruct administrative staff in accessing and evaluating information (information literacy), and participate directly in campus planning teams. These functions closely parallel librarians' roles in campus instruction and research.

Further Administrative Support by Librarians

In institutional planning, quick access to previous planning efforts and information on outcomes of earlier decision-making can be invaluable, since relying on personal recall is insufficient, given normal turnover rates among top-level administrators. A sound records-management program administered by a trained archivist can meet this need. Such programs involve training office staff across the campus to retain appropriate records, systematically collecting files from administrative offices, evaluating the future value of such files, and organizing the selected materials for ease of future access.[19]

Other materials valuable to campus planning might be news clippings on the institution, reports by the higher education governing board and pertinent legislative reports, student publications, records of student organizations, faculty publications, and instructional development resources.[20] The collection and archiving process should avoid duplication of effort. External affairs offices, for example, usually collect campus news articles but seldom organize them for future research. A cooperative effort between external affairs and the library could meet the need for both current awareness and future reference with but a small increase in investment over the cost of ongoing public relations activities.

Beyond such special collections and archives, the regular library collections can provide a wide range of information valuable for planning, decision-making, and fundraising. At the California Maritime Academy for example, the library director, Carl Phillips, encourages campus administrators to use the library resources, but in practice they usually ask library personnel to find information for them. Requests have included the following variety:

- For the search for a director of public relations, Phillips did a review of newswires, newspapers, the Web, and other publication channels to get a sense of the finalists' work and successes in using the media.

- When administrators were looking into the possibility of partnering with a private sector simulation company to receive federal grant funding, the library was able to find information about simulation companies and the federal grant program, which were useful for their deliberations.

- When the campus was considering reformulating its smoking policies and possibly incorporating a program for smoking cessation, the library was asked to search for articles that would indicate the experience of other campuses with smoking policies, as well as providing information on smoking cessation programs and their varying degrees of success or failure—particularly among college students. The literature review was of great use in the creation of new campuswide smoking policies and a new smoking cessation program.[21]

Coordinating administrative and library purchasing can produce a better campus information resource base, which can be used for both faculty and administrators. For example, do those who coordinate library collection management know what materials the development office is already purchasing? Are materials in the development or faculty research offices used so heavily that they should not be made accessible to all campus personnel? Are materials in these offices listed in the library online catalog? Do development officers make effective use of library resources? For example, are they familiar with searching the *Foundation Directory Online*, business-related databases, and other sources of company information?

The availability of hundreds of online databases and thousands of online journals has not only significantly expanded the information available for campus planning purposes but also the speed at which it can be obtained. This can be quite useful to top campus administrators who need information to respond to questions raised by community leaders. The increasing use of online catalogs, databases, and other resources also makes it possible for faculty and administrators to search holdings from either office or home, both for personal and administrative research. The challenge today is not the lack of information for planning purposes, but how to find efficiently the information that best addresses the issue or concern at hand. This should not be the task of already overburdened administrators, but rather of trained information intermediaries, that is, librarians.

Librarians can also support administrative planning by coordinating and performing "environmental scanning," a management technique of monitoring current publications to keep track of changing or emerging trends that may affect the institution. As the major collection point for current information in all formats, the library is the obvious operational base for this planning function. Ongoing monitoring of information about distance education, for example, could help administrators keep up to date with this burgeoning field. *Ulrich's Periodicals Directory* online lists close to 1,300 magazines and journals in higher education,[22] while OCLC's *WorldCat* lists over 4,700 books, 482 videos, and 46 conference proceedings, speeches, and lectures on distance education.[23] As campus leaders identify areas of concern for planning purposes, they can either ask the library to undertake a focused retrospective research effort or request ongoing scanning of current materials until that aspect of the planning process is completed.

A president should ensure that campus efforts to monitor community or state activities are comprehensive but not redundant. Every dean and director may have similar monitoring efforts underway, differing only in focus and comprehensiveness. Librarians working with administrative personnel and perhaps a representative from the business or public affairs program should be able to design an effective information management system that includes an efficient environmental-scanning component.

As any experienced fundraiser knows, the basis for effective development rests on good research. Knowing the history of an organization, the professional and philanthropic connections of its board members, and what neighborhoods and age groups constitute the firm's major market can make or break the effectiveness of a proposal. Much of this information can be obtained by questioning personal contacts familiar with the firm, but more in-depth information can be obtained from the library, and this is often more efficient as well. Presidents who encourage informed library use by both their own staffs and the advancement office can expect increased productivity from both.

Besides such ongoing activities, involving librarians in planning for any nonroutine occurrence can pay real dividends. For example, in preparing for campus linkages with other higher educational institutions, businesses, or governmental agencies abroad, campus libraries can provide access to a gold mine of background material. Besides information on current economic, political, social, technological, and educational trends in particular countries, they can also provide information on business customs and protocol.[24]

All intellectual property policy and IT planning efforts should include appropriate library representation. Not only can librarians quickly assemble examples of already existing policies, but they also have a customer service orientation that is important to achieving academic goals. For example, some campuses such as Wichita State University have looked to library personnel to take the lead in developing university-wide Internet policies.[25]

Just as little appears in the literature regarding KM on campuses, little is also found on the strategic use of librarians in supporting administrative decision-making. Moreover, where such services have been documented, such as at California State University (CSU) Chico[26] and Eastern Kentucky University,[27] initial successes have not resulted in sustained services. The real question is why presidents would not want such a support service and explore its possibility with their library deans.

Information Literacy and University Staff Productivity

In keeping with the KM model, all university employees should be given opportunities and encouragement to develop information literacy abilities. Librarians should be invited to conduct workshops for various staff. Presidents could provide an important role model by promoting the development of such skills among the personnel in their own offices, while encouraging other campus officers to do the same. A good practice in preparation for a scheduled workshop would be for library faculty to interview members of a particular administrator's staff to identify recent projects, then use these projects as case studies to document what relevant information the staff could have easily obtained from the library. Consideration should also be given to setting up profiles of key areas of concern so that staff will be notified when new resources on those topics are received by the library.

Such workshops could increase productivity throughout the campus, because they offer a good way to reduce "information 'float' by decreasing the delay and uncertainty associated with information."[28] Librarians can hold regular workshops for faculty assistants and departmental secretaries to demonstrate how library resources and services can help them perform their jobs more effectively and efficiently. A side benefit of academic administrative assistants attending such workshops is that they learn how to schedule library information literacy workshops, contact library liaisons, request purchase of library materials and other processes that can save both classroom instructors and library personnel a great deal of time and frustration.

Two examples of library-initiated efforts to promote information literacy abilities among administrators and staff illustrate the coverage that instructional programs can provide. In both cases, the services were described as offering special (corporate-like) library services.

The Catherwood Library at Cornell's School of Industrial and Labor Relations extended its client orientation efforts to include administrators. Training sessions for Cornell's Office of Human Resources and other administrative units were held to accomplish several goals.

> In an effort to bring the library's strengths in line with the mission of the university, administrators are being taught how to use the latest information tools, including leading databases, Internet services, and existing print and electronic practitioner materials provided by the library. The idea behind the training sessions is to
>
> - increase the productivity of administrators by empowering them with the ability to use sophisticated information sources. This includes training in library research methods and multitasking (how to cut and paste from one or several sources into word processing or e-mail programs), with an eye toward production of reports and memoranda;
> - enhance administrators' creative alternatives by acquainting them with an enlarged scope of information sources, ideas, and communication processes; and
> - demonstrate that the library can be an active player in making the university more competitive by providing training and consulting services.[29]

The library that serves the colocated University of Washington Bothell and the Cascadia Community College initiated a series of orientations for administrators, faculty, and staff when the new campus opened in the fall of 2000.

> This orientation program intended to present the library and media center's services and resources to this user group, to encourage them to make use of their services and resources, and to offer them some

basic skills to begin to address their information needs independently. Additionally, library staff wanted the academic administration,
faculty, and support staff to be able to

- locate service points in the library;
- become familiar with the library's physical and virtual spaces;
- be able to search the online catalog and databases;
- order resources from other branch libraries;
- feel comfortable approaching library staff for help; and
- become aware of the ways the library can assist them with their
  information needs.[30]

Survey responses over the first year indicated that "all respondents felt
more comfortable and familiar in their ability to use the resources and
services after attending the orientation sessions."[31] This plus other positive responses led to consideration of enhancements to the orientation
program, such as the following:

- Casually tracking administration, faculty, and support staff library use;
- Providing attendees with bibliographies of sources they might find of
  use in their particular departments;
- Offering advanced, more in-depth sessions for those with library skills
  surpassing the basic level;
- Offering subject-specific sessions, by department, for example;
- Offering the session quarterly; and
- Working with Human Resources departments at both institutions to
  make this session a standard part of new employee orientations.[32]

The instructional role of libraries can also include grantsmanship
workshops that introduce faculty to relevant library resources and give
them tips on how to write good grant proposals. Plagiarism workshops
could help administrative staff and faculty deal more effectively with this
problem. (See further discussion on this topic later in this chapter.) The
library could also offer workshops on how to use newer research technologies or how to use library resources for environmental scanning. All
such instructional efforts could empower campus employees to work more
efficiently and effectively.

Librarians on Administrative Planning Teams

In further considering the administrative support librarians can provide, administrators should not overlook the possibility of direct in-

volvement of librarians in planning. Just as librarians can be valuable members of faculty research teams, they could also make a useful contribution to administrative planning teams internally and as part of campus service efforts. For example, when the Wayne State University (WSU) president, Irvin D. Reid, chaired a city/university Academic Achievement Task Force to address the challenges facing the Detroit Public Schools, the WSU dean of the libraries, Sandra Yee, served on the task force, and a senior librarian, Paul Beavers, served on its Faculty Advisory Committee. The WSU dean of education, Paula Wood, also a task force member, credits Beavers with the quality of the well-documented research undergirding the report as well as for drafting several of its sections. Wood stated that the White Paper on Academic Achievement of the Youth of the City of Detroit[33] "would not have been as strong or as well referenced without the work of Beavers. While faculty from the academic departments had much to offer in their content areas, the literature searches completed by the librarian enriched each segment of the report and helped us reflect a very current representation of the research on urban education."[34]

Even before the emergence of KM practices, the business, scientific, and industrial research communities increasingly recognized that librarians (or information managers) could be valuable members of their management teams. As William A. Moffett points out in *Priorities for Academic Libraries*, "The same should be true of colleges and universities. I've seen so much time wasted simply because no one bothered to search the literature—something librarians would have done right away."[35] The remainder of this chapter highlights how campuses have achieved increased productivity and more effective operations by strategic use of their library personnel and services in key areas such as faculty development, school relations, student recruitment and retention, and related efforts.

ENHANCING FACULTY DEVELOPMENT

The general issue of library support for campus administrative priorities brings us back to the need for further growth in technical and information skills among faculty, and this has led to a growing appreciation of the interplay between information literacy and faculty development. Already there are a number of collaborations between libraries and campus organizations focusing on enhancing faculty teaching to demonstrate how beneficial such partnerships can be.

One of the first campuses to capitalize on this knowledge was Florida International University (FIU) in Miami, where a partnership between

the library and the Academy for the Art of Teaching got underway in
1998. Academy director Leora Baron saw the information literacy/faculty
development relationship resulting in widespread and tangible benefits.

> The benefits of information literacy permeate the entire teaching
> and learning process. For institutions, the benefit is compliance with
> changing requirements of accreditation. For individual colleges and
> department, the benefits are compliance with professional accredit-
> ing requirements and the enhanced quality of graduates. For teach-
> ers, the course of study they have designed and facilitated enables
> their students to learn and produce on a higher level. And for the
> students, there is the very tangible benefit of acquiring skills that
> will support their future success, as many of the skills embedded in
> information literacy are also skills necessary in the workplace.[36]

Baron's library counterpart, Patricia Iannuzzi, was equally a champion
of the partnership; and they saw their efforts as directly supporting FIU
president Mitch Maidique, who had stated that "when ubiquitous computing arrives, we will be limited, not by the quantity of information but
by its quality, and our ability to retrieve, manipulate, and analyze it."[37]
Identifying four campus initiatives (SACS accreditation, the strategic
plan, student retention, and technology in the classroom), the partners
developed a multifaceted program that addressed each of these concerns
(e.g., a freshman experience to address retention concerns). Iannuzzi
summarizes the win/win partnership as follows:

> As the library and the Academy for the Art of Teaching began a col-
> laboration to form the Information Literacy Initiative, a model de-
> veloped that reflects both parties' interests in faculty development
> as related to information literacy. Information literacy occurs at the
> intersection of teaching, thinking, and learning, within the broader
> environment of technology. Both the academy and the library en-
> courage faculty to develop the critical thinking skills of students. In-
> formation literacy provides the vehicle for developing those critical
> thinking skills.[38]

An even broader successful campus collaboration in support of faculty
development can be found in the UWired working group at the University of Washington. This collaboration's mission is "to promote and support access to technology, fluency in information technology and
resources, and innovation in teaching and learning through technology."[39] The UWired Web site documents its activities, which includes fif-

teen campus units and the active involvement of library personnel. One project, focused on the integration of information and computer use into the curriculum, won the 1995 Association of College & Research Libraries Bibliographic Instruction section's Innovation in Bibliographic Instruction Award.

> [UWired] targets both faculty and students, and has developed tools and content for distinct audiences. . . . The program employs active learning techniques in its tutorials and also develops the learner's technical skills. UWired includes an outreach dimension as well, designing programs carried out within "commons" facilities in libraries, faculty symposia, and workshops; for-credit seminars; ties with freshman curricula; and programs with the community, the school system, and international partners. This program has clearly served as a catalyst for creating partnerships and for extending the library's reach beyond the campus-based curriculum.[40]

Other educators point to the value of greater information literacy abilities among faculty as critical to more effective use of technology in the teaching/learning process. Jamie McKenzie, editor of *From Now On*, an educational technology journal, summarizes the situation on campuses as well: "Information literacy is the key to a successful technology initiative. By moving past technology to literacy, we are able to mobilize a greater proportion of teachers to make frequent use of the network and are able to achieve more impressive student achievement."[41] He suggests a careful consideration of investment of at least 25 percent of a new technology project budget for professional development. Campuses where technology-focused faculty development is separate from pedagogical support will be wise to ensure that consideration is given to the management and evaluation of content to enhance faculty appreciation of the technology.

The library at Cleveland State University has been actively involved in faculty development both in partnership with the Office of Assessment and the Center for Teaching and Learning. According to George Lupone, associate library director,

> The [assessment] council is composed of associate deans and faculty from teaching departments, the associate director of the library, and representatives from various administrative departments. The library . . . is the only campus unit that assesses both student learning and student services. The library, therefore, is able to assist with the overall campus assessment effort in addition to tending to the assessment of library instruction and services.

For example, at a campus assessment seminar, the associate library director served on a panel with three associate deans to share experiences on assessment. The director of assessment chose a library representative for the panel, because "the faculty understand the library." The library, which has a long record of successful assessment, can assist academic units because they feel an affinity toward the library. The assessment office considers the library assessment report a model and has included the report on its web site for others to copy. Subsequently, the Physics Department, encouraged by the campus assessment office, emulated the library's assessment report.

The library has also formed a partnership with the university center for teaching and learning to assist faculty with their teaching. The partnership was strengthened when, because of a retirement and reorganization, the library assumed responsibility for instructional media services, including interactive video distance learning (IVDL). With the center, the library invited faculty using IVDL to a luncheon to share their experiences and concerns. It became immediately apparent that the faculty were eager to learn more about the IVDL equipment and the pedagogy of teaching a class from a distance. . . . The library played a key role in reengaging the faculty in interactive video distance learning. The library staff set up electronic mailing lists to communicate with faculty who teach using IVDL and those who express interest in doing so in the future. The library director and director of the center for teaching and learning now have a vehicle for communicating with these faculty regularly. Together they planned a seminar series for interested faculty.[42]

Wayne State University created a home for this coming together of information literacy and faculty development. The campus launched its faculty development center in September 1996, and the completion of a new undergraduate library allowed the center to quickly relocate to a beautiful area designed to house the operation—complete with kitchenette to allow for coffee making to add to the ambience of the meetings. Locating this faculty learning center in an undergraduate library committed to student retention and academic success created a true learning center for the campus.

Efforts such as those at Florida International, Cleveland State University, and Wayne State University can provide a vision for the future to many campuses, but where such collaborations do not exist, academic leadership from presidents and provosts may be needed to ensure that librarians' expertise and services are not being overlooked. For example, a study conducted at Texas A&M in 1999 surveyed faculty rankings of services provided by the library liaisons to their departments. Of the eleven services included, all were ranked as important by 62 percent of the faculty, with "updating the faculty on the services available in the library . . . unanimously regarded as the overall *very important* service."[43] What is of particular concern—and quite likely is the case on all campuses—was the number of library services of which a significant percentage of faculty were unaware. These are indicated in the following table.[44]

Librarian Services	*% Faculty Unaware*
Served as consultants in library's resources to graduate students	52.6%
Conveyed faculty's opinions/suggestions of the library to the library administration and gave a timely report back to the faculty on any actions taken by the library	40.6%
Conducted bibliographic instruction for students	36.1%
Came to the department (or invited faculty to the library) to demonstrate databases to the faculty	23.1%
Provided a faculty current awareness service based on the faculty member's field of research and teaching interest	22.2%

Another example of the less than ideal use of library services is highlighted in the May/June 2004 issue of *Change*, which focused on the question, "Who are the educators outside of the classroom?" One article laments that many teaching faculty are not aware of many campus educators who interact with, encourage, and assist student learning most frequently outside the classroom. The primary author of the article is Patricia M. King, who is professor and director of the Center for the Study of Higher and Post Secondary Education at the University of Michigan. She urges that "the work of faculty and administrators will similarly be enhanced when they know how to fit together the puzzle pieces of expertise of other educators on campus"; and, among those hidden "pieces," she lists librarians.[45]

> Although the role of librarians still includes assisting students in locating information, this information is increasingly available online. Librarians, therefore, are called upon to help students navigate their way through a plethora of information clearinghouses to access the materials they need.
>
> In the process, they help students clarify their assumptions about how a body of knowledge is organized, and how to evaluate the validity of the information they retrieve. These skills not only assist students in dealing with their class-related activities, but also . . . help them become resourceful when responding to the demands of work and civic life.[46]

Faculty with retention, tenure, and promotion concerns and campus leaders with concerns for faculty productivity and student success will want library services and resources to be better known and more extensively used. This will not happen without thoughtful and deliberate action on the part of campus leadership.

ENHANCING CAMPUS/HIGH SCHOOL RELATIONS

The value of good campus/school relationships has been highlighted in a number of educational reform reports.[47] Collaboration between local high schools and academic libraries can be particularly fruitful in strengthening this relationship. In fact, high school class visits to local academic libraries were common long before building school/college relations became a priority for academic leaders.

By their junior or senior year of high school, many college-bound students have academic abilities and interests that far exceed the scope of their local school libraries. When they are ready to do more in-depth research, these students naturally look to nearby academic libraries to provide the richer resources they need. Traditionally, both publicly-supported and some private institutions have offered library orientation tours and instructional packages to high school classes. Scheduling such tours helps control reference desk demands generated by a whole class of students unable to find their way around the library. Librarians usually require advance notification of pending class visits so they can avoid scheduling visits during heavy academic use periods, arrange for adequate staffing, and offer instruction that will complement class assignments. The active participation of the classroom teacher helps ensure a successful visit. Depending on institutional policies, high school students may use their high school library cards to check out materials, obtain free college library cards (or in some cases purchase them), or obtain college library materials through interlibrary loan services through their high school library.

Organized use of local academic libraries can help give students a taste of college life and, in some cases, even inspire students who are not sure if college is for them. In this controlled environment, high school students can be college library users for a day. They can explore information technologies unavailable at their local schools and observe college students working individually and in small groups to do research for class assignments. Just how effective such visits could be in motivating students can be seen in an excerpt from a reflective journal students were assigned to keep by their high school teacher when they visited the library at San José State University in November 2003:

I personally thought that this was going to be a waste of time, but
it was great. This library mesmerized me because it was so huge. It
has everything in it, and the catalogs are really cool. I felt like it is
a place that I would enjoy studying in. I felt good that I got a card
and some books, and made this a useful trip. I don't know if I will
read them, but at least they are here. I felt great about learning about
Beethoven and Steinbeck because they are important figures in history from the art perspective. I did not even know that there was
this exhibit here. I felt great about the whole trip. Christina and I
got [to] philosophize a little bit about our lives, and we got to learn
about this place. I felt that this trip opened a new place for me to
use.[48]

Academic officers at institutions committed to building ties with local
schools can find out what current library policies are and explore with library personnel how campus outreach efforts can be strengthened. Building on this existing tie may well produce better results with less effort
than developing a program for improving campus/school relations from
scratch and then selling it to local schools.

Beyond orchestrated visits, creative and successful college/school library collaborations continue to emerge to meet local situations. Some
of the ones documented in the earlier edition of our book continue to
thrive, but the variety and range in what two universities have done in
recent years will be highlighted here. Some campuses have made multiple school outreach efforts through their libraries, thus providing good
models for other institutions.

Wayne State University

Wayne State University (WSU) has maintained a commitment to
first-generation students, has a strong College of Education, and a commitment to the schools in Detroit. Among the projects in recent years
focused on outreach to the schools through its libraries are the following
efforts.

- Feeder high schools were approached to work with personnel from the
  WSU undergraduate library to facilitate high school students improving their information literacy abilities. Teams from the schools consisted
  of an administrator, teacher, and librarian. Together with the WSU library personnel, they developed a definition of information literacy, decided how best to incorporate information literacy learning in their
  respective curricula, and held workshops for teachers to enable them to

facilitate such learning. A local bank donated funds to allow for teacher release time and other needed expenditures. The bank saw this project as valuable for producing a better-prepared, information age workforce from which it would be hiring.[49] This project was rated successful by school administrators, school library media specialists, and teachers and led to good insights for undertaking additional information literacy partnerships.[50]

- The Ameritech representative on the library dean's external advisory group worked with library personnel and the Michigan Association for Media in Education (MAME) to produce a PowerPoint presentation emphasizing the value of school libraries staffed by school library media specialists. Ameritech's considerable contribution was explained as the result of years of installing technology in schools and then receiving complaints that the technology investment was not "paying off." Ameritech's experience was that schools with a school media specialist were the ones where fruitful use was made of the technology. The presentation was made available for showing at meetings of principals, superintendents, PTA groups, and other appropriate groups. MAME prepared practical supplementary material on characteristics of good school library media specialists, how to locate and hire such people, and other practical advice for principals.

- WSU's Vera P. Shiffman Medical Library regularly brings in cohorts of eleventh- and twelfth-grade students from the Detroit Public Schools' Crockett Career and Technical Center to spend eight hours per week in the library for six weeks. Students are provided with medical smocks to wear and spend half of their time doing work for the library (e.g., assisting with interlibrary loan activities, including processing patron requests from locating items to delivery of material). The other half is spent in learning "the latest biomedical information databases and resources through hands-on information literacy instruction and work study experience."[51] The final project for each student is to research a particular disease or medical problem and create a flyer on that topic, which the library makes available to the public. Students gain lifelong learning skills, self-confidence, and have a taste of careers in both the medical and library fields. The pride generated by their accomplishments is clearly evident in the students and their family members who often take off from work to attend the concluding ceremonies at which students receive certificates of achievement.[52]

San José State University

San José State University (SJSU) was a teacher's college at one time and has strong teaching programs. The opening of its new Dr. Martin

Luther King, Jr. Library in partnership with the San José Public Library literally created an inviting pathway through the library from its city-side into the heart of the campus. Its message to potential first-generation college students is clear: "You can do it. You can get a college education. It is only one step beyond your public library." The nature of the new library has encouraged the initiation of other collaborations, including the following:

- It was not long before the Enrollment and Academic Services Office began tours in the city-side lobby of the library and it next created a student welcome center off the lobby. Relations with the library expanded to other recruitment and retention efforts described later in this chapter.

- Even before the library opened, a vision for library programming to benefit school learning emerged from focus groups that included both campus and community personnel. The vision was to bring together all the California-approved curriculum material, the best in children's literature, the best in continuing teacher and curriculum development materials, and materials on information literacy and school libraries into a single location. This placement allows parents, teachers, future teachers, and other interested people to see in one convenient place quality K–12 resources. In addition, there is an ongoing town/gown advisory committee, the Education Resource Center (ERC), that advises library personnel on programming and projects that can enhance K–12 learning in ways in keeping with the library's mission and that go beyond the class visits and story hours already offered by the public library's children's room personnel. (These latter activities provide ongoing opportunities for university student internships from both the College of Education and the graduate-level School of Library and Information Science.)

  The first project suggested by the ERC Advisory Committee was for the library to create and maintain a database of award-winning teachers and programs within San José's thirty-three school districts. This allows, for example, a teacher in one district who wants to incorporate a service learning component in a class to be able to identify other successful nearby programs. This database was soon mounted on the King Library's Web site along with other helpful K–12 information, such as lesson plans, technology resources, and standards-based education resources.

- The second major project the University Library undertook within its first year of operations was to respond to a major foundation's suggestion that the library apply for a grant that would promote science and environmental learning in the region. The first step in deciding whether or not to pursue this opportunity was a brainstorming session with the ERC Advisory Board. The project as subsequently designed involved partnering among the King Library staffs, the SJSU College of Science Resource Center, and the County Department of Education. The project has a number of components:

- The creation of an online science resource hub to provide information on all the science learning opportunities in the county and link their activities to state science standards. Also to be included in the database and linked to standards are the King Library and branch library resources.

- The creation of online science lesson plans linked to K–6 state science standards, including video clips of local teachers using different pedagogies in offering such learning.

- Training for teachers and future teachers in using these resources.

The audience for these collaborations would be anyone concerned about science learning, for example, teachers, future teachers, school administrators, home schoolers, parents and other child care personnel. In addition, the collection of information on community science programs (e.g., museums, science camps) would also help identify which of the standards have little or no enrichment programs to support their learning, making it possible for nonprofit and/or for-profit organizations to fill the gap.

At the time of writing, it is not known whether the project will be implemented, but it is clear that SJSU library staff in conjunction with its public library partner have much to contribute to K–12 learning and that the university/city library offers fertile ground for town/gown collaboration in enhancing local schools.

University of California at Los Angeles

At UCLA, the College Library, in partnership with the Graduate School of Education & Information Studies and the Los Angeles Unified School District School/Universities Partnerships Program launched two programs aimed at helping K–12 teachers and librarians incorporate information literacy and technology concepts into their curricula. College librarians worked with teachers and administrators in the Venice Westchester Cluster, an ethnically, culturally, and economically diverse school cluster that sends a disproportionately small number of students to UCLA. The resultant projects, the Information Literacy Instructional Pipeline Program and the Technology and Information Literacy Initiative, are train-the-trainer programs involving teachers and librarians in Southern California.

Vanderbilt University

Vanderbilt University offers two programs to high school students. The first is to students who participate in the International Baccalaureate (IB) programs at two local high schools. The IB program requires that students write an in-depth research paper, and for these students, Vanderbilt provides an "Introduction to Research" session and a tour of the library. The research session covers how to use the library catalog, where to find articles (online and in print), how to tell the difference between popular and scholarly articles, and where to find style guides for information on how to properly cite an article found in an online database. In addition, the students are given access cards good for one year.

Vanderbilt also provides an "Introduction to Academic Libraries" session for students in other local high schools. These sessions are initiated when a high school teacher calls to request a tour of the library. A basic orientation to academic libraries is provided, and the main focus of the presentation is on electronic resources to which students will still have access after they leave the library. When these visits are tied to a specific assignment, classroom space is made available so the students and their instructor have a "home base" from which to work.[53]

These above examples suggest some of the many ways academic libraries could help build strong college/school relationships. To encourage outreach programs to schools to make use of this important resource, presidents can ensure that library representatives are included in planning teams and ask that library involvement be addressed in any questionnaires or discussions held with local school representatives.

STUDENT RECRUITMENT AND THE CAMPUS LIBRARY

Standard publications that advise high school students on how to prepare themselves for college life frequently mention the importance of knowing how to use a library,[54] and libraries are stressed as a factor in selecting a college. The Carnegie Foundation Report *College* suggests how prospective college students (and their parents) should evaluate a library.

> The number of volumes in a library is often given, but circulation numbers can offer better information about how academically challenging the college is. Having a large number of books on library shelves has little relevance to students who don't use them. And how does the library budget compare with other college expenditures—intercollegiate athletics, for example?[55]

The popular press also emphasizes the library as an indication of institutional quality. *Changing Times*, for example, gives parents and students the following advice:

> Take a good look at the library. Is it doing a brisk business, or is it nearly deserted? The library won't be much help to you unless what's in it is appropriate for your studies and in sufficient supply.[56]

To these criteria, we would today add criteria such as access to computers and other appropriate technology, the availability of small group study rooms, and whether the library has online and phone reference services.

Having a strong academic library is in itself an obvious asset to institutions trying to recruit quality students. Yet the library can also play a more active role in recruitment. Most of the activities cited under school/college relations can be used as recruiting devices, and librarians experienced in outreach to local schools can serve as effective spokespersons for the campus. The library at Augustana College in Sioux Falls, South Dakota, has actively supported recruitment for its campus by changing its approach to meet changing opportunities. During high school class visits,

> guides to the library and handouts about specific research tools are now distributed to each student in an attractive packet with general information about the college, supplied by the Admissions Office.
>
> The session ends with the distribution of a "Thank You for Visiting the Library" discount coupon. Support from a campus idea fund resulted in funding to distribute these coupons to each high school student participating in a class visit to our college library. The coupon is worth a one dollar discount on a purchase in either the campus food service or the campus bookstore. To use the coupon, the student must provide his name, address, high school, and class status. Admissions staff then follow up with letters encouraging the students to consider Augustana when selecting a college.[57]

When funding was no longer available for discount coupons, the Admissions Office made a different offer,

> to host a study break in the nearby commons to encourage high school groups to see more of the Augustana campus. When area teachers call to schedule their visits, the librarian extends this invitation so that teachers and Admissions staff can plan accordingly. For those groups anticipating a longer stay, lunch in the Commons is suggested and the teacher offered a complimentary meal voucher.

The study break includes cookies and a bottle of "Augie" water, as well as an opportunity to pick up an Augustana admissions packet. Those students choosing to register for a packet are eligible for an immediate drawing of an Augie product—t-shirt, lanyard, or Nalgene water bottle.[58]

Having a wonderful new university/city library at San José State University led Marshall Rose, the associate vice president for Enrollment and Academic Services, to partner with university library personnel to capitalize on new opportunities that can provide a competitive edge. Even before he had a small space off the city-side lobby refurbished for a welcome center, most campus tours for student prospects and their parents began in the library, and he ensured that tour guides had the right information to share. In addition, building on the Augustana College model, a letter from the university library dean was sent out in a mailing to all accepted students early in the summer. The mailing briefly addressed the importance of "university-level research skills" to academic success and provided a brief self-test with encouragement to use a series of self-paced online modules if the self-graded test results indicated the need for upgrading research skills before the start of classes. At the least, the mailing was an additional indication of SJSU's commitment to students' success. For some incoming students, the incentive to enhance such skills could make a difference in their successfully making it through that first crucial semester.

Campus personnel who arrange tours for prospective students and their parents can work with library staff to design a library presentation that will reinforce a campus image that balances concern for academic quality with sports and eating facilities. A campus-developed great books list that mentions the importance of reading and using the library for quality education can be used as a handout for visits or mailed to prospective students. Libraries are among the largest campus employers of students; since visiting prospective students may well be employed there someday, a few comments by a current library student worker could highlight this possibility in positive terms. The academic library is also a traffic center for displaying recruitment posters and distributing recruitment handouts.

Recruitment publications can also be library-based. Some years ago, the academic vice chancellor at the University of Colorado–Denver prepared the brochure "Students' Guide to Graduate Education" as a low-key recruitment device aimed at campus undergraduates. Besides basic information on choosing graduate schools and descriptions of graduate programs on the Denver campus, the brochure included an annotated bibliography that sends the students to their campus library and/or their computers for information on graduate and professional programs.[59]

When recruiting adult learners, learning programs that highlight individualized learning in a hands-on, self-paced setting can be particularly attractive. Usually found in community colleges, such programs encourage a positive approach to learning for nontraditional students. Because libraries offer a flexible range of learning materials in a variety of formats and levels of difficulty, many learning programs are located in the library and administered as part of the learning resources program.[60]

LIBRARY USE AND STUDENT RETENTION

While libraries are a definite plus in recruitment, they are an even more powerful asset in student retention efforts. Campus libraries can be involved in orientation programs, academic success programs, and in programs targeted at retaining particular groups, such as part-time, international, or academically disadvantaged students. In fact, when some California State University library deans were asked what they most wished their presidents better understood about their libraries, they agreed that the role academic libraries play in student retention is far undervalued.

Orientation Programs

Orientation programs help incoming freshmen learn how to cope with the problems of college life and to exploit its opportunities. One goal of such programs should be to reduce or eliminate academic library research shock. Funded by a federal research grant, the Ohio Department of Education identified major areas of library intimidation for college freshmen and developed a pre-graduation orientation program for high school seniors. They found that students were intimidated by physical factors—multilevel distribution of the collection throughout the building(s); the size of the collection(s); the Library of Congress Classification System; and the diversity of the collection and available formats.[61] The research also showed that students were hesitant to ask librarians for assistance.

Since that study, the situation has become even more problematic. Major state budget deficits in the early nineties and again early in the new millennium have led to high school libraries being severely cut back in many states. This is of particular concern since a longitudinal study, based on data from the National Study of Student Learning conducted by the National Center on Postsecondary Teaching, Learning, and Assessment during the 1992–1995 academic years, documented a strong relationship between high school use of libraries and undergraduate use of libraries.

> Although background characteristics such as gender, race, and initial critical thinking scores initially correlated with library use during the freshman and sophomore years, they were no longer statistically significant by the junior year. However, high school library use continued to have a strong relationship with undergraduate academic library use during all three years of the study. The finding that high school library use remained a predictor of undergraduate academic library use after three years in college indicates the importance of assisting undergraduates to develop their library skills during secondary school.[62]

At the same time, public libraries, which in funding priorities always come in far behind police and fire demands on city budgets, have also suffered significantly. The result is that students in many locations are far less familiar and comfortable in libraries than they were in earlier decades. In addition, concerns for getting students to write better have led in many cases to favoring narrative papers over the traditional research paper. As a result, many students coming into campuses today are even more intimidated and less prepared to do research than their predecessors.

Another contributing factor to research limitations relates to varying levels of technology competence. A study on "Technological Preparedness Among Entering Freshmen: The Role of Race, Class, and Gender," published in 2001, arrived at the following conclusions:

> Using data from a nationwide survey of college freshmen, this study demonstrates that students' level of technological preparedness varies by such key factors as race, class, gender, and academic background. Further, racial/ethnic differences in experience with technology persist despite controls for key explanatory variables including parental income, parental education, and high school type. Institutional awareness of these inequities is critical at a time when colleges and universities are rapidly incorporating computers into nearly all aspects of the college experience, including admissions, the curriculum, class registration, and student life in general. We suggest that these pre-college disparities in the use of electronic mail and the Internet, if not attended to, may seriously compromise some students' ability to navigate through and benefit from college.[63]

Although not cited in the study, such lack of technology preparedness also significantly impacts students' abilities to use today's technology-rich libraries.

Despite all this, much progress has been made on many campuses in establishing flexible library services and programs to accommodate students at whichever level they are in their intellectual development and to systematically prepare them to do college-level research. Public libraries have long been acknowledged as the poor people's university (i.e., if you could not afford to go to college, you could prepare for a job at the public library or could tool up for a new job if needed). What few people appreciate is that academic libraries play a similar equal opportunity role in promoting student preparation on campuses. Certainly, in community colleges and four-year institutions alike, there is great inequality in student preparation for doing college-level research. Many students still come to college without having computers in their homes, or even books or magazines. They may or may not be first generation college students, but if they are to succeed, they need to become comfortable in their academic library and be able to access and effectively use both the information technology and the more traditional research materials housed there.

Libraries as Social Gathering Places

Libraries can also give students a place to belong or hang out, a place where they are always welcome, where they can go with friends, or even maybe make a friend. Increasing numbers of academic libraries, in fact, are located and organized to capitalize on meeting student needs for someplace outside the classroom or cafeteria to congregate and to study. For example, at George Mason University, the library was built into a student union.[64]

At Wayne State University when the new undergraduate library opened, weekly "cultural" events were held in an open atrium area that had molded seating along one wall. The programming was planned with the knowledge that students who become involved with some activity on campus besides their studies are more likely to stay in school. Cultural events were broadly interpreted to include, for example, an annual visit and demonstration from the award-winning WSU fencing team. The team always arrived with flyers to pass out to students explaining why they became members of the fencing team. Often, students would be lured from their studies to stand at the balconies overlooking the area to hear a musical presentation or some other event.

In like fashion, exhibits in libraries can whet the appetite of students to explore other resources on campus. Many students, for example, will not go out of their way to visit an art gallery on campus, but if art is displayed in the library, it may entice them to give some thought to art outside of a required humanities course. The whimsical artwork in the San José State University King Library is all related to the library and its collections. It is not uncommon to see students dragging a friend behind them to come and see a particular piece that intrigues them, such as the hidden revolving bookcase in the mystery section of the library.

Moreover, libraries should be places that are just pleasurable to be in. A library that has students' comfort in mind will have a variety of seating arrangements: places where students can work together in small groups, overlook a pretty scene, be able to sit and watch the world go by, hide away in a quiet corner, access media in a carrel or any other seating arrangement that suits their fancy. Libraries that are fortunate enough to have special events rooms and/or auditoriums can often entice students into the library for the first time to attend an event of particular interest to them. Once there, hopefully the atmosphere in the library is such that they will want to come back. Of course, nothing works better than having classroom faculty members encourage student use of the library—particularly in beginning freshman classes. Freshman research courses are ideal for making this student-library connection early and leading students to a potential intellectual home base on campus.

Special Uses of Libraries

Other means to bring students into the library include using it as a voting place for student elections or, in the case of California State University–San Francisco, even for national elections. When the campus became large enough to have its own precinct, the library volunteered to have the voting take place on its premises. Central to all of these ideas is the vision of the library as a multifaceted, welcoming, and nurturing center for student learning.

On many campuses, library contributions to student academic achievement extend beyond the walls of the library building. Academic success centers, writing centers, or other tutorial opportunities can also be points at which the opportunity to effectively develop research skills are made available to students. In recent years, academic success centers have become more common on campuses. Certainly, there needs to be a close tie between the academic library and any such center. All programs helping students develop speaking and writing skills should incorporate research skills; it makes sense that one can speak with more authority and write a better paper when one has good factual information on which to base the speech or the paper. Just as adult literacy programs are incomplete without people knowing how to find the information they need to read in order to have a better life, just so writing courses and speech courses need to help students get grounded in how they develop an adequate and compelling information base.

The library can also provide a bridge for bringing other support services to students. For example, at California State University–Sonoma, faculty advisors from the Advising Subcommittee responded to the Associated Students Resolution on Advising, which was passed because students were frustrated with the lack of advising in their majors. In keeping with the spirit of the campus Charlie Brown Café and the Jean and Charles Schulz Information Center University Library, they decided to set up a Lucy's Advising Booth in the library. The intent, as explained by the managing director of Advising, Career and Testing Services, Joyce Chong, was to improve both general and academic major counseling to all students on campus, but particularly to the more than 1,000 undeclared students seeking majors. Lucy's booth was set up in the lobby of the library right before registration week. Faculty volunteered to staff the booth. The Advising Subcommittee was very pleased with the results of the two-week effort and reported an "extremely positive response" from students.[65]

The concept of having the library serve as a bridging place between students and retention-promoting services has been well implemented at Loyola University in New Orleans. As part of a planned approach to increase retention rates, President Bernard P. Knoth "suggested that an existing lab located within the Library could be redesigned to serve as a resource clearinghouse—to represent all of the different academic support services on campus."[66]

> The new facility for academic support services at Loyola is named "The Academic and Career Excellence Center" or ACE Center. It is located adjacent to the reference room in the J. Edgar and Louise S. Monroe Library. At its fundamental core, the ACE Center is a word processing lab, but its mission is to be a highly visible, one stop student resource for referral to the appropriate academic assistance: counseling, tutoring, career guidance, academic assessment, disability services, as well as research and reference services. While the core services retain their respective identities, the ACE Center creates an environment where old geographic boundaries are blurred and activities move smoothly across multiple departments. The ACE Cen-

ter is staffed with peer tutors representing all of the support service departments. The tutors must go through an intensive period of cross training. Tutors learn the main points of each service and more importantly they understand that the center is a point of referral to the home bases of the various services. The peer tutors are trained not only as tutors in their subject areas, but also as generalists with the skills and knowledge to provide seamless delivery of services in all areas. "An important dimension of integrated information service on-site is efficient and effective referral to the next level of expertise, when appropriate."[67]

In addition to the ACE center, library personnel at Loyola have launched a new collaboration to replace term paper clinics with a series of workshops.

With the inclusion of all of the support services and other peripheral departments, these workshops target more than paper writing. In teaming with the campus colleagues the ACE Center will host sessions that target specific courses and audiences. The sessions will range from paper writing (offering tips from writing experts and research and bibliography assistance), presentation creation (creating a presentation using PowerPoint, media tips from experts and research assistance), to resume writing and interview preparation (offering business and industry research tips). All of these sessions are fluid and will be augmented and modified according to the needs of the target groups.[68]

Such creative linking of library and academic support units is an excellent model for other retention-conscious campuses to emulate.

Almost all academic libraries promote student retention through their heavy employment of students. Besides the general benefits of working on campus, many students increase their own research skills through their library experiences and the encouragement of library staff. In some cases, students are specially trained in research skills to serve as peer information counselors, to assist at information or reference desks, or in some fashion help other students feel more at ease in the library. In these cases, both the students working in the library and the students they assist benefit from the experience.

On other campuses, librarians have been actively involved in first-year learning communities, as these provide a promising venue to address research inadequacies, as well as what some have analyzed as cognitive development challenges for many beginning students (i.e., they have "not yet developed the skills necessary to ask the right questions or to know when they need information."[69]). These first-year efforts by librarians have ranged from collaborating with some or all faculty teaching these courses to teaching the courses themselves.[70] In light of the lack of research skills of most freshmen, the problem with the latter approach is the time commitment involved to reach small number of students.

Two more promising approaches are the required freshman Information Power course initiated by Wayne State University in 1997 (see description later in this chapter) and an approach developed by Margit Misangyi Watts at the University of Hawaii at Manoa. Her textbook, *College: We Make the Road by Walking*,[71] is used in a foundation course on her campus and has recently been adopted by Harvard for its freshmen. A first year experience leader, she has collaborated for over a decade with librarian Randy Hensley, and information literacy concepts are integrated throughout the textbook. The approach is designed to help students learn what the world of scholarship is and how to be a successful part of it. Manoa is also one of a growing number of campuses that are beginning to experiment with information literacy study centers in dormitories.

Information Literacy and Student Retention

Besides libraries being major contributors to the successful acculturation of the students to an academic environment in general, information literacy can play a significant role in students' classroom success. Campuses involved in student assessment programs need to ensure that information literacy skills are clearly accounted for in assessing critical thinking and academic skills. With the availability of national information literacy standards at both the school[72] and college[73] levels and the development of an information communication technology (ICT) test by the Educational Testing Services (ETS), assessing incoming students' skill levels will increasingly become more practical—allowing for targeted remedial work as appropriate.

The best measure of successful instruction in library use and research skills development is, of course, retention and academic performance, and research documenting a positive correlation between these factors goes back as far as 1972 at Brooklyn College.[74] A later synthesis of findings from sixty evaluation studies also indicates that such programs for high-risk students have had positive effects.[75] Significant relationships between library use and academic performance were also documented in unrelated retention studies in California. These include a 1960s study that revealed a statistically significant correlation between library use and persistence among first-year students at California State Polytechnic Col-

lege in Pomona,[76] and a 1980s study at the University of California–
Irvine, which evaluated the impact of a two-unit course entitled "Biblio
Strategy" on student academic success as measured by grade point average, student persistence, and graduation rate.[77] (The California State
University libraries stay involved in major student learning outcomes assessment efforts, including one on what CSU students know about finding, evaluating, and using information undertaken in partnership with
the Social and Behavioral Research Institute at CSU San Marcos,[78] and
the Educational Testing Services ICT skills test discussed in chapter 2.)

A recent longitudinal study conducted at Glendale Community College (California) found that information literacy instruction "has significant impact on student success (defined as retention and grades)."[79]
Efforts on this campus focused on two different approaches in two different disciplines and was initiated because of earlier research that had
shown library classes and workshops impacting students' success as defined by their GPAs in the following semester in comparison with a
matched group of students. Further research focused on a pairing model
of a one-unit library course with a three-unit English course and on in-
fusing information literacy instruction into two entry-level nursing
courses. Both approaches "proved successful and are being expanded."[80]

As campuses respond to pressures to assess student competence in basic
academic skills, they should look not only at students' progress in learning skills but also at the effect of skill levels on persistence and academic
success. Along with grade point averages, persistence, and graduation
rates, measurable elements might include the quality of bibliographies
and research papers, demonstrated skill in constructing and implementing search strategies (students could be asked to record their research efforts in a journal), effectiveness of oral arguments, and quality of senior
research projects or theses. Campus personnel concerned with student
retention should encourage more controlled experiments in all academic
skills areas and incorporate successful approaches into ongoing academic
programs.

DETERRING PLAGIARISM

These days no discussion about student retention and academic success can be complete without discussing the serious problem with plagiarism that exists on most campuses. Plagiarism is now so widespread in
both academic and business settings that plagiarism detection is a growing business, and even the U.N. Security Council has begun to use such
technology to ensure the originality of commissioned reports.[81] One re-

searcher admonishes that "every experienced teacher must be aware that at least half of American students confess to cheating of one sort or another, and that copied or purchased papers are among the easiest and least detectable forms of cheating." He urges universities "to deal with plagiarism on two fronts: prevention through education as well as punishment for violations."[82]

At Vanderbilt and on many other campuses, library faculty have taken the lead in addressing prevention through education in keeping with the Association of College & Research Libraries Information Literacy Competency Standard Five, which states that "The information literate student understands many of the economic, legal, and social issues surrounding the use of information and accesses and uses information ethically and legally."[83]

The Vanderbilt effort has focused on workshops to meet the needs of both faculty and graduate students and includes a student "assignment" that participants analyze to detect plagiarism clues.[84] California State University's information literacy initiatives

> place a high premium on helping students to learn correctly how to represent the language, thoughts, and ideas of others when writing a paper, creating a project, working in the laboratory, growing a crop, raising an animal, or engaging in any other type of creative or research activity; how properly to cite sources; how to understand and respect copyright laws and intellectual property rights in a physical and a virtual world; and how to avoid unethical behavior.[85]

How this is implemented on the various CSU campuses varies. At San José State University, for example, a self-paced online module, similar to existing research skills modules, can be assigned by faculty members or taken at students' own initiative. SJSU librarians offer workshops for faculty on how to use the module, as well as how to detect plagiarism. At Vanderbilt University where professors have indicated that plagiarism is a problem among their students, the Peabody Library regularly offers a two-hour seminar in the fall semester that is team-taught by two Peabody College professors: "Tools of Academic Integrity." They demonstrate relevant Web sites and discuss what plagiarism is and when it is necessary to cite sources.

At Hofstra University, Margaret Burke, reference librarian in the Axinn Library, provided the leadership for the campus move to using the program Turnitin when requests from faculty to help detect plagiarism grew from three to four a month in the spring of 1999 to 25 a month by December 2000. Under her guidance and with assistance from the university's legal department, it was determined that Turnitin "does not appear to be a threat to students' intellectual property rights and that the benefits derived from the service far outweighed the argument that students' rights might be jeopardized."[86] The new service caused the incidence of online plagiarism to drop by 34 percent at the end of December 2001 to 12 percent by the second year. Faculty are encouraged to inform students that Turnitin may be used to detect plagiarism, thus avoiding students' claims that their rights have been infringed. Librarians now offer "an elective one-credit class that introduces students to library information and technology. In these classes, librarians explain the research process, demonstrate how and when to cite sources, and we offer a detailed explanation of what constitutes plagiarism. We also describe how Turnitin.com functions."[87]

Given the above examples, it seems evident that as campuses work to create a climate of academic integrity, the potential contribution of library personnel, resources, and services should be integral to planning and implementation efforts. Researching the best that is already in place on other campuses is a good way to start.

WORKING WITH SPECIAL POPULATIONS

Campus libraries also support retention and academic success efforts targeted at specific subgroups of students, such as international, minority, academically and economically disadvantaged students, and off-campus students.

Needs of International Students

Successful programs for international students, for example, take students' cultural adjustment and coping skills into account. These factors are important to their library work.

> Many of these students were accustomed to very traditional styles of learning based on memorization and the use of a single text, and to libraries in which they were handed the book that they needed. They had had little or no opportunity for critical thinking and independent study. Furthermore, they were unaccustomed to American professors' expectations and methods of teaching. Coming from different cultural backgrounds, they were striving to adjust to entirely new and confusing social mores, including the western sense of time. In addition, many of them were mature individuals with important responsibilities in their own countries. Their inability to

function effectively in our culture, for example, their dependence on the librarians, was upsetting and embarrassing to them. Their lack of facility with English intensified all of these problems.[88]

Libraries in the United States also operate very differently from libraries elsewhere, particularly those in Asian, Latin American, and African countries. "Students have little familiarity with basic sources, little expectation of reference help, little experience in independent research. Even open stacks are an unfamiliar concept to many who are used to having their materials paged. This makes the needed one-to-one contact, almost an inevitability for the American library user, hard to come by for the foreign student unless the library staff makes the effort to overcome the strangeness felt on both sides."[89] Libraries actively involved in meeting the needs of international students emphasize the following important elements:

- Clear, informative signs;
- Specially designed library and orientation programs carefully integrated into selected course offerings;
- Immediate practice of concepts learned;
- Information compiled specifically for international students (for example, lists of local people fluent in foreign languages and lists of campus services designed for foreign students);
- Emphasis by both teacher and librarian on asking librarians for help; and
- Multiple copies of materials in heavy demand (international students often need extra time with audiovisual materials because of linguistic accents and other problems).

Librarians can also help international students by collecting materials that feature life outside the United States so that students may do research on more familiar topics, by hiring international students for library jobs, and by educating library staff on cultural differences.[90]

Needs of Ethnic Groups

The same elements are as important to library programs for specific ethnic groups as they are for international students. Library staff who are sensitive to cultural differences will not lump all Spanish-speaking or all Asian students together in their thinking and planning.[91] Student service personnel with responsibility for particular ethnic groups must not overlook library staff in training campus personnel to respond positively to special student needs.

Libraries generally employ many student workers. At one time, Cleveland State University used library employment practices to promote minority student retention. Minority students with sophomore standing and a grade point average of 2.5 or above were identified and trained in basic and advanced library and information skills. They then serve as reference/information service assistants and also work on specific research projects under the guidance of librarians. This supportive environment helped student employees develop a positive attitude toward higher education and improve their research skills, while strengthening academic performance and, for some, becoming positive role models for other minority students.

Library personnel can refer to successful programs across the country when designing responses to particular student needs. As far back as 1969, UCLA created one of the first library instruction programs designed specifically for Chicano students, and the model developed there was often adapted to meet a wide variety of student needs both at UCLA and on other campuses. This program was phased out in 1981 and replaced with a series of other activities designed to actively support recruitment and retention of students from underrepresented groups or those who are otherwise disadvantaged, including information literacy outreach. Esther Grassian and Stephanie Brasley, from the UCLA College Library, summarize current efforts focused on particular sets of student needs.

- Summer Transfer Enrichment Program (STEP), run by the UCLA Community College Partnerships Office. This is a nonresidential summer bridge program for community college students transferring to UCLA, which often involves underrepresented minorities or disadvantaged students. The library has developed a program of two-hour, one-shot information literacy sessions to support their research needs and introduce them to UCLA libraries (one to two sessions, usually June or July).

- Summer Intensive Transfer Experience (SITE), run by the UCLA Community College Partnerships Office. This is a summer bridge program for incoming UCLA freshmen, generally identified as underrepresented minorities or disadvantaged students. The College Library developed a program of two-hour, one-shot IL sessions to support their research needs and to introduce them to UCLA libraries (about eight sessions, usually June or July of each year).

- Freshman Summer Program/Transfer Summer Program (FSP/TSP) is another summer bridge program for incoming UCLA students, both freshmen and transfers from community colleges and CSUs, primarily. Again these students are underrepresented minorities or disadvantaged students. The College Library provides between 20 and 35 information literacy instruction sessions in August each year.

- The college library has also developed a liaison role with the Office for Students with Disabilities (OSD), providing information through the OSD newsletter, *New Horizons*, and through in-service presentations to staff. Students identified through OSD may arrange for individualized research appointments with college librarians.

- Migrants Engaged in New Themes in Education (MENTE), a program that has been in existence for 20 years, is funded out of the federal Migrant Education Programs. The program serves as an academic bridge that sharpens and expands the intellectual skills of migrant students by providing rigorous academic coursework. In 1999, the program was held at UCLA. The college library developed an information literacy/research skills session for students in the program.[92]

Needs of Academically At-Risk Students

Library support programs for academically disadvantaged students usually need to serve students from a wide range of backgrounds. Libraries should be encouraged to rethink their priorities in light of the growing numbers of students who are academically at risk.[93] Unfortunately, creative use of academic libraries in facilitating the success of such students is still rare.[94]

To help academically disadvantaged students succeed, librarians and academic personnel who have primary responsibility for these students need to develop good working relationships so that they can jointly determine what library learning and research experiences are needed and how best to implement them. To accommodate lower reading levels, libraries can supplement college titles with materials usually provided by public libraries (such as pamphlets on current issues and popular journals) and acquire multiple copies of paperback books. If numbers justify this commitment, specific library personnel can be assigned to work directly with high-risk students and to ensure a welcoming atmosphere in the library.[95]

The goal should be empowerment, "giving these young people confidence in themselves, which in turn will help them learn and will inculcate in them that they have a magnificent contribution to make to society."[96] Library instruction limited to traditional library orientation tours or one-time class sessions that try to cover all resources in a particular discipline in fifty minutes could have a negative impact on high-risk students' attitudes and performance[97] by increasing library research shock rather than by improving skills.

One experienced worker with academically disadvantaged students suggests that new instructional approaches should make practical distinctions among the needs of beginning and advanced students. Following an approach modeled on athletic instruction, she recommends "establishing minimum competencies or fitness skills at development levels (such that basic library survival techniques are mastered early and become part of the nontraditional students' set of operational skills regardless of whether they stop out, drop out, or graduate), and advanced level, competitive information retrieval skills for those who aim to complete their degrees and establish careers in the information marketplace."[98] Critical to both levels are sufficient learning opportunities and the integration of library use into classroom assignments.

Wayne State University's unpopular freshman survival course, "The University and Its Libraries," was significantly revamped in 1997. It was designed to take advantage of its award-winning debate team coach by building the course around a team debate format. Students who would normally settle for any information on a topic for a paper, thought more carefully about doing more thorough research when they knew that their classmates would be preparing to refute their arguments. In team debates, students learned how to speak more effectively, organize their thoughts, and do better research, all while enjoying a little friendly peer competition. The new course, which was entitled Info Power, was taught by classroom faculty who were provided with quality videotapes and PowerPoint materials to support their instruction. In addition, librarians conducted two of the sessions that particularly focused on information searching and evaluation techniques. In this new configuration, 89 percent of students in the various course sections said "yes" when surveyed as to whether they could use what they learned in the course.[99]

Bringing All Students Up to College Level

As noted earlier, academic libraries can play a key role in providing equity of learning opportunities for economically disadvantaged and/or first-generation college students. For these students, library access to information resources is essential to their academic success. In many cases, even where students have had access to computers, they are not

likely to have developed the skills they need to complete research assignments. In a 2002 Benton Foundation transatlantic roundtable on
the topic, "Toward Digital Inclusion for Underserved Youth," it was
noted that, although there is more use of technology in communities,
"it's not just about access, it's got to be about outcomes. If all [a teen-
ager] does with that technology are the things he or she can do with a
newspaper or a television, if he or she is not getting new skills [or] . . .
contributing to the community, then what's the point of this technology?"[100] At a time when many colleges and universities are seeking to
rid themselves of remedial responsibilities regarding students' writing
and math skills, it may seem counterintuitive to declare information
literacy a core competency that is not adequately addressed in K–12
classrooms; however, the fact remains that the great majority of students are coming to college without adequate skills to successfully complete their academic responsibilities, much less to be prepared for
lifelong learning and critical thinking in today's information society.
Our choice is—as in other core competency areas—either to work with
the K–12 sector to improve information literacy mastery there or to accept the responsibility for institutionalizing the assessment and remedial work needed on our campuses.

SPECIAL FOCUS AREAS IN INFORMATION LITERACY

Globalization

Earlier in this chapter, the role of libraries in meeting the special needs
of international students was discussed. Additional attention should also
be given to other ways in which academic library personnel and resources
can support campuses' growing interests in globalization. Of particular
value may be well-developed information literacy programs; internationally, there is increasing concern that people be able to acquire such abilities. For example, researchers from the International Literacy Institute
and the National Center on Adult Literacy at the University of Pennsylvania emphasize throughout a 2003 paper[101] that the "what" of the digital divide continues to shift, initially referring to access to computers,
then to the Internet, and now to appropriate information and learning
opportunities. Communities around the globe continue to make strides
toward improving the first two items, as these are the "easy" components
for government agencies, private organizations and companies to provide.
It is the third, the information and learning opportunities, that is the

most difficult, yet most critical, for achieving basic and advanced literacy skills.

In addition, UNESCO's Strategic Orientation to the World Summit on the Information Society (WSIS), which was held in Geneva in December 2004, describes the power of the Information Society:

> The emergence of the Information Society is a revolution comparable to the deep transformation of the world engendered by the invention of the alphabet and the printing press. A new culture is emerging, based on symbols, codes, models, programs, formal languages, algorithms, virtual representations, mental landscapes, which imply the need for a new "information literacy." Information and knowledge have not only become the principal forces of social transformation. They also hold the promise that many of the problems confronting human societies could be significantly alleviated if only the requisite information and expertise were systematically and equitably employed and shared.[102]

This same concern, particularly as related to developing countries, led to UNESCO's partnering with the U.S. National Commission on Library and Information Science and the National Forum on Information Literacy in bringing together information literacy experts from twenty-three countries in Prague in September 2003. The "Prague Declaration: Towards an Information Literate Society" appears in Appendix E, and more than thirty papers commissioned for the conference, covering the role of information literacy in economic development, education, human services, and policy making, are available at http://www.infolit.org/Inter national_Conference/index.htm. Recommendations in the Declaration include the need to consider information literacy as a basic human right.

Other indications of both national and global recognized needs for lifelong learning workforces are seen in coalitions focusing on information and communication technologies (ICT) literacy. For example, the Web site, "The Essential Digital Literacy Skills for the 21st Century Global Citizen" represents "a fast growing international movement focused on promoting Information and Communication Technologies (ICT) Digital Literacy." Its goal is to build an international consensus for advancing meaningful educational initiatives, for training a highly skilled workforce, and for understanding issues related to economic development. This Web site provides a rich, centralized portal for the repository of ICT literacy resources, highlights innovative efforts and partnerships promoting ICT literacy, and facilitates the interaction between researchers, business, government and educational segments.[103] Some of these efforts concentrate more narrowly on technology skills, but, increasingly, ICT skills incorporate technology skills with critical thinking skills to enable people to obtain, evaluate, and use information effectively. Other writers particularly concerned with the "have-nots" of the world also point out the need for information literacy:

> The potential benefits of advanced technologies for millions of people, many of whom are in desperate need, will not be realized unless they are seen in the context of a wider programme to alleviate or cancel unsustainable debt.
>
> Specifically in regard to the use of information and communications technologies, there is also scope to initiate a programme of free provision of hardware and software, training and education, targeted initially at the Highly Indebted Poor Countries.
>
> Better access to information is a key to development, and here we can see some synergy with other areas such as health and disability. Here we start to need to consider the issue of "information literacy."[104]

Given the growing importance placed on information literacy at the international level, campuses developing ties with universities in other countries may find that overseas partners view their campus programs and standards for information literacy as attractive additions to their portfolios. In addition, cooperative research programs may also open doors— particularly in developing countries where information literacy efforts may just be getting underway.

Library resources can also provide information useful to campus personnel to facilitate doing business within different cultures. As for the internationalization of American students, adequately funded acquisitions can provide a wide range of multimedia information resources from other countries that can enrich both classroom and more informal learning opportunities.

Information Literacy in Healthcare

At campuses with medical school and hospitals, librarians can offer health-related services. We have already discussed earlier in this chapter the program the Wayne State University medical library initiated for at-risk high school students, and the director there was also heavily involved with the transformation of the medical curriculum into a problem-based approach.

No aspect of information literacy is more emotionally charged than the area of health information. Campus responsibilities in this regard are twofold. First, there is the need to ensure that future healthcare workers apply information literacy in their work. Unfortunately, there is a gap between literature and practice, as noted in an editorial in 2000 in the *Annals of Internal Medicine*, despite more recent commitments by medical schools to evidence/problem-based learning. "[T]he medical profession falls far short in its efforts to make the critical link between the huge body of information hidden away in the medical literature and the information needed at the point of care. This failure means not only that many opportunities for improved patient care and continued learning are missed but also that much of the effort, creativity, and money that go into biomedical research is simply wasted."[105] One approach to addressing this dilemma is to have campus medical librarians play a role in supporting medical decision-making. Documentation of the value of clinical medical librarians and training programs for them goes back to the very early 1970s.[106]

At Vanderbilt University, librarians at the Eskind Biomedical Library serve as "informationalists." These librarians after special training serve as clinical librarians going on rounds in the Vanderbilt Medical Center. Their role is to "focus on patient-specific questions, so as they're debating about care for a particularly challenging case or a condition that's a little bit rare, there's an opportunity for [them] to jump in and take a look at the literature to see what else it might offer."[107]

Campuses with schools of medicine, nursing, and strong health sciences programs might also consider running these programs in collaboration with the library so that healthcare information is made available to campus and community members. Many current examples exist, often from public libraries, as this example from Williamsburg, Virginia, illustrates:

> A diagnosis of cancer raises many questions for patients, their families, and their friends. To help people in the community meet the challenge of cancer, the Williamsburg Regional Library and the Williamsburg Community Hospital formed a partnership to develop the Phillip West Memorial Cancer Resource Center. The Center, located in both the Williamsburg Library and the James City County Library, provides access to understandable, current, and accurate cancer-related information in both written and computerized formats. The collection includes circulating books, videos, and audiotapes, reference materials and cancer-related magazines for in-library use, and free informational pamphlets. The center also offers a web

site, www.westcancer.org, developed and maintained by the Library's Reference Department. To complement the Center's resources, educational programs are offered throughout the year at the libraries.[108]

No matter what programs your campus offers or what the size of the enrollment, the challenge for all campus leaders should be to ensure the alignment of library resources and services with campus goals, whether they be better college/school relations, improved instruction, student retention, increased research, or improved community service. More direct involvement of library resources and personnel can truly be a strategic tool in achieving all of these and other institutional priorities.

NOTES

1. Lewis Guodo Liu, "The Contribution of Library Collections to Prestige of Academic Programs of Universities: A Quantitative Analysis," *Library Collections, Acquisitions, & Technical Services* 25 (spring 2001): 49.

2. Brian Hackett, *Beyond Knowledge Management: New Ways to Work and Learn* (New York: The Conference Board, 2000), 38.

3. Ibid., 51.

4. Don Cohen, *Managing Knowledge in the New Economy* (New York: The Conference Board, 1998), 7.

5. Ibid., 15.

6. Julie N. Oman, "Information Literacy in the Workplace," *Information Outlook* 5 (June 2001): 33.

7. Angela Donnelly and Carey Craddock, "Information Literacy at Unilever R&D," *Update Magazine*, December 2002. Retrieved on 11 April 2005 from http://www.cilip.org.uk/publications/updatemagazine/archive/archive2002/december/update0212c.htm.

8. Daniel A. Wagner and Robert Kozma, *New Technologies for Literacy and Adult Education: A Global Perspective* (Philadelphia: University of Pennsylvania, 2003).

9. Angela Abell, "Corporate Information Literacy: An Essential Competence or an Acquired Skill," *Records Management Bulletin* 99 (October 2002). Retrieved 16 April 2001 from http://www.rms-gb.org.uk/99%20Abell.html.

10. Ibid., 13–14.

11. Cohen, *Managing Knowledge in the New Economy*, 21.

12. Alex Bennet, "Information Literacy: A New Basic Competency," *CHIPS Magazine*, fall 2001: 1. Retrieved 5 August 2004 from http://www.chips.navy.mil/archives/01_fall/information_literacy.htm.

13. *The Knowledge Proposition: Developed by the Participants of the CKO Summit, 5–7 October 2003* (London: TFPL Ltd., 2003), 9.

14. Oman, "Information Literacy in the Workplace," 35.

15. Todd Kulik, *Knowledge Management: Becoming an E-Learning Organization* (New York: The Conference Board, 2000), 21.

16. Robert Grover and Jack Glazier, "Information Transfer in City Government," *Public Library Quarterly* 5 (winter 1984): 26.

17. Peter G. Watson and Rebecca A. Boone, "Information Support for Academic Administrators: A New Role for the Library," *College & Research Libraries* 50 (January 1989): 66.

18. Ibid.

19. William Saffady, "A University Archives and Records Management Program: Some Operational Guidelines," in *College and University Archives: Selected Readings* (Chicago: Society of American Archivists, 1979).

20. Roger Crane and Wallace Poole, "Project Retrieval: The Banking of Instructional Development Resources at Brock University," *Educational Computer Magazine* 2 (March/April 1982): 46–47.

21. Carl Phillips, e-mail correspondence to Patricia Breivik, 7 October 2004.

22. *Ulrich's Periodicals Directory*, http://www.ulrichsweb.com/ulrichsweb/.

23. *WorldCat*, http://www.oclc.org/worldcat/.

24. Marc Katy, "AT&T Long Lines: Building a High Volume Information Research Center in Just 5 Years," *The Information Manager* 1 (September/October 1979): 23.

25. Beth A. Smith, "The Library Takes the Lead: Wichita State University Library Proposes a University-Wide Internet Policy," *C&RL News* 63 (July/August 2002): 509.

26. Watson and Boone, "Information Support for Academic Administrators."

27. Marcia Myers, "Special Library Services for Academic Administrators," *Kentucky Libraries* 59 (spring 1995): 9.

28. Martha Boaz, *Strategies for Meeting the Information Needs of Society in the Year 2000* (Littleton, Colo.: Libraries Unlimited, 1981), 86.

29. Stuart M. Basefsky, "The Other Client: Information Training for Administrators Pays Dividends for the Library," *C&RL News* 61 (February 2000): 100.

30. Leslie Hurst, "The Special Library on Campus: A Model for Library Orientations Aimed at Academic Administration, Faculty, and Support Staff," *The Journal of Academic Librarianship* 29 (July 2003): 233.

31. Ibid., 235.

32. Ibid.

33. Academic Achievement Task Force, Wayne State University and City of Detroit, "White Paper on Academic Achievement of the Youth of the City of Detroit," 19 November 2003. Submitted by Irvin D. Reid.

34. Paula Wood, telephone conversation with Breivik, 18 October 2004.

35. William A. Moffett, "What the Academic Librarian Wants from Administrators and Faculty," in *Priorities for Academic Libraries*, ed. Thomas J. Galvin and Beverly P. Lynch (San Francisco: Jossey-Bass, 1982), 17.

36. Leora Baron, "Why Information Literacy?" *NEA Higher Education Advocate* 18 (August 2001): 8.

37. Patricia Iannuzzi, "Faculty Development and Information Literacy: Establishing Campus Partnerships," *Reference Services Review* 26 (fall/winter 1998): 101.

38. Ibid.

39. University of Washington, *UWired Index*. Retrieved 20 March 2005 from http://www.washington.edu/uwired/.

40. Wendy Pradt Lougee, *Diffuse Libraries: Emergent Roles for the Research Library in the Digital Age* (Washington, D.C.: Council on Library and Information Resources, 2002), 18.

41. Jamie McKenzie, "Winning with Information Literacy," *Technos: Quarterly for Education and Technology* 9 (spring 2000): 1. Retrieved 6 June 2002 from http://www.findarticles.com/cf_0/m0HKV/1_9/65014442/print.jhtml.

42. George Lupone, e-mail correspondence to Patricia Breivik, 28 February 2005.

43. Zheng Ye (Lan) Yang, "University Faculty's Perception of a Library Liaison Program: A Case Study," *The Journal of Academic Librarianship* 26 (March 2000): 125.

44. Ibid., 126.

45. Patricia M. King and Nathan K. Lindsay, "Teachable Moments, Teachable Places: Education Beyond the Classroom," *Change* 36 (May/June 2004): 55.

46. Ibid., 52.

47. See, for example, Claire L. Gaudiani and David G. Burnett, *Academic Alliances: A New Approach to School/College Collaborations*, Current Issues in Higher Education, no. 1 (Washington, D.C.: American Association for Higher Education, 1985–1986). Other examples of university/school partnerships focused on information literacy can be found in the appendix of the *Blueprint for Collaboration*, a 2000 report of the American Association of School Librarians/Association of College & Research Libraries Task Force on the Educational Role of Libraries. Available at http://www.ala.org/ACRLtemplate.cfm?Section=whitepapers&Template=/ContentManagement/ContentDisplay.cfm&ContentID=14514.

48. Student journal entry provided by Patricia Randazzo, teacher at Accel Middle College, which educates high school students at Evergreen Valley College, San José, California, 23 November 2003.

49. Janet Nichols, "Building Bridges: High School and University Partnerships for Information Literacy," *NASSP Bulletin* 83 (March 1999): 75–81.

50. Nichols, "Sharing a Vision: Information Literacy Partnerships (K–16)," *C&RL News* 62 (March 2001): 275–77, 285.

51. "Team at Wayne State University's Shiffman Medical Library Wins National Award," *Wayne State University Library System Newsletter* 44 (spring/summer 1998): 1.

52. Lothar Spang, Ellen Marks, and Nancy Adams, "Rx for Learning: Information Tools 2000," *American Libraries* 29 (November 1998): 56. Retrieved 18 July 2004 through Expanded Academic ASAP.

53. Melinda F. Brown, e-mail correspondence to Patricia Breivik, 23 September 2004.

54. *Academic Preparation for College: What Students Need to Know and Be Able to Do* (New York: The College Board, 1983), 10.

55. Ernest L. Boyer, *College: The Undergraduate Experience in America* (New York: Harper & Row, 1986), 24.

56. "Good Colleges That Cost Less," *Changing Times* 36 (November 1982): 77.

57. Ronelle K. H. Thompson and Glenda T. Rhodes, "Recruitment: A Role for the Academic Library?" *C&RL News* 47 (October 1986): 576.

58. Ronelle K. H. Thompson, e-mail correspondence to Patricia Breivik, 16 September 2004.

59. John S. Haller, Jr., "A Student's Guide to Graduate Education," versions prepared at California State University at Long Beach, 1986, and at the University of Colorado at Denver, 1987.

60. D. Joleen Bock and Ernest W. Tompkins, *Learning Laboratories: Individualized Adult Learning*, Library Journal Special Report, No. 14 (New York: Library Journal, 1980).

61. Juanita W. Buddy, "Orientation to the University Library—The Missing Link," *NAASP Bulletin* 66 (December 1982): 100.

62. Ethelene Whitmire, "The Relationship Between Undergraduates' Background Characteristics and College Experiences and Their Academic Library Use," *College & Research Libraries* 61 (November 2001): 536.

63. Linda J. Sax, Miguel Ceja, and Robert T. Teranishi, "Technological Preparedness Among Entering Freshmen: The Role of Race, Class, and Gender," *Journal of Educational Computing Research* 24, no. 4 (2001): 363.

64. "George Mason Creates New Center of Learning," *C&RL News* 57 (May 1996): 277–78.

65. Joyce Chong, telephone conversation with Patricia Breivik, 3 September 2004.

66. Elizabeth Orgeron, "Integrated Academic Student Support Services at Loyola University: The Library as a Resource Clearinghouse," *Journal of Southern Academic and Special Librarianship* 2, no. 3 (2001). Retrieved 14 June 2004 from http://southernlibrarianship.icaap.org/content/v02n03/orgeron_e01.htm.

67. Ibid.

68. Ibid.

69. Nancy H. Seamans, "Student Perceptions of Information Literacy: Insights for Librarians," *Reference Services Review* 30, no. 2 (2002): 123.

70. See, for example, Tammy S. Sugarman and Laura G. Burtle, "From 50 Minutes to 15 Weeks: Teaching a Semester-Long Information Literacy Course

within a Freshman Learning Community," in *Integrating Information Literacy into the College Experience* (Ann Arbor: Pierian Press, 2003), 187–98; and Burtle and Sugarman, "The Citizen in the Information Age: Georgia State University's Creation of a Librarian-Led Freshmen Learning Community," *C&RL News* 63 (April 2002): 276–79.

71. Margit Misangyi Watts, *College: We Make the Road by Walking* (Upper Saddle River, N.J.: Prentice Hall, 2003).

72. See American Association of School Librarians' *Information Literacy Standards for Student Learning* at http://www.ala.org/ala/aasl/aaslissues/aaslinfolit/informationliteracy1.htm.

73. See the Association of College & Research Libraries' *Information Literacy Competency Standards for Higher Education* at http://www.ala.org/ala/acrl/acrlstandards/informationliteracycompetency.htm.

74. Patricia Senn Breivik, *Open Admissions and the Academic Library* (Chicago: American Library Association, 1977), 57–59.

75. Chen-Lin C. Kulik, James A. Kulik, and Barbara J. Shwalb, "College Programs for High-Risk and Disadvantaged Students: A Meta-Analysis of Findings," *Review of Educational Research* 53 (fall 1983): 397–414.

76. Harrold S. Shipps, Jr., "A Pre-College Program in Library Skills for Minority Students," *Library Journal* 95 (15 September 1970): 2887.

77. Lloyd A. Kramer and Martha B. Kramer, "The College Library and the Drop-Out," *College & Research Libraries* 29 (July 1968): 310–12.

78. *CSU Information Competence Assessment Task Force Phase II Report Summary.* Retrieved 1 April 2005 from http://www.csupomona.edu/~kkdunn/ictaskforcearchive/Phase%20II%20Summary.htm.

79. Deborah Moore, et al., "Information Competency Instruction in a Two-Year College: One Size Does Fit All," *Reference Services Review* 30, no. 4 (2002): 300. Retrieved 12 September 2003 from Emerald Insight database.

80. Ibid., 305.

81. May Wong, "Plagiarism Detection a Growing Field," *San Jose Mercury News*, 11 April 2004, 1F–2F.

82. Edward M. White, "Student Plagiarism as an Institutional and Social Issue," in *Perspectives on Plagiarism and Intellectual Property in a Postmodern World*, ed. Lise Buranen and Alice M. Roy (Albany: State University of New York Press, 1999), 205–6.

83. *Information Literacy Competency Standards for Higher Education* (Chicago: Association of College & Research Libraries, 2000).

84. Melinda F. Brown, e-mail correspondence to Patricia Breivik, 10 February 2005.

85. Ilene F. Rockman, "The Importance of Information Literacy," *Exchanges: The Online Journal of Teaching and Learning in the CSU.* Retrieved 14 May 2002 from http://www.exchangesjournal.org/print/print_1100.html.

86. Margaret Burke, "Deterring Plagiarism: A New Role for Librarians,"

Library Philosophy and Practice 6 (spring 2004): 6. Retrieved 22 March 2004 from http://libr.unl.edu:2000/LPP/burke.pdf.

87. Ibid., 8.

88. Johnnye Cope and Evelyn Black, "New Library Orientation for International Students," *College Teaching* 33 (fall 1985): 160.

89. Terry Ann Mood, "Library Services to Foreign Students in Colorado," *Colorado Libraries* 8 (September 1982): 10.

90. See, for example, Cope and Black, "New Library Orientation," 159–62; Mood, "Library Services to Foreign Students in Colorado," 8–11; and Elaine P. Adams, "Internationalizing the Learning Resource Center," *College Board Review* 119 (spring 1981): 19, 27, 28.

91. Arnulfo D. Trejo, "Library Needs for the 'Spanish-Speaking,'" *ALA Bulletin* 63 (September 1969): 1077–81.

92. Gary Strong, e-mail correspondence to Patricia Breivik, with information provided by Esther Grassian and Stephanie Brasley, University of California, Los Angeles, College Library, in an attached document, 8 September 2004.

93. Donald T. Rippey and Carol Truett, "The Developmental Student and the Community College Library," *Community College Review* 2 (winter 1983–1984): 41–47.

94. For a useful discussion of how libraries can be of assistance, see ACRL, CJCLS Committee on Services to the Disadvantaged, "Libraries Services to the Academically Disadvantaged in the Public Community College," *C&RL News* 48 (April 1987): 189–91.

95. See, for example, E. J. Josey, "The Role of the Academic Library in Serving the Disadvantaged Student," *Library Trends* 20 (October 1971): 432–43; Thomas W. Shaughnessy, "Library Services to Educationally Disadvantaged Students," *C&RL News* 36 (November 1975): 443–48; and Sylvia Hart Wright, "A Pre-College Program for the Disadvantaged," *Library Journal*, 15 September 1970, 2884–87.

96. Josey, "Role of the Academic Library," 443.

97. Breivik, *Open Admissions and the Academic Library*.

98. Collette Wagner in consultation with Augusta S. Kappner, "The Academic Library and the Non-Traditional Student," in *Libraries and the Search for Academic Excellence*, ed. Patricia Senn Breivik and Robert Wedgeworth (Metuchen, N.J.: Scarecrow Press, 1988), 51–52.

99. "UGE 1000 Extends Its Reach," *Wayne State University Library System Newsletter* 46 (winter 1999): 4.

100. Benton Foundation, *Toward Digital Inclusion for Underserved Youth: A Transatlantic Roundtable Summary and Next Steps* (Washington, D.C.: Benton Foundation, 2002), 8.

101. Daniel A. Wagner and Robert Kozma, *New Technologies for Literacy and Adult Education: A Global Perspective* (Philadelphia: University of Pennsylvania, 2003).

102. Cited in *Information Literacy, the Information Society and International Development: Report of a Meeting*, 6. Retrieved 11 April 2005 from http://www.ideography.co.uk/wsis-focus/meeting/InfoLit_21jan2003.pdf.

103. Information and Communication Technologies (ICT) Literacy, *Research Information Communication Technologies ICT Literacy*. Retrieved 1 April 2004 from http://www.ictliteracy.info/.

104. John Lindsay and Brian Layzell, *ICTs, Information Literacy, Health & Development*. Retrieved 17 August 2004 from http://www.epsg.org.uk/dcsg/docs/infacclit.pdf.

105. F. Davidoff and V. Florance, "The Informationist: A New Health Profession?" *Annals of Internal Medicine* 132 (20 June 2000): 996–98.

106. Carolyn E. Lipscomb, "Historical Notes: Clinical Librarianship," *Bulletin of the Medical Library Association* 88 (October 2000): 393–95.

107. Danianne Mizzy, "Informationists: Making Rounds Make a Difference," *C&RL News* 64 (March 2003): 176.

108. American Library Association, *ALA Information Literacy Community Partnerships Assembly, July 6, 2000*. Retrieved 21 October 2004 from http://www.ala.org/ala/ourassociation/governanceb/pastpresidents/nancykranich/informationliteracyassembly.htm.

CHAPTER

Libraries in Transition

Since the advent of the Internet, the library has become one of the most transformed departments on most campuses. It may look very much the same on the outside, but the resources and services have been and continue to be significantly altered. In fact, it is safe to say that few faculty and fewer campus administrators realize just how different things are, and this may in many cases cause a gap between expectations and reality, as well as underutilization of resources and services by both faculty and their students. What is the nature of these changes?

Technology advances constitute a major factor in the rapid change in libraries. Expansion of reference services to providing virtual services 24/7 is a fairly obvious change to users. For many, the impact of technology has been so extensive that by 1999 some libraries needed to be characterized as digital libraries, as defined by the Council on Library and Information Resources:

> organizations that provide the resources, including the specialized staff, to select, structure, offer intellectual access to, interpret, distribute, preserve the integrity of, and ensure the persistence over time of collections of digital works so that they are readily and economically available for use by a defined community or set of communities.[1]

For most academic libraries, the challenge has been to remain all that they have been plus becoming highly digitalized.

But the changes that have been occurring go even deeper. An August 2002 report commissioned by the Council of Library and Information Resources (CLIR) analyzes the significant challenges facing libraries while sustaining still-needed traditional functions.

> The changes under way reflect an evolutionary path in which, as distributed and collaborative models emerge, libraries are taking on far more diffuse roles within the campus community and beyond. That is, libraries are becoming more deeply engaged in the creation and dissemination of knowledge and are becoming essential collaborators with the other stakeholders in these activities.
>
> The roles emerging through this evolution are based in part on extrapolations of existing functions, yet they also represent fundamentally new roles for academic libraries. We see these changes reflected in the library's shift from
>
> • emphasizing the value of collections to emphasizing the value of expertise,
>
> • supporting information description and access to taking responsibility for greater information analysis,
>
> • serving as a support agency to serving as a collaborator,
>
> • [changing from] a facility-based enterprise to a campus-wide enterprise.[2]

A major conclusion of this report is that collaboration with a growing array of partners will be of greater importance in the development of tools, services, and capabilities.[3] Such collaboration requires institutional negotiations and some loss of control in decision-making, but it is increasingly successful in terms of expanding services while minimizing expenditures.

If you add to all of the above the many possible expansions of roles that this book suggests for libraries in serving as strategic tools to accomplish campus priorities, it is clear that libraries truly are one of the most rapidly changing departments on campus. This reality often leads to staff and faculty discomfiture and certainly calls for library leaders to be facilitators par excellence of change.

So the question is not *whether* libraries will change, but *how* they will change. Will libraries evolve haphazardly, reacting to a host of external pressures, or will presidents and academic vice presidents guide their evolution in order to further institutional goals and objectives? Will libraries respond piecemeal to needs and opportunities, or will presidents and librarians develop a plan for growth that integrates campus goals and objectives?

Academic administrators who wish to ensure effective use of their libraries need to appreciate the major changes occurring in academic libraries. They need to separate the myths of academic librarianship from today's realities. Clearly, presidents and academic vice presidents cannot and should not oversee the daily workings of their libraries any more than governing boards should manage the daily operations of campuses. Yet to place library planning in a meaningful context and to establish a realistic basis for judging the adequacy of their library's performance in meeting institutional goals and objectives, presidents and academic vice presidents need some familiarity with the major challenges faced by libraries in transition.

The next four chapters provide that background. We provide no easy answers, for there are none; rather, we offer a realistic glimpse into the complex environment in which information management must occur today. This chapter will detail aspects of library operations that are largely internal to the library: changing relationships with campus computer centers, changing technology, changing external relationships, and changing facilities. Chapter 8 will address shifting patterns in information management and the importance of technology in increasing campus access to information. Chapter 9 will look at people issues: the hiring and evaluation of library directors, changes in personnel and organizational structures, and faculty status for librarians. Chapter 10 will discuss finances.

INTEGRATING LIBRARIES AND COMPUTER CENTERS

The relationship between libraries and computer centers continues to be a topic of serious discussion in higher education, library, and technology literature. Increasing use of information technology by faculty and students coupled with limited resources requires change and points

> to the need for the library and IT organizations to work together to support today's scholars and students in a much more seamless fashion. Most institutions already have some level of cooperation and collaboration between these functional areas, but a greater potential for integration exists on all campuses. The difficult economic realities faced by higher education require each institution to make the best use of the staff and budget resources devoted to these costly enterprises.[4]

Ideally, faculty and students should have access to all academic support services through a single source and have that access 24/7. Whether an initial inquiry is made in person or from a home, dormitory, or office, there should be access to the full range of services and resources. Increased integration of all academic support services also provides a natural home base for effective faculty development programs.

A 2002 EDUCAUSE summary report of 621 campuses found that "the library and IT organizations have been merged in about one out of six institutions."[5] Still, on many campuses libraries, media centers, and academic computing centers are both administratively and physically distant. Often, their respective personnel have little knowledge of the resources and services available at other centers. This lack of common knowledge and the differences in training for the three areas create significant stumbling blocks on campuses that wish to merge such operations.

There is, however, a growing consensus on the value of such integration into a seamless service, both from a service standpoint and from an administrative efficiency perspective. A 2004 EDUCAUSE Review article articulates a strong justification for undertaking such steps and presents a compelling list of resulting benefits.[6] Moreover, Warren Arbogast, "a consultant who specializes in information technology at colleges and universities, about avoiding wasteful spending on IT,"[7] when interviewed by The Chronicle of Higher Education as to whether merging IT and library services could have an impact on avoiding wasteful spending, stated the following:

> There's no question that efforts at some colleges to merge library and IT services have had a large impact.
>
> I'm often asked where IT should fall within the organizational structure of a college. Unfortunately, there really is no one answer. . . . I can see, in the right circumstances, library and IT services coming together and aligning efforts. After all, library professionals and IT professionals have a great deal in common: At heart, they are all information professionals. . . .
>
> Since I think libraries are important, central cores for every college community, I see a great opportunity for libraries to house highly innovative, specialty spaces such as immersion classrooms, research studios, black-box labs, etc.—the kinds of facilities that are too expensive to equip and manage in every academic building on campus.[8]

We believe that the case is firmly made for the importance of close collaboration, if not merger, of libraries and IT services. The need is urgent today, and, as implied in the quotation above, even more so for tomorrow. To accomplish this is not an easy task, given the very different backgrounds and cultures of library and IT personnel. Their differences have been characterized as involving organizational culture, social distinctions, compensation differentiation, subcultural patterns, and dissimilar professional backgrounds.[9] Any efforts to integrate two such disparate groups will require thoughtful planning and investment in staff development.

In addition, time and again it has been found that critical to the success of such integrative efforts is "pressure from senior administrators," with a clearly articulated goal of providing the best possible service for the least cost.[10] Even with such direction from the presidential level and with a clearly articulated goal, rushing into a merger would be unwise on most campuses because of the fears of the people involved. A number of intermediate steps should be considered instead. A positive first step might be for the library to have library and computer center personnel jointly staff an information desk in the library or to collaborate for round-the-clock student support during finals. Any mutually-produced successes can begin a good foundation for future cooperative efforts.

Mutual planning efforts, however, may prove an even more promising tool for effectively linking library, media, and academic computing services. Structuring the planning process so that the units must together consider campus needs for instruction, research, and service is one way to increase understanding of what each operation contributes. Such efforts can be reinforced through structured input from service users (e.g., faculty, student service personnel, and students) and a combined committee or task force charged to enhance academic resource support. An excellent planning guide for integrating library and IT services was produced by CAUSE in cooperation with the Coalition of Networked Information in 1998 and is available at http://www.educause.edu/ir/library/pdf/PUB3018.pdf.[11] It can be a useful planning tool for any campus undertaking cooperative planning.

Successful outcomes of such planning efforts will vary in keeping with particular campus situations. An example of successful integration can be found at the University of Southern California, where the library and information technology division "have been so completely merged that staff members no longer carry titles such as librarian or information technology specialist. They are now 'public services staff' (whose members help patrons locate an article or load new software on their computers), or they are 'technical staff' (whose members wire the campus or add bibliographic records to the online catalog)."[12]

At the other extreme, Hamilton College in New York took a separate but collaborative approach that works well for this 1,750-student campus. The Library and Information Technology Services (ITS) are located in the same building but decided not to merge the two units. Instead, they adopted "a policy of aggressive collaboration" by which they seek out opportunities to collaborate together in supporting campus priorities. Their initial undertakings included the following:

- The establishment of a multimedia presentation center targeted at providing "integrated services to students and faculty to support presentations and class assignments;"[13]
- Working with Oral Communications, the establishment of a support team that supports "faculty in the identification, selection, and use of technologies and content applicable to their teaching or research needs;"[14]
- The establishment of a service desk jointly staffed by reference librarians and instructional technologists.

One major hurdle in structuring integrated academic support units is determining who will direct the operation. When considering candidates for chief information officer, academic leaders must decide what is the most desirable background for candidates. Rarely will they find a person with significant experience in all academic resource areas.

We still believe a stronger case can be made for the value of library education and experience over media or computer backgrounds in providing leadership for integrated units; indeed, the success in which cutting-edge technology has been successfully integrated into libraries since our earlier book provides good testimony on behalf of our belief. Librarians have a primary commitment to the learning outcomes of individuals and the information provided them, as exemplified by the aggressive posture their profession takes in regard to information literacy and intellectual freedom. On most campuses, librarians are actively involved with curriculum and research efforts. Many teach regularly as part of information literacy programs and actively help faculty keep up-to-date for teaching in their fields. Either they have academic status or they are usually seeking it. Librarians remain on the cutting edge of information technology, yet their primary concerns remain the service, access, and content issues of information. Computing personnel and media personnel, in contrast, tend to be more concerned with hardware for the delivery of information.

Administrative experience is another reason for emphasizing a library background. "Most computer-center directors are hired for their technical skills, not their management or interpersonal abilities, so it should come as no surprise that many have problems as managers," explains one university director of computer services.[15] Librarians' training for reference work is heavily people oriented, and given the larger staff size of library versus computer operations, talented librarians tend to move rather quickly into increasingly responsible managerial positions.

Of course, there are wonderful exceptions. Joy Hughes, vice president for Information Technology at George Mason University, has been a successful chief information officer (CIO) on more than one campus. She states, "A CIO has to be passionate about the library for it to work." In her own case, she credits the public library in Philadelphia for saving her when she was there growing up poor.[16]

While titles for campus CIOs vary widely and reporting lines differ, what is deemed important from a survey of existing operations is access to campuswide decision-making. "The ability to sit on the president's cabinet, executive committee, or whatever the top policy forum is called is far more important, in that this seat allows the top IT leader to actively engage in campus-level discussions about strategic directions and policy and to work with other senior officers in understanding the role that IT can play in the various functional areas on campus."[17]

A good description for a top information officer on the campus would include being the "senior executive responsible for establishing institutional information policy, standards, and management control over all institutional information resources." A good job description might include these requirements:

- Help educate others on campus about more effective uses of information resources and services.
- Provide leadership in developing better and more efficient delivery systems.
- Bring information to those who need it, when they need it, and in a form they can use.
- Communicate a vision of technology as a tool rather than as an end in itself.
- Direct all information services on campus and promote their effective interfacing with the academic programs.[18]

It is a big job. To facilitate the success of the information officer, the campus needs to have a campus philosophy, clear goals for including integrated academic support services, and the support of faculty for both.

CHANGING TECHNOLOGIES AND SERVICES

Everyone loves a simple solution. The more complex the situation, the more attractive the simple solution becomes. Americans have also typically prided themselves on progress and on their ability to develop a "better mousetrap." These two tendencies have made a realistic, clear-eyed evaluation of new information technologies difficult. Americans expect newer information technologies to replace older ones, despite the lesson of history that they almost always become additions rather than replacements. Academic administrators and state legislators who believe in a simple high-tech solution to library acquisition and space needs are a fairly familiar—if unwelcome—reality. "Computers and their technological siblings have most dramatically affected libraries, and especially so during the 1990s. The evidence is everywhere—card catalogs gone, teaching styles sharply altered, full books and articles in digital form, multimedia products with sound and motion pictures, abundant hookups for PCs and laptops, and the World Wide Web providing us hypertext links to open a universe of instant information."[19]

Moreover, technology is changing so rapidly that new libraries often find aspects of their IT infrastructure outdated before the doors open for service. This reality increasingly intimidates authors, like ourselves, from writing on IT topics of concern. Certainly, we could never have predicted the impact of the Internet, which celebrated the tenth anniversary of its becoming open to the general public in 2001. Nor does anyone understand yet how "the Internet influences the social, political, and economic behavior of users and non-users,"[20] despite a growing body of research on this topic. What we do know is that the Internet, wireless technology, and a host of other innovations have forever changed the face of learning and of libraries. For example, a 2002 report out of the EDUCAUSE Center for Applied Research found that "libraries and classrooms are cited most often as having wireless coverage today and are most likely to benefit from wireless networks in the future."[21] (At the same time, the dreaded microform machines continue to be hated and be used, as much information is not accessible in other formats.)

Technology has blown out the walls of the library to serve students in their homes and workplaces. More and more time is spent developing comprehensive but intuitive Web pages that can support broad-based student learning needs anywhere and at any time of the day or night. It is not just off-campus students who need such access services, but it is also the preferred means for meeting many students' research needs. To further support such access, libraries must also offer reference and computer assistance services by phone, e-mail, and instant messaging.

Two other technological advancements of recent years that hold significant efficiency values for libraries are self-checkout machines and the radio frequency identification (RFID) technology for collections control. Originally marketed to public libraries, academic libraries are also finding self-checkout machines to be preferred by many users as well as being a staff time-saver. A goal of 80 to 90 percent self-checkouts is quite feasible and can be well worth the financial investment.

RFID technologies and materials handling have existed for many years and have been used by retailers and others needing to handle large inventories or other purposes such as automatically paying highway tolls. Their ability to enhance essential library services and for significant savings of staff time once installed, has been recognized more recently. An August 2004 article in *The Chronicle of Higher Education* reported that at that time more than 300 libraries in the United States were using this technology.[22] The article pointed out that some privacy advocates fear the potential of RFID for invasion of people's privacy. While caution in regard to privacy is always good, in this case it does not need to be a deterrent to achieving the benefits of RFID technology.

What is certain is the operational value of this technology coupled with materials-handling technology and the potential for freeing staff time for increased service to the public rather than laboriously checking in each item and later sorting it by hand for reshelving. RFID technology also allows quicker self-checkout since the patron does not need to carefully align the bar code with the reader, and it allows a wand to read shelves for items lost or out of place.[23]

In other areas, technological enhancements raise more serious concerns. One is out-of-library use of commercial databases and how to provide access to campus personnel as defined in vendor contracts but at the same time prohibit access by others. This usually involves a log-in name and password that can be cumbersome to difficult for many to use, often requiring telephone support help. Until recently, such authentication was not needed for on-campus use, often allowing anyone who came into the library to access the Internet and all campus-provided databases. But concerns for Internet-related crime, hacking, and limited resources to meet student needs are causing some campus security personnel and some librarians to rethink open access policies.[24]

Changing Services

New and enhanced services made possible by evolving information technologies are here to stay and are increasingly enriching learning, research, and service activities. There is not, in fact, a library service that has not benefited from some technology advancement. While technology's impact on information or collection management will be dealt with in the next chapter, good examples of technology's reshaping of how libraries operate are seen in changing reserves and reference services.

Electronic Reserves

Earlier we urged a more reflective use of reserves since they do not encourage students' development of lifelong information literacy abilities. One historical reason for discouraging the use of reserves was that they so infrequently were used by the designated classes; in the meantime they were not available in the collection for ease of access by other students. Electronic reserves may be the answer to this problem—at least to some degree.

Electronic reserves are a collection of course-related materials that have been digitized so as to be made available over a computer network. In 1993, San Diego State University was the first to report an experiment with such a service. In an Association of Research Libraries survey of fifty-six research libraries several years later, a majority of the libraries were offering electronic reserves to some extent. "The five most common types of material placed in electronic reserves systems were instructors' course notes and sample tests (94 percent); instructors' exercises/problem sets (88 percent); journal articles (69 percent); and book chapters (59 percent). Materials such as links to Web pages, syllabi, homework solutions, and student materials were also mentioned. Four libraries specified that they place only public domain materials on their systems."[25]

The chief advantage of electronic reserves is flexibility of access to the materials from anywhere a student has Internet access and at any time of day or night. A study of students at Penn State found 87.3 percent of students using the course material as opposed to an early study of traditional reserves at the University of Virginia, in which as many as 50 percent of students in courses with assigned materials may not be reading them.[26] In similar research findings at the University of Illinois, it was found that "students accessed electronic reserves from a variety of places, by far the most popular being from off campus. A significant number of respondents also indicated that the ability to access reserves online led them to read more reserve material than they had in the past."[27] Certainly, electronic reserves are a particular boon to distance education students. Electronic reserves also have other advantages, including precluding loss or damage of materials, saving space, and some saving of staff time after materials are on reserve.[28]

Reference Services

Until fairly recently, it could be argued that "basic approaches to reference service have not altered in recent decades despite dramatic changes in user needs, customer service technologies, and transformations in other areas of the library."[29] Certainly, the goal of reference services both pre- and post-Internet is "to understand users' information seeking behaviors and to support those behaviors effectively."[30] The coming of the Internet has, of course, greatly changed people's information-seeking habits. Where physical access was the major obstacle in the past, information overload is the major obstacle today. Moreover, so many options for approaching research mean that the biggest challenge is knowing where to start. Research through use of five focus groups of faculty and students at the University of Idaho found that participants

> were largely knowledgeable about current electronic sources. They were aware of the need for exercising discretion in selection and use of sources (especially the Internet), and they valued traditional non-electronic resources such as printed and human sources of information. Still, frustrations abound: overwhelming numbers of often irrelevant hits when searching the Internet, lack of standardization in search systems, and lost, missing, or inaccessible information (whether in printed or electronic form). Needs that emerged through discussions were for more familiarity with starting points and strategies in searching for information, more skill at sifting through vast amounts of information (better search techniques), and better ability to find particularly good sources for the search at hand.[31]

The other not surprising finding was that "time is an overriding criterion in the choice of information selection and delivery."[32]

Reference services have changed significantly and are continuing to adapt to new technology-based opportunities to respond to concerns of where to start and to demands by users that research efforts have to fit into their time schedules. Telephone and e-mail reference services were significant steps toward addressing reference needs of off-site faculty and students. They were followed by more carefully constructed Web pages and help services built into the online catalog. The latest efforts have been focused on 24/7 virtual or electronic reference services, which although possible to staff on a single-campus basis, much more frequently involve collaboration with other institutions.

The evolution of electronic reference from single to multi-institutional services creates a more complex framework for virtual assistance. In these models, reference services are collaboratively staffed and mechanisms are developed to profile staff and institutional specializations in systematic and structured ways. In addition, the services often incorporate capabilities for real-time discussion and knowledge databases to store the results of reference transactions for future use.[33]

By summer 2002, a survey of its membership by the Association of Research Libraries found that slightly more than half of the respondents provided chat reference service, which was defined as "synchronous or real-time text-based messaging between computer users on the Internet."[34] These efforts are so new that the guidelines and standards for e-reference are just emerging,[35] and the patterns of best practices in electronic reference/eight-hour services are still unknown. To date, however, e-reference or chat reference is far from being a success, either through campus libraries or through commercial vendors. The one apparent exception to the downward slide of commercial online reference services in recent years is fee-based Google Answers, which has paid attention to quality in its answers. However, "Google Answers does not seem to be going anywhere. As of January 2004, it averaged about 60–70 questions per day, down over 50 percent from the 200+ questions per day the service got in the late Spring of 2002, just after it opened. Even using the higher usage figure, you're still only talking about 0.0001 percent of the 200 million searches done every day on the regular Google site."[36]

In fact, a 2004 analysis of e-reference provides strong evidence for the advantages of telephone and e-mail reference over chat technologies.[37] The number of campuses (including Vanderbilt) that have tried chat services and dropped them, plus the fact that even the busiest academic library e-reference services only average one question an hour,[38] indicate that the latest technology is not always the best or the most cost-effective means for meeting users' needs for reference services. Others believe that such services can be more cost-effective when done collaboratively and worry that younger users will be lost to library use if such technologies are not used.[39] Librarians will, of course, continue to experiment with emerging technologies, and some like the General Libraries of the University at Buffalo are now exploring the use of instant messaging.[40] So it is conceivable that someday,

some forms of reference service will be outsourced in a manner similar to the outsourcing of other library functions, such as copy cataloging. If for instance, an outside provider can adequately address simple reference questions at one-fifth the cost of doing so in-house, why duplicate the service? Reference librarians need to analyze more thoroughly how much time is spent by function performed. By freeing themselves from more routine tasks, they can focus their efforts on aspects of complex information discovery and use in which they clearly excel.[41]

But for now, the challenge is not just to extend the reach of reference service through technology, but also to better self-assess the quality of reference responses. "Just as public school teachers evaluate each other's performance throughout the school year, reference librarians could improve their services through peer review. In addition, Google Answers' practice of encouraging users to rate and publicly post evaluations of responses received should be considered. A similar precedent already occurs in the academy as student ratings of professors' classes are posted with the course description at some institutions."[42]

What should not change is the addressing of individual needs, whether the faculty member or student is physically present at the reference desk or on the other side of the world. "In an increasingly impersonal world, the librarian will continue to provide personalized service to patrons. Personal service is what will differentiate the library from other providers."[43]

Other Service Considerations

The list of enhanced services could be much longer, but the above examples should be sufficient to make the point that it is not business as usual in the library. It is better, more customer-focused business in the library. But each enhancement comes at a price in terms of dollars and staff investment—though some technologies, such as RFID coupled with material-handling technologies, may ultimately result in staff savings. Before that time arrives, there will be start-up costs, ongoing maintenance contracts, and more complex infrastructures requiring more staff to maintain them and to provide for security. Presidents and faculty leadership need to determine what quality of service they want for their students and ensure resources for providing that level. Leadership in the library should be held accountable for keeping the campus informed of how it uses resources efficiently and what enhancements are possible at what costs.

This brief look at how emerging information technologies are enhancing library services needs to end by acknowledging that the rapid onslaught of technology-driven changing opportunities have left far too little time for research, much less reflection, on resulting practices.

> Making library services available online is not only expensive; it is also very risky. The library's roles there are not at all clear. Neither are its relationships with users or with other information services. There is little information about how library users behave in a network environment, how they react to online library services, and how they combine those services with others such as search engines like Google, bookstores like Amazon, Internet gateways like Voice of the Shuttle, instructional technologies like WebCT or Blackboard. Digital libraries are still relatively immature—most are still at a stage where limited experimentation is more important than well-informed strategic planning. While libraries have excelled at assessing the development and use of their traditional collections and services, comparable assessments of online collections and services are more complicated and less well understood.[44]

Fortunately, serious efforts to address needed research are underway through a number of national organizations. For example, the Digital Library Federation (DLF) has committed to leading a research process that will provide information needed to inform library development in a networked era. The goals of this process are twofold:

- to develop better understanding of methods effective in assessing use and usability of online scholarly information resources and information services, and
- to create a baseline understanding of users' needs to support strategic planning in an increasingly competitive environment for academic libraries and their parent institutions.[45]

Shaping the Future

Technology offers no simple solution to the problems posed by the continuing exponential increase in information and its inherent cost. Well-informed academic leaders realize that the newer information technologies are an element of the information explosion, not a solution to the challenges it poses. Presidents and academic vice presidents must ensure that campus adoption of technologies is directed at meeting institutional priorities, not pursued blindly as a magical solution to ongoing library budget and space problems. Before making commitments to new technologies, they need to know what they hope to achieve, develop a clear and comprehensive plan, and then determine how quickly the campus can afford to implement the plan. This challenge is all the greater, because at this point, the magnitude of the effects of the changes brought about by the evolving technology are still unknown.

CHANGING FACILITIES

Just as technology has brought about major changes in library services and management of collections, so too does technology dictate major changes in how academic library buildings should be designed. Not surprisingly, many projects are driven in part by the need to upgrade the technology infrastructure in the building. However, early beliefs that the digitization of collections would negate the need for library expansions have proven to be the wrong answer to the wrong issue. There is a growing consensus that the chief function of academic libraries is not as a storage facility but as an important center for learning. This is not to say that print and media collections are not important, but there are other and less costly alternatives to building bigger warehouses in the center of campuses. (For example, see comments later in this chapter regarding OhioLINK.)

Nor has there been a slowdown in library renovations or new construction. Between 1995 and 2002, more than 400 campuses undertook library building projects.

> Academic library building activity has not diminished in recent years. In fact, the pattern of activity was remarkably stable during the study period, with identified activity reaching its highest point in 2002.
>
> The most common project types were new facilities (43.1 percent, including 13.3 percent in multipurpose buildings) and addition/renovation projects (42 percent). Addition-only and renovation-only projects were less frequent. Also, the University of Maryland and several other institutions have "re-purposed" existing facilities to permit new uses. Despite some writers' contentions that space requirements have diminished, the size of improved library facilities has increased in all cases except renovations, with the doubling or tripling of existing building size common in many smaller institutions.[46]

Before looking at how libraries are being designed, a president might well wonder if a major expenditure for libraries is warranted, since students and faculty can get so much information off the Internet. How many students never go into the library at all—either because they take off-campus courses or because their assignments do not require library use? Indeed, a 2001 article in *The Chronicle of Higher Education*, entitled "The Deserted Library," raised this question.[47] However, a January 2003 survey of campuses that had recently opened new libraries or had significantly enhanced their libraries found a very different reality.

> This study confirms that *the great majority of new and improved libraries have experienced sustained increases in usage of the physical facility following project completion. In addition, some libraries have experienced profound increases in usage, with 25.6 percent of survey participants reporting postproject usage gains exceeding 100 percent. In short, a high-quality building does make a difference,* and students continue to use an improved facility even after the novelty of a new library has worn off.[48]

This study also identified a number of specific facility attributes associated with postproject usage gains, including:

- number of data ports;
- percentage of seats with wired network access;
- number and quality of public access computers;
- quality of library instruction lab;
- quality of telecommunications infrastructure;
- quality of natural lighting;
- quality of user work spaces;
- quality of layout (including location of service points);
- quality of collection storage space;
- quality of HVAC system;
- quality of overall facility ambience.[49]

Certainly, such findings can be of significant value for planning on other campuses.

A major report on redesigning libraries for learning authored by Scott Bennett, Yale University Librarian Emeritus, found that library projects during the 1990s were still largely driven by the need for space for growing collections. The second greatest motivation was to provide new types of student study space. In general, however, he judged most planning to be based on prior experiences even while including more social space and accommodating the need for more technology.[50] He urged that "library design should not be dominated primarily by a concern for information resources and their delivery. . . . Library design should incorporate a deeper understanding of the independent, active learning behaviors of students and the teaching strategies of faculty meant to support those behaviors."[51]

A 2001 *New York Times* article explored how architects are rethinking libraries. Architects report focusing on collaborative spaces "because of interdisciplinary teams and workplaces,"[52] and because students see the library as less a place to get information than as a place for social academic experiences.

> Shopping is a recurrent image. "The library is an intellectual marketplace," says Mr. Freeman, who has worked on libraries at Brown, Yale, Princeton, Cornell and Columbia and lectures on how architecture affects the teaching and learning process. "Look at the souks in Middle Eastern marketplaces, where all the wares are out in the open." Right upon entering, Mr. Freeman continues, "I want to see the service points, the collections, see other people producing and doing things. I want to see activity, not rows of quiet tables.
>
> "You'll still have quiet reading spaces, and all of the things that were in the library of the past," he continues, "but we're adding a whole other layer, this discovery activity."[53]

Information Commons

One of the clear trends in library design that reflects the growing commitment to having libraries serve as learning and social centers for campuses is the "information commons" (IC). The term can be applied to any merger of computing and library services, and the general definition is one-stop shopping to seamless integration of high tech and high touch. It is a campus response to the need for having integrated library and technology support services for students and faculty—preferably twenty-four hours a day, seven days a week.[54]

> Students need to take their research (much of which is done using electronic resources) and write papers, create web pages, develop multimedia presentations, collaborate with others, and more. The model of the past—get the needed information from the library and go home to complete the research and write a paper—no longer holds true. These changed outcomes are prompting libraries to re-examine the services they are offering, especially technology-based

services. Therefore these "new" information commons go beyond the basic computer lab—they merge and integrate tools and services from traditional computer labs, media production areas, and library information resources, especially electronic resources.[55]

Some campuses, however, have carried this model much further to create highly visible centers for learning. One of the earliest of these was an outgrowth of a vision by George Mason University (GMU) President George W. Johnson. In 1989, he asked university librarian Charlene Hurt to think about having the library in a student union. Johnson was seeking solutions for several problems.

- It was very hard to develop a sense of community at GMU when many of our commuter students couldn't find anywhere to sit before or after classes except in their parked cars; and
- The Commonwealth of Virginia was disinclined to build any traditional space on our campus except in small increments (generally 100,000 square feet at a time).

   It was also a serious attempt to address a long-standing concern of the president's, which he described as the "egg carton" problem, whereby the various parts of academic life were isolated from each other, making it impossible for students to make connections between classroom learning and the rest of their lives. He wanted a building that would help integrate all aspects of student life, demonstrating that learning takes place in many ways.[56]

By May 1990, the task force charged to address this issue adopted the following proposal for its university center:

   We are disavowing the cloistered notion of a library separate from the rest of the university. In the University Center students and faculty will be able to read, do research, collaborate, and socialize in one unified space.
   The University Center is designed to encourage active engagement in the academic enterprise by all elements of the university. The architectural design will encourage interaction with the resources provided throughout the building, and with others engaged in the learning process. The small book and materials collection of the library will be pertinent to the general education core. These resources will support a common core of knowledge around which students and faculty can interact throughout their academic careers.
   The design of the University Center is informed by the work of the General Education Committee of the University, which has de-

veloped a core curriculum to help students develop verbal, reading and mathematical abilities, critical thinking abilities, multi-cultural understanding, content related understandings, and resource utilization abilities. Since learning is continuous, and significant portions take place outside the classroom, the University Center integrates library resources and student activities designed to encourage those outcomes.

The library in the University Center will be a model Library of the Future, serving as the central node of an information system that reaches outward to the wider world of information. The latest in technological systems will maximize access to information for students and faculty. . . . The system design also will enable researchers to contact other students and faculty interested in the same research areas, thereby encouraging the human collaboration so important to effective learning.[57]

A year and a half after opening, the library could report that the "building is busy all the time," and "the Campus underground newspaper, which seldom finds anything to praise, reported the Spring after we opened that students seem happier, and are staying on campus longer."[58] Moreover, service demands and circulation of materials had significantly increased. Of course, there were some challenges that needed to be addressed; chief of these had to do with security for library materials and effective management of the service desk. Despite the challenges, the Johnson Center Library at George Mason University not only documented how library space and facilities can be tailored to meet a presidential vision for campus improvement, but also set the stage for a growing number of other campuses to develop their versions of an information commons.

Another well-established model for an information commons can be found at the University of North Carolina at Charlotte (UNCC). At this campus, the information commons was developed "as a shared venture with staff from the library, the University Teaching Center, and the Center for Computing and Information Technology.[59] We have already discussed the benefits of close ties between library and faculty or teaching development centers in and having close ongoing interaction of these operations plus computing and media service personnel within the setting of an information commons can only help all units, as at UNCC, to "develop resources and support structures as well as expand, update, and evolve these to meet the changing needs of our patrons, especially as they affect the teaching-learning-research enterprise."[60]

A campus committed to enhancing teaching and learning and/or to creating an intellectual home for students will do well to think creatively regarding the location and organizational relationships among their libraries, academic computing, and faculty development centers. Presidents can help this process by asking questions about such relationships that challenge the status quo.

This emphasis on making libraries a place where people want to be and want to learn was taken several steps further at Davidson County Community College in North Carolina, and it started with a much-needed renovation of existing facilities. Although what Davidson staff is doing may not be appropriate in many academic settings, their mission "to empower individuals to identify, locate, and evaluate information while promoting the value of reading and research as a means of lifelong learning and personal fulfillment"[61] is being addressed by the staff's creativity and passion for getting students into the library. The attractive new setting and addition of forty state-of-the-art computers with access to the Internet and other electronic resources quickly resulted in increased use. Staff noticed that, "Yes the computers were busy, and yes there were more and more students at the workstations. But what was astonishing was that all of our tables and chairs, sofas, and love seats were continually occupied. It was a true library: a place to get information, to give information, and to use information. Students came there to study, to meet with other people, and to read and check out books."[62]

But that was only the beginning. Library staff introduced games; a program of "Coffee Hour@the library" (cosponsored by Student Services and the Cultural Events Department) featured book signings, musical programs, and other events; and eventually a bookmobile cart that for ninety minutes two days a week brought new books, videos, and DVDs into staff areas on campus. The library is meeting many needs for its students and faculty, from supplying a place to relieve stress between classes to building a comfortable home base where a sense of community exists. On top of that, weekly gate counts and circulation statistics continue to grow.

Nor is the model of academic libraries serving as a catalyst for the intellectual life of the campus—something of particular importance on commuter campuses—restricted to community college libraries. At the Melvin Gelman Library of George Washington University, librarians partnered with students to transform periodically a twenty-four-hour study room into an evening coffee house. The first Café Gelman was held in 1992.

> Library staff and students transformed the room into a café with tables, tablecloths, and candles. Paper over the lights faintly colored

the room and gave it a warm glow. A faculty and student ensemble provided jazz. A stool and microphone awaited those who would choose to read poetry or other literature. The refreshments arrived, and we waited anxiously. Would students really come to such an event? Indeed, they would and they did. They read their own poetry, their favorite poetry, and passages from books. One student read her favorite childhood poem in Russian and translated it. Two students improvised a dance to poetry. It was an unqualified success.[63]

Planning Facilities

Planning for a new library or expansion should start by establishing a planning partnership that brings together faculty and students with library staff. "This partnership should construct a shared understanding throughout the campus community of key issues in learning and teaching and their implication for library space. . . . Such partnerships will necessarily be at the heart of any effort to design library buildings that are primarily about people as learners, rather than about the information 'stuff' that supports learning."[64] Then, to assist in developing an effective and efficient building design, library staff can provide essential data on service patterns and trends, level of collection use, networking activities, the trade-off in services and costs for a decentralized versus a centralized collection, and other needs. Planning efforts should ensure ongoing and adequate input from the library staff during all planning and construction phases. There are far too many examples of libraries that are attractive structures but that fail to adequately meet users' needs and/or are not designed for efficiencies in operations.

Another important preplanning step is to view as many good examples of buildings as possible. Since 1963, the American Institute of Architects and the American Library Association (ALA) have jointly given library building awards. Photographs of the building designs are available on loan from ALA or may be purchased on microfiche. The ALA also maintains a list of library building consultants. Each December issue of *Library Journal* features library buildings completed during the preceding year; these architectural issues can be useful for identifying suitable architectural firms as well as for developing initial building concepts. In addition, visits to other campus libraries with similar institutional missions and new library facilities can help the planning team decide among options.

Among the books on planning for library buildings, the most encyclopedic is the revision of Keyes D. Metcalf's *Planning Academic and Re-*

search Library Buildings,[65] which also covers possible alternatives to a new library building. Another useful tool for making sure that nothing falls "between the cracks" and that covers initial planning steps through the dedication ceremony is the often revised *Checklist of Library Building Design Considerations*.[66] For an up-to-date consideration of changes in the design of library space due to the movement of libraries beyond information storage sites, consult the February 2005 report of the Council on Library and Information Resources, entitled *Library as Place: Rethinking Roles, Rethinking Space*.[67]

Start with listening to students' and faculty's hopes for the new library, and match those desires with the best of what you find in other libraries that address their interests. Remember, for example, the high value users place on natural lighting and the ambience of the space. Adequate infrastructure for technology and built-in flexibility for what comes next must be carefully considered. In addition, the construction of library buildings and extensions should normally be planned to accommodate approximately fifteen years of collection growth and enrollment changes. Despite the Internet, collections will always grow, but also remember that there are alternatives for housing parts of the collection so as to keep the primary focus of the library on learning.

Many states have provided guidelines or standards for publicly supported academic library buildings. Academic leaders contemplating expansion of existing or new library facilities should check that these guidelines have been updated recently enough to reflect changes necessitated by the newer technology and a growing understanding of library use patterns. It is far better to identify and challenge space standards in advance than to seek an exception or waiver when a building plan goes forward.

While guidelines are important to state-supported institutions, far more important is a clear, written philosophy for the library that can serve as a basis for architectural planning. Is library use integrated into undergraduate instruction? Is the library to serve as the major computer access point for the campus? Are media services and production to be integrated into library holdings and services? Will the faculty development office be housed in the library? Will there be a twenty-four-hour study area? Will the campus encourage the use of libraries by the business community? Will it build extensive special collections and archives? Is off-site storage of materials acceptable? Would branch or undergraduate libraries complement or harm educational goals? Will there be a café? How many small group study rooms? Would the campus benefit from a 24/7 information commons? The list could go on, but the basic issue is how the president sees the role of the library in promoting institutional goals and objectives. The president's vision should find expression in a statement of philosophy for the library that will guide not only physical expansion but all of the choices librarians face in an era of rapid change.

Mission-Driven Libraries

While all libraries should be planned around the campus mission and the particular needs of their faculty and students, sometimes a library can be a dynamic expression of the heart of the institution's character. This chapter will end with a look in some depth at two such libraries.

The focus on the retention and academic success of freshmen and sophomore students at Wayne State University (WSU) dictated some building design issues for its new David Adamany Undergraduate Library, which opened in September 1999 to provide a friendlier face to beginning students than did its four research libraries. Fortunately, the architect was using a build/design approach that allowed internal building changes far into the construction project. This was important since serious program and service planning did not get underway much before groundbreaking. Among the design issues addressing the mission were the following:

- A round, welcome/reference desk straight ahead of the entrance;
- An open cultural event center in which a wide range of weekly events (e.g., fencing to concerts) was offered to encourage student involvement, with the knowledge that students are more likely to stay enrolled if involved with an activity on campus besides their studies;
- Three types of seating interspersed throughout the library (i.e., lounge, open tables, and carrels), all providing for computer hookups, except for part of one floor for students who want things really quiet;
- Space for housing a freshman survival course, entitled "Information Power" (for more information on this course, see chapter 6);
- A 100 seat computer/study lab that could be open after normal library hours, with an adjacent vending area that offered school supplies and food; and
- A large faculty development center to provide for faculty teaching and research enhancement.

The success of this facility seemed remarkable, since by this time, undergraduate libraries had largely been considered failures at other major research universities. The clearly articulated mission made the difference.

Its success in supporting freshman and sophomore retention and academic success is testified to in part by these facts: students quickly availed themselves of the after-hours study area; the entire library needed to be open during exams; and students quit using the general computer labs in favor of the new library (student dollars from the labs were transferred to the library). In addition, with the desire of a new president for an academic success center a few years later, it was decided that the library had already provided the foundation for such a center.

Some years later, another campus reached out to its community through its library. More than 21,000 people showing up to celebrate the opening of an academic library is unusual, to say the least, as was the wealth of local news coverage that San José State University received in August 2003 when the Dr. Martin Luther King, Jr., Library began service. The brainchild of SJSU president Robert L. Caret and San José Mayor Susan Hammer, this unique collaboration between the campus and the city was the strongest manifestation to date of Caret's vision of SJSU as a metropolitan university. Not only was the intent to meet the need of both organizations for new libraries, but it was seen as a significant step back to a time of strong engagement between the city and the campus.

> In the early years, the city and university got along harmoniously, said Walsh, author of a new interpretive history of San José State University from 1950 to 2000.
>
> Then came the tumult of the Vietnam War era. Swept up in campus anti-war and anti-racism protests of the 1960s, San José State strained to keep up with an expanding student population and battened down against the crime and blight downtown.
>
> The city and university drifted into an arms-length relationship as California emptied its mental institutions and the fraternity and sorority system collapsed under the wave of student activism. Boarding and halfway houses took over many of the big houses downtown as students began commuting from farther away.
>
> "The University felt besieged by the criminal element of [the] community and fewer faculty wanted to live downtown because the public schools were going downhill," Walsh said.
>
> By the end of the 1970s, there was little reason for students and faculty to spend much time off campus.
>
> . . . San José State took shelter behind a line of tall, inward-facing buildings dubbed "the Great Wall" of Fourth Street.
>
> "The University turned its back on downtown because there wasn't a lot to open your arms to," said Scott Knies, a 1979 graduate who now heads the San José Downtown Association.[68]

To gain support for the "joint" library project, there were several architecturally related givens:

- The library had to be built on the corner lot of the campus closest to downtown and close to the site for the new city hall.[69]
- The library had to have "equal" entrances on the city and university sides.
- The library had to be large enough to house all the libraries' holdings (by that time, the university collection was housed in two different locations) and have room for twenty years of collection growth.
- All people—whether from the campus or the community—were to have equitable access to all resources.

In addition, the prolonged campus negotiations needed to gain faculty support for the project identified a series of anticipated problems that needed to be addressed first in the operating agreement and then in the design of the building. Among these issues were the following:

- *Anticipated unacceptable noise level:* The children's room was located next to the public entrance, and other heavy traffic areas were located on the first through fourth floors. Escalators were provided for floors one through four. Thirty-nine small group study rooms were provided.
- *Anticipated increase in loss of university materials:* In addition to undertaking a complete inventory of materials prior to relocating in order to accurately measure resource losses, staffed security stations were provided at both exits to monitor security gate alarms. In addition, eighty-nine security cameras were installed and are regularly monitored from a security point in the library.
- *Anticipated unavailability of academic resources when needed by students because they were checked out by public users:* The solution to this concern could not be built into the design of the building. Rather, it is being addressed by the shared use of an online library management system, which has a specially developed software capability allowing both libraries to know whether it is SJSU or public users who have checked out materials placed on hold by academic users—or vice versa. Both libraries are committed to purchasing duplicative materials as needed.

The benefits accrued to the campus were significant. Politically, it would have been impossible to have achieved a new library building for a decade or more if not for the opportunity created by leveraging dollars with the city. The campus gained a much larger facility than it could have had otherwise, and to some degree, contrasting high-use periods between the campus and the public library users means greater seating options for all users. Campus programs, which had always been open to but poorly attended by the public, are now more accessible to and more frequently attended by the public. In like fashion, several special collections (i.e., the Beethoven and Steinbeck Centers, the University Special Collections, and the California Room) are now handsomely provided for in attractive venues that are much more obvious to both campus and community people.

The building design even facilitated the coming together of previously isolated University Library units. Sharing workspace and a programming room, three ethnic collections have adjacent spaces that flow into each other to create the Cultural Heritage Center (CHC). This new arrangement encourages collaborative initiatives among Africana, Asian-American, and Chicano groups but still allows each to maintain their identities. The disappearance of the silo mentality was highlighted by a collaborative initiative to honor the birthday of Dr. Martin Luther King, Jr., six months after the library opening. One newspaper columnist noted that it was "about time" that a multicultural event was planned to honor King and "about time" that it was being held on King's actual birthdate.[70] In addition, the CHC nurtures a small-collection home base for students in these programs while preparing them to expand their research efforts to the larger collections.

What is clear from the San José State University situation is that facilities can be an exciting means of bringing together a campus and its community. Not only did library use go up significantly by both campus and community members, but the obvious success of the effort quickly brought city leaders back to SJSU seeking potential areas for collaboration related to economic development. With the building of the new city hall only a block from the campus, more instructional opportunities are also likely to emerge.

COLLABORATION

While library collaboration and resource sharing are still to some degree unnatural acts in the highly competitive sphere of higher education, developments in information technology are making such activities far more attractive. Historically, neither the campus nor the state has rewarded such activities, and frequently, cooperative efforts have elicited a great deal of suspicion among campus officers, for network participation requires that libraries give up some local autonomy in decision-making and management and sacrifice some budgetary flexibility. Neither accreditation standards nor funding mechanisms foster cooperative activities. Despite these detriments, collaborative efforts among academic and other libraries are at an all-time high.

Examples of collaboration in order to better meet student, faculty, and administrative needs have already been mentioned in regard to electronic reference, information literacy programs, and other services. Consortial arrangements among libraries have existed for decades in some cases, but those long-established relationships are significantly enriched by the newer technologies and the Internet. As many as 200 library consortia have sprung up over the past decade to negotiate volume discounts with electronic publishers,[71] and it seems safe to predict that "new economic realities will drive most campuses towards establishing consortia to make networked information resources economically accessible."[72]

Examples of Consortia

Historically, there have been different motivations for starting consortia. OhioLINK is the result of a library space crisis in the late 1980s. Attempting to deal with an insupportable level of need for more library space,

> The regents appointed a Library Study Committee, which made two recommendations that changed the way libraries operate in the state. They also laid the groundwork for OhioLINK.
>
> First, the committee called for an offsite storage and delivery system for library materials. Ultimately, the state built six depositories in different regions of Ohio, each with a capacity of roughly 1.5 million volumes. . . . What made the book depository system work, and later proved to be the cornerstone for statewide cooperation, was the regents' commitment to develop a unified electronic catalogue. Under the new system, individual users could access bibliography records from any library online and request direct delivery to their home library. In November 1992, the catalogue was activated with six libraries online. Today the system's 83 member libraries hold 7.9 million unique entries.[73]

OhioLINK now includes eighty-three public and private campuses and is supported by dedicated state funds. It has continued to enhance services to provide access to researchers. "One of the fastest growing areas on OhioLINK is also one of the most accessible to the general public. Most of the wide variety of material on the Digital Media Center is not password protected. OhioLINK has effectively become a publisher for professors and institutions willing to digitize materials. The holdings include foreign language and physics videos."[74]

The collaboration of the California State University (CSU) libraries was initiated by an early technology "crisis" in the mid-1970s. It began with the formation of a unit in the Chancellor's Office called Learning Services Development. Its focus was the systemwide implementation of an early library automation system, specifically the CLSI circulation system. Because the state took positions from the libraries in return for its investment in library automation and because the system was imposed centrally, the effort was highly controversial among library directors.

In the years since then, the Council of Library Deans and Directors (COLD) from the now twenty-three CSU campuses have voluntarily collaborated for successful outcomes in areas ranging from information literacy programming, implementation of cutting-edge information technology software, joint purchasing of electronic resources, establishing a union catalog with over 13 million holdings (4 million titles), offering 24/7 online reference services, and more recently, working with the Educational Testing Service (ETS) on a national initiative for assessment of information communication and technology (ICT) skills. It is a formidable record of collaborative accomplishments that is often lauded by the Chancellor's Office as a model for other systemwide units. In 2005, COLD completed its third strategic plan in which it continues to collaboratively address library efforts in support of CSU's mission in learning, research, and service.[75]

Besides these long-standing consortia, many others are now operating to the benefit of their member institutions. Some have been created out of consortial arrangements of their parent institutions. For example, the Center for Library Initiatives (CLI) was established in 1994 to support the members of the Committee on Institutional Cooperation (CIC), the academic consortium of the Big Ten universities and the University of Chicago.

> The primary goal of the CLI is to establish and maintain a cohesive consortial organization guided by a vision of the information resources in the CIC as a seamless whole, whether those resources are developed or owned individually or collectively. The cornerstone of these efforts is the Virtual Electronic Library (VEL), which links the thirteen online catalogs into one virtual union catalog, supports patron-initiated borrowing of library materials, and provides full-text access to a variety of scholarly content.[76]

Consortial arrangements can be as large as the more than 100 libraries in the University of California[77] or as small as two libraries in Kansas sharing the salary of a preservation expert.[78] Wise presidents will support and encourage the library's involvement in appropriate consortial arrangements. There are expenses involved and a certain diminishing of autonomy, but in this day of soaring materials and technology expenses, such arrangements cannot only leverage limited dollars, but also enrich services.

Commentary: "Libraries Collaborating for Success"

Gordon W. Smith
Director, Systemwide Library Programs
Office of the Chancellor, California State University

Academic libraries have a long and rich tradition of collaboration. The most obvious manifestation of that collaboration is resource sharing, a reflection of the reality that no one library can own every book or journal its users might want to examine. Interlibrary loan continues to be an important service in academic libraries, even as journals and books become increasingly available electronically. Many libraries, to increase the effectiveness of resource sharing, have also entered into consortial agreements with other libraries to coordinate their collection building. Such agreements permit individual libraries to concentrate on purchasing resources in subject areas of particular strength and sharing those, rather than trying to build comprehensive collections across all subjects.

While the time-honored traditions of resource sharing among academic libraries will continue into the foreseeable future, dramatic changes that have swept the information and educational landscapes over the past twenty years have opened up new avenues of collaboration that libraries are just now beginning to fully appreciate. New opportunities are emerging for libraries to work together more effectively to contribute to the success of the teaching and learning missions of their institutions.

Technology and its vicissitudes serve as both opportunities for collaboration and as challenges that make combining libraries' efforts ever more necessary. Advances in information and library technology have greatly expanded the scope of information resources libraries offer, and have greatly enhanced libraries' abilities to share resources and collaborate in their acquisition. At the same time, however, this increasingly complex information environment is challenging librarians and faculty to find new ways to equip students to navigate this environment. Academic libraries working together can combine the talents of their personnel and their investments in information resources and technology to succeed in meeting the challenges and opportunities technology presents.

For many years, the administration of the California State University has recognized the importance of this collaboration among its twenty-three libraries. The CSU system has encouraged and supported the development of systemwide library strategic planning to advance a wide range of collaborative initiatives aimed at strengthening the libraries' role in supporting the instructional and scholarly missions of the institutions. In a climate of increasingly scarce resources, supporting this planning and investing in its resulting initiatives has been an easy decision for administrators in the systemwide Office of the Chancellor.

Academic library collaboration may be viewed as falling into three broad dimensions: content, access, and instruction. The metaphor of the three-legged stool comes to mind. All three legs are necessary for the stool to succeed in serving its purpose; all three dimensions of operation are essential for the success of the libraries' mission.

The first of the three, content, lends itself most readily to multi-library, consortial cooperation. The accelerating shift by publishers from print to electronic delivery means library consortia can band together to negotiate contracts with information providers in a way that was not possible in the print environment. Consortial purchasing enables libraries to better cope with the costs of the ever-growing assortment of journals and other information resources, not to mention the sharp yearly price increases for which publishers have become noted.

An example of successful consortial purchasing can be found in the Electronic Core Collection of the California State University. The libraries of the CSU have agreed that if a minimum of fifteen campuses consider a particular electronic resource to be worth purchasing to support their academic programs, the systemwide office will undertake to negotiate and fund acquisition of the resource for the entire system. The Electronic Core Collection thus mirrors the core curricular offerings of the CSU campuses.

Given the ever-expanding assortment of information resources libraries must attempt to provide, the technology of access in a collaborative environment must play a central role. Technology can be used to create a combined online catalog of the holdings of all the libraries in a consortium. With a user-friendly direct interlibrary requesting application, such a catalog can, in effect, create one large collection from the users' perspective. This is a very powerful and much-used feature for cooperating libraries, particularly in regional or statewide settings.

Technology is emerging that can also make sense of the information universe for the student and can serve as an important resource for learning. Web-based library information "portals," which can guide students though the search process and greatly simplify the task of finding relevant information, are being implemented by many libraries. With a single search, the user can retrieve information and find resources available locally, regionally or even worldwide. This portal technology is becoming the academic library's answer to Google; librarians select the underlying resource for searching based on authority and appropriateness. Another technology that is becoming widely used provides direct linking between a bibliographic database citation and the full text of the article referenced. All of these technologies become more powerful in a collaborative setting; they permit the broader leveraging of the investments individual libraries make in information resources and in the talents of professional staff.

These new technologies represent dizzying advances in how information is organized and accessed, and accordingly, the instruction mission of the academic library is becoming critical. Information literacy—the ability to find, retrieve, evaluate, and effectively use information—is increasingly important for success in the academic environment, the world of work, and life in general. Instruction in information literacy is a central role for the academic librarian. Both faculty and librarians are coming to recognize the importance of information literacy throughout the curriculum; partnerships between librarians and faculty are increasingly common as information literacy is infused as a learning outcome in both lower and upper division courses. The downside of this recognition is that librarians find themselves under enormous pressure. Simply put, there are not enough of them to go around.

In an ideal academic world, there would be enough librarians to partner with faculty when courses are designed and delivered, to offer instruction in information literacy to every incoming freshman and transfer student, to work closely with faculty in selecting and deselecting library information resources, and to offer assistance to students in the library every hour it is open. Of course, the reality is that even in the most generously funded academic library, such a world is unattainable. While collaboration among libraries cannot come close to a remedy for this situation, at least some mitigation can be achieved with a bit of creative thinking.

With a modest investment of funds, library consortia can serve as ideal vehicles for bringing together librarians and faculty to share models of successful integration of information literacy throughout the curriculum. The CSU, for example, has brought librarians and faculty together in workshop and conference settings. Grouped by discipline specialties, participants have raised awareness of the importance of information literacy as a learning outcome and have exchanged creative approaches to building information literacy into course curricula.

Development of means of assessing student abilities in information literacy is another example of the value of libraries collaborating to accomplish a task far too complex for a single institution. In a notable example, librarians and faculty from several universities, together with the Educational Testing Service, have created a sophisticated scenario- and Web-based assessment instrument to measure how well students actually go about using technology and information resources to solve problems and make decisions. Results of this assessment can be used to guide institutions in designing effective information literacy instruction as well as certifying students' readiness for advanced learning and the workplace.

As the examples above illustrate, academic libraries continue to find new avenues for collaborating for success. The longstanding culture of library cooperation is now reaching beyond librarians to join with faculty, administrators, and others to advance the success of students and faculty in an ever-changing information and educational environment.

Shared Libraries

One form of inter-institutional collaboration remains to be discussed: the sharing of a library facility and/or the integration of the campus library with another library. One of the very first joint libraries involved Vanderbilt University and two other academic institutions that were located nearby, George Peabody College for Teachers and Scarritt College. By 1928, the three schools were separated only by a city street.

An initial attempt to plan a shared library in 1930 failed to reach agreement, but by the mid-1930s, a joint self-survey launched a number of collaborative initiatives, and special attention was placed upon the interchange of courses and sharing of libraries. These efforts were reinforced by a survey of the American Council on Education regarding the facilities for graduate work.

> It brought to light the inadequacy of facilities for graduate work in the south . . . [this report] provided a favorable climate for the joint self-survey of Peabody and Vanderbilt. This survey made their faculties and administrative officers aware of many opportunities for increasing and improving the educational offerings and services of the three institutions through cooperative efforts. In this atmosphere the concept of Nashville as a regional University Center, based upon voluntary cooperation of Peabody, Scarritt, and Vanderbilt, emerged. As a result, a detailed program for the expansion of educational offerings, especially on the graduate level, the interchange of courses, the elimination of unnecessary duplication in offerings, and for a joint university library enterprise was projected and was submitted to the educational foundations in the spring of 1936.[79]

The full story of the planning and fundraising for this first-of-its-kind collaboration was documented in the alumni publication of the George Peabody College for Teachers upon the twenty-fifth anniversary of the Joint University Library. In it, David Kaser, the library director, made a statement that is equally true today: "Genuine cooperation between neighboring institutions of higher learning in the United States is rare. When and where it is undertaken, it is fraught with difficulties; it requires patience and good will. But its rewards can be significant, and we do well to keep them in mind in this University Center."[80]

Joint libraries are not new, but there has been a recent increase in the number and type of such efforts—with a growing number of them involving academic libraries. Australian Alan Bundy has studied the development of joint-use libraries globally and concludes that "worldwide, the number of such libraries, and experimentation with them, is growing. In Sweden, 40 percent of public libraries are joint-use, as are 40 percent in South Australia, 9 percent in Australia, and 8 percent in Canada (but less than 2 percent in the United States)."[81]

While some proclaimers of joint-use libraries see such collaborations as necessary but in less than optimistic terms (i.e., "keeping from being marginalized in the digital age"[82]), others see them as an opportunity to provide enhanced services. In March 2000, College & Research Libraries editor Donald E. Riggs summarized current joint-use facilities that serve academic and public constituents. While he notes that "it is uncommon to find any two joint-use libraries that are identical in the way they operate," he does predict that they "will become more common in the twenty-first century" and that their emphasis will be "more focused on improving services, rather than boasting about a library's inventory count."[83] Indeed, the literature on joint-use libraries has grown to the point that in 2002, ALA created a bibliography on what it termed "combined libraries."[84]

A watershed event in collaborative libraries occurred in June 2004 with the awarding of the prestigious Gale/*Library Journal* 2004 Library of the Year Award to the Dr. Martin Luther King, Jr., Library in San José, California, and things will never be the same again. This complex, highly visible, and initially highly suspect project establishes once and for all that two existing libraries with their different missions, different clients, and different bureaucracies can do more than just share a building; they can successfully integrate operations. (For more information on the King Library, see chapter 1.)

Both the Vanderbilt and the San José State University joint libraries are examples of extensive integration, with the intent of better supporting their parent institutions' missions. Other joint libraries are less ambitious in their goal, but nonetheless are a means of benefiting their institutions. For example, the Nova Southeastern University Library in Florida, which opened its current library building in 2001, has contracted with the county public library to staff and operate the county library out of the new facility. In this case, the libraries are on different online systems, and the collections are separately housed. In 2004, a new library was opened to serve the Metropolitan State University and local patrons of the St. Paul Public Library. Here the organizations are not merged in any respect though they share a building.

Yet for every joint library planned or already open functioning, a far larger number has been considered but not implemented. Most often, the reason for not proceeding is the same as the one that brought the first attempt at merger to a standstill in the Nashville Higher Education Center, that is, the inability of the institutions "to agree on a plan of joint ownership, control, and management for a cooperative library project."[85] Conversely, the success of the King Library in San José can be attributed to the extensive and comprehensive nature of the "prenuptial agreement" developed by the university and city and their lawyers.[86] However, such written agreements alone cannot guarantee success.

The other essential ingredient for the success of the King Library was that top leadership from both sides committed to serve on a Senior Leadership Team. The original membership included the director of the San José Public Library, the dean of the university library, the SJSU provost and vice presidents for Administration and Finance and Advancement, the city manager, and the director of the San José Redevelopment Agency. With the completion of construction and the capital campaign, membership has decreased. The team now brings together on a quarterly basis the library leadership with the city manager and the university vice president for administration and finance, plus whoever else is needed (e.g., the city budget director). This high-level oversight and support for the project are major reasons why it has worked so well and continues to do so. This team has acknowledged that the King Library could not function if it had to adhere to every city and every university rule and regulation.

A campus with a mission that includes service to its surrounding community and that needs a new library facility would do well to see whether a logical partner exists and to explore the possibility of a joint effort. Such considerations should be predicated upon potential benefits for each partner—benefits that might include a bigger and better building than would otherwise be obtainable, the richness of the combined collections, service enhancements and/or better ability to obtain resources. It will require a lot of extra work up front, but as David Kaser said so many years ago in Nashville, "the rewards can be significant."[87]

NOTES

1. Donald J. Waters, "What Are Digital Libraries?" *CLIR Issues* (July/August 1998). Retrieved 15 April 2005 from http://www.clir.org/pubs/issues/issues 04.html.

2. Wendy Pradt Lougee, *Diffuse Libraries: Emergent Roles for the Research Library in the Digital Age* (Washington, D.C.: Council on Library and Information Resources, 2002), 1–2.

3. Ibid., 22.

4. Chris Ferguson, Gene Spencer, and Terry Metz, "Greater Than the Sum of Its Parts: The Integrated IT/Library Organization," *EDUCAUSE Review* 39 (May/June 2004): 46.

5. Brian L. Hawkins, Julia A. Rudy, and Joshua W. Madsen, *EDUCAUSE Core Data Service 2002 Summary Report* (Washington, D.C.: EDUCAUSE, 2003), 4.

6. Ferguson et al., "Greater Than the Sum of Its Parts," 39–46.

7. "Colloquy in Print: Ensuring Effectiveness in Information Technology," *The Chronicle of Higher Education* 50 (4 June 2004): B20.

8. Ibid.

9. Chris Ferguson and Terry Metz, "Finding the Third Space: On Leadership Issues Related to the Integration of Library and Computing," in *Leadership, Higher Education, and the Information Age*, ed. Carrie E. Regenstein and Barbara I. Dewey (New York: Neal-Schuman, 2003).

10. Peggy Seiden and Michael D. Kathman, "A History of the Rhetoric and Reality of Library and Computing Relationships," in *Books, Bytes, and Bridges*, ed. Larry Hardesty (Chicago: American Library Association, 2000), 10.

11. Arnold Hirshon, "Integrating Computing and Library Services: An Administrative Planning and Implementation Guide for Information Resources," CAUSE Professional Paper Series, vol. 18 (Boulder, Colo.: CAUSE, 1998). Retrieved 23 February 2005 from http://www.educause.edu/ir/library/pdf/PUB 3018.pdf.

12. Deanna B. Marcum, "Bright Future for the Academic Library," *Priorities* 13 (winter 2000): 6–7.

13. Randall L. Ericson, "Living and Thriving with Library/ITS Collaboration," *C&RL News* 65 (October 2004): 511.

14. Ibid.

15. Judith Axler Turner, "Role of the Computing Director Is Increasingly Managerial," *The Chronicle of Higher Education* 33 (17 September 1986): 15, 18.

16. Joy Hughes, e-mail correspondence to Patricia Breivik, 22 June 2005.

17. Brian L. Hawkins et al., *EDUCAUSE 2002 Summary Report*, 2.

18. Linda H. Fleit, "Choosing a Chief Information Officer: The Myth of the Computer Czar," *AAHE Bulletin* 38 (April 1986): 7–9.

19. Philip D. Leighton and David C. Weber, *Planning Academic and Research Library Buildings*, 3rd ed. (Chicago: American Library Association, 1999), xix.

20. USC Annenberg School, *The Digital Future Report: Surveying the Digital Future, Year Four; Ten Years, Ten Trends* (Los Angeles: University of Southern California, 2004), 9. Retrieved 15 April 2005 from http://www.digitalcenter.org/downloads/DigitalFutureReport-Year4-2004.pdf.

21. *ECAR Respondent Summary: Wireless Networking in Higher Education in the U.S. and Canada* (Washington, D.C.: ECAR, 2002), 2. Retrieved 23 February 2005 from http://www.educause.edu/ir/library/pdf/ERS0202/ekf0202.pdf.

22. Scott Carlson, "Talking Tags," *The Chronicle of Higher Education* 50 (6 August 2004): A29.

23. Laura Smart, "Making Sense of RFID," *Library Journal* (15 October 2004). Retrieved 23 February 2005 from http://www.libraryjournal.com/article/CA456770.

24. Scott Carlson, "To Use That Library Computer, Please Identify Yourself," *The Chronicle of Higher Education* 50 (25 June 2004): A39.

25. Cindy Kristoff, *SPEC Kit 245: Electronic Reserves Operations in ARL Libraries* (Washington, D.C.: Association of Research Libraries, 1999). Retrieved 23 February 2005 from http://www.arl.org/spec/245fly.html.

26. Anna Klump Pilston and Richard L. Hart, "Student Response to a New Electronic Reserves System," *The Journal of Academic Librarianship* 28 (May 2002): 147–51.

27. Mary S. Laskowski and David Ward, "Creation and Management of a Home-Grown Electronic Reserves System at an Academic Library: Results of a Pilot Project," *The Journal of Academic Librarianship* 27 (September 2001): 369.

28. Brice Austin, "A Brief History of Electronic Reserves," *Journal of Interlibrary Loan, Document Delivery & Information Supply* 12, no. 2 (2001): 1–15.

29. Chris Ferguson, "'Shaking the Conceptual Foundations,' Too: Integrating Research and Technology Support for the Next Generation of Information Service," *College & Research Libraries* 61 (July 2000): 300–311. Retrieved 13 April 2004 through WilsonWeb.

30. Soo Young Rieh, "Changing Reference Service Environment: A Review of Perspectives from Managers, Librarians, and Users," *The Journal of Academic Librarianship* 25 (May 1999): 185.

31. Nancy J. Young and Marilyn Von Seggern, "General Information Seeking in Changing Times," *Reference & User Services Quarterly* 41 (winter 2001): 165.

32. Ibid., 164.

33. Lougee, *Diffuse Libraries*, 14–15.

34. Jana Ronan and Carol Turner, *SPEC Kit 273: Chat Reference* (Washington, D.C.: Association of Research Libraries, 2002). Retrieved 20 May 2003 from http://www.arl.org/spec/273sum.html.

35. Thomas A. Peters, "E-Reference: How Consortia Add Value," *The Journal of Academic Librarianship* 28 (July 2002): 248–50.

36. Steve Coffman and Linda Arret, "To Chat or Not Chat—Taking Another Look at Virtual Reference, Part 1," *Searcher* 12 (July/August 2004). Retrieved 8 July 2004 from http://www.infotoday.com/searcher/jul04/arret_coffman.shtml.

37. Coffman and Arret, "To Chat or Not Chat—Taking Yet Another Look at Virtual Reference, Part 2," *Searcher* 12 (September 2004). Retrieved 9 September 2004 from http://www.infotoday.com/searcher/sep04/arret_coffman.shtml.

38. Coffman and Arret, "To Chat or Not Chat, Part 1."

39. Brenda Bailey-Hainer, "Virtual Reference: Alive & Well," *Library Journal* 130 (15 January 2005). Retrieved 21 January 2005 from WilsonWeb database.

40. Marianne Foley, "Instant Messaging Reference in an Academic Library: A Case Study," *College & Research Libraries* 63 (January 2002): 36–45.

41. Anne R. Kenney et al., "Google Meets Ebay: What Academic Librarians Can Learn from Alternative Information Providers," *D-Lib Magazine* 9 (June 2003): 12. Retrieved 17 October 2003 from http://www.dlib.org/dlib/june03/kenney/06kenney.html.

42. Ibid.

43. David Tyckoson, "On the Desirableness of Personal Relations between Librarians and Readers: The Past and Future of Reference Service," *Reference Services Review* 31, no. 1 (2003): 15. Retrieved 15 April 2005 from Emerald database.

44. Denise Troll Covey, *Usage and Usability Assessment: Library Practices and Concerns* (Washington, D.C.: Council on Library and Information Resources, 2002), 1.

45. Ibid.

46. Harold B. Shill and Shawn Tonner, "Creating a Better Place: Physical Improvements in Academic Libraries, 1995–2002," *College & Research Libraries* 64 (November 2003): 460–61.

47. Scott Carlson, "The Deserted Library," *The Chronicle of Higher Education* 47 (16 November 2000): A35–A38.

48. Shill and Tonner, "Does the Building Still Matter? Usage Patterns in New, Expanded, and Renovated Libraries, 1995–2002," *College & Research Libraries* 65 (March 2004): 149.

49. Ibid., 148.

50. Scott Bennett, *Libraries Designed for Learning* (Washington, D.C.: Council on Library and Information Resources, 2003).

51. Ibid., 39.

52. Patricia Cohen, "Spaces for Social Study," *New York Times*, 1 August 2004, sec. 4A, 19.

53. Ibid.

54. Jennifer Burek Pierce, "Grassroots Report: Next Stop, Information Commons," *American Libraries* 35 (April 2004): 87.

55. Billie Peterson, "Tech Talk: Information Commons," *Library Instruction Round Table News* 25 (December 2002): 9.

56. Charlene Hurt, "The Johnson Center Library at George Mason University," in *Building Libraries for the 21st Century: The Shape of Information*, ed. T. D. Webb (Jefferson, N.C.: McFarland & Company, 2000): 86–87. © 2000 by Terry D. Webb, by permission of McFarland & Company, Inc., Box 611, Jefferson, N.C. 28640. www.mcfarlandpub.com.

57. Ibid., 88–89.

58. Ibid., 101.

59. Donald Beagle, "Conceptualizing an Information Commons," *The Journal of Academic Librarianship* 25 (March 1999): 82–89.

60. Russell Bailey and Barbara Tierney, "Information Commons Redux: Concept, Evolution, and Transcending the Tragedy of the Commons," *The Journal of Academic Librarianship* 28 (September 2002): 277–86. Retrieved 14 June 2004 from Wilson Web database.

61. Linda Burke, "The Saving Grace of Library Space," *American Libraries* 35 (April 2004): 76.

62. Ibid., 75.

63. Deborah C. Masters, Jessica Arneson, and Hank D. Lutton, "Café Gelman: An Innovative Use of Library Space," *The Journal of Academic Librarianship* 19 (January 1994): 388.

64. Bennett, *Libraries Designed for Learning*, 40.

65. Leighton and Weber, *Planning Academic and Research Library Buildings*.

66. William W. Sannwald, *Checklist of Library Building Design Considerations* (Chicago: American Library Association, 2001).

67. Council on Library and Information Resources, *Library as Place: Rethinking Roles, Rethinking Space* (Washington, D.C.: Council on Library and Information Resources, 2005).

68. Becky Bartindale, "How City, SJSU Made Peace to Become Library Partners," *San José Mercury News*, 10 August 2003, 1A. Retrieved 15 April 2005 from NewsBank database.

69. This location had a long history of campus/city collaboration associated with it. Originally, the city had donated the land to have the university locate in San José. The campus donated the corner lot back to the city for the location of a Carnegie Public Library, which opened exactly 100 years prior to the opening of the King Library. When the city outgrew the Carnegie Library, the land was transferred back to the campus, which used the building as a student union until it was torn down in order for a new academic library to be built.

70. Leigh Weimers, "Talk of Space Travel Has Valley Fired Up," *San José Mercury News*, 12 January 2004, 2B.

71. Ron Feemster, "Volume Discounts," *CrossTalk* 11 (summer 2003): 6–7, 14.

72. Richard N. Katz, "Managing Academic Information Resources in the Future," in *The Mirage of Continuity: Reconfiguring Academic Information Resources for the 21st Century*, ed. Brian L. Hawkins and Patricia Battin (Washington, D.C.: Council on Library and Information Resources, 1998), 176.

73. Feemster, "Volume Discounts," 7.

74. Ibid., 14. (For more information on OhioLINK, see http://www.ohiolink.edu/.)

75. For more information on COLD, see http://seir.calstate.edu/acom/cold/index.shtml.

76. Committee on Institutional Cooperation, *Center for Library Initiatives (CLI): About This Program*. Retrieved 26 February 2005 from http://www.cic.uiuc.edu/programs/CenterForLibraryInitiatives/aboutThisGroup.shtml.

77. See the University of California Libraries Web site at http://libraries.universityofcalifornia.edu/.

78. Brian J. Baird, "Consortial Preservation Management: A New Model for Library Preservation Administration," *C&RL News* 63 (September 2002): 572, 573–74.

79. A. F. Kuhlman, "A Quarter Century of Service," *The Peabody Reflector* 34 (July–August 1961): 103.

80. Ibid., 104.

81. Alan Bundy, "Joint-Use Libraries: The Ultimate Form of Cooperation," in *Planning the Modern Public Library Building* (Westport, Conn.: Libraries Unlimited, 2003), 146.

82. Charles Kratz, "Transforming the Delivery of Service: The Joint-Use Library and Information Commons," *C&RL News* 64 (February 2003). Retrieved 14

June 2004 from www.ala.org/ala/acrl/acrlpubs/crlnews/backissues2003/february1/ transforming.htm.

83. Donald E. Riggs, "Joint-Use Libraries: Thinking Out of the Box," *College & Research Libraries* 61 (March 2000). Retrieved 17 August 2004 from http:// www.ala.org/ala/acrl/acrlpubs/crljournal/backissues2000b/march00/candrl-march2000editorial.htm.

84. American Library Association, "Combined Libraries: A Bibliography," ALA Library Fact Sheet Number 20 (2002). Retrieved 17 August 2004 from http://www.ala.org/library/fact20.html.

85. Kuhlman, 103.

86. See the Dr. Martin Luther King, Jr. Library Web site at http://www. sjlibrary.org/legal/.

87. Kuhlman, 104.

CHAPTER 8

Collections and Access

J ust as technology has radically changed how libraries offer services, it has also had a profound impact on what has historically been known as collection development. Today librarians no longer do collection building so much as they do information management. Working in collaboration with classroom faculty, librarians must constantly monitor the availability of information in different formats, at different costs, with differing access possibilities and differing preservation considerations—all of which increasingly involve the purchase or licensing of electronic resources. In addition, campus expectations must also be considered for accessing library resources through wireless technology and cellular phones that with each generation become more like computers.

The question could well be asked as to why, with more and more information available electronically from home or office, the library must continue as a source of information. Granted, library services can be helpful in getting students' research skills up to par, managing reserve collections, and facilitating access to hard-to-find information that is not in digital form. However, given budget limitations and users' preference for electronic materials, have not libraries outlived their usefulness as depositories of information? Some people think so.

Take, for example, when a new California State University (CSU) campus was planned for the Monterey Bay area. In the January 30, 1995, issue of *Newsweek*, CSU Chancellor Barry Munitz envisioned a bookless library and stated his belief that "you simply don't have to build a traditional library these days."[1] No one else seemed to share his belief, however, and on opening day, the collection—besides electronic resources—had 18,000 volumes and has continued to grow since.

Today, libraries must be perceived by academic personnel less as physical entities and more as the means of access to all information; by necessity, libraries have expanded their role beyond developing and managing discrete collections housed in physical facilities located on their campuses. To implement this expanded role, the deans, faculty, and staffs of libraries must devote time and resources to establishing a framework for efficiently sharing resources with other libraries.

The reign of the "fortress library" has ended. Such libraries were characterized by "their lack of involvement with other libraries, lack of contribution to the wider community, and restrictive practices towards their users."[2] At one time, cooperating in local networks seemed to some a distraction from a library's primary responsibility to its "own" faculty and students. Now, cooperative ventures are essential to provide access to the larger scholarly network beyond the confines of the campus library buildings. The technology services and facilities issues discussed in the previous chapter are all heavily influenced by a library's ability to establish effective information networks.

Libraries have, in fact, worked together to share resources for many years. The three major goals this cooperation accomplished were to extend the capability of individual libraries to deliver information to users; to reduce demands on their acquisition budgets by relying on other collections to supply needed items; and to ensure that such tasks as cataloging of particular items need not be repeated over and over by different libraries.[3] Many campuses have also added a fourth goal: to ensure campus-level quality in courses taught off campus.

PRINT VS. ELECTRONIC RESOURCES

The importance of collaboration continues to grow, because making provision for access to electronic resources—often through consortial arrangements—is at the heart of information management today.

This does not imply that print materials are a thing of the past. The reality is that one million new titles were published worldwide from 2003 to 2004,[4] and new books in the United States, estimated at 120,000 in 2004, were up from 40,000 in the 1970s.[5] This level of productivity is not surprising when one considers the expansion of programs and faculty during this period. Electronic resources will never meet all the scholarly needs of the campus, nor will the Internet. However, the Internet does require a rethinking of the criteria and the very nature of collection building; and it is desirable that faculty and student leaders should be in-volved in rethinking the management of scholarly materials, both to pro-vide a user perspective in the planning and so that they understand the necessary trade-offs. Questions to be considered include the following:

- What must be bought and held?
- What can be secured through some assurance of access short of physi-cal possession?
- How do questions of medium (paper or electronic formats, for example) connect with choices of subject areas to be covered?
- What does the availability of electronic information tell as about the urgency of buying (or replacing, repairing, and otherwise tending) printed books on those topics?[6]

Whether or not campuses are carefully rethinking their information management efforts, they are making significant changes in how they spend their materials budget. A 2001 survey found the following pattern:

> remarkably similar purchasing behaviors among all academic li-braries—namely, a palpable shift in the collection and usage of dig-ital resources from traditional print resources. And even though books and other print resources still account for the lion's share of library spending, nearly every respondent said he or she expected spending on digital resources to continue to rise sharply over the next three years. . . . Perhaps the most noteworthy finding of the 2001 survey is the staggering popularity and usage figures of full-text aggregated databases. . . . Roughly nine out of ten purchased their aggregated databases with the help of state consortia.[7]

To put this into shifts in spending costs, the survey report gave two ex-amples:

> In 1998, the University of Texas at Austin (UT–Austin) spent roughly five percent of its annual materials budget on electronic re-sources and 30 percent on monograph purchases. But just three years later, in 2001, 20 percent of its $10 million annual materials budget went to electronic resources and only 15 percent to monograph pur-chases. Meanwhile, a junior college library in Michigan spent nearly 50 percent of its $375,000 materials budget on electronic resources in 2001—more than 15 times the three percent devoted to elec-tronic resources in 1998.[8]

There is little question that most faculty and students prefer getting their information electronically. Having information available 24/7 from on or off campus is a plus for everyone, and allowing more than one person to access a particular journal at one time is also an important plus. Most of all "readers report that they spend much less time locating and obtaining library-provided articles when they are available electronically."[9]

Librarians and scholars rightly worry about publishers maintaining back-runs when they are no longer profitable, but this issue seldom concerns any but the most sophisticated of users. This means—since almost always dollars must be reallocated within existing funds—that acquisitions dollars need to be reallocated from print to electronic resources. Such a change will be painful for some classroom and library faculty, and there will always be the exception that must be retained in print because of inherent qualities in the publication or high-use patterns.

Even the largest libraries have been forced by escalating costs to reduce journal holdings (see chapter 10). Normally, the progression of cuts is as follows:

- Eliminate print journals that are low use and are available electronically;
- Eliminate journals that are high use but available electronically;
- Eliminate electronic journals.

Where titles are eliminated, efforts should be made to provide document delivery services for the journals that are cut. This is what was done at Appalachian State University when budget cuts forced the library to cancel 730 of its 3,400 journals. There, "the library will make up for the lost journals through a commercial document-delivery service, paid through the library budget. The service charges $35 to deliver a copy of an article to a professor's desk. In the case of expensive journals, the service can provide a real savings."[10]

Care must also be taken to protect reasonable levels of funding for monographs, video, and other one-time purchases. Far too often, libraries must sacrifice such one-time purchases because of the timing of payments for subscriptions. Since the resultant gaps in collections are seldom if ever filled in (each year brings its own set of new publications), the humanities and social sciences are particularly disadvantaged. "Many scholars worry that as library budgets shrink, book collections will become 'less deep, less interesting, and less inspiring.' There is concern that libraries will no longer collect in order to preserve the cultural record for future generations."[11]

It should be noted that faculty and students' enthusiasm for electronic journals and databases has not carried over to e-books despite high expectations for their use and educational benefits such as those described below.

> Electronic books offer creative possibilities for expanding access as well as changing learning behavior and academic research. Content can always be accessible, regardless of time or place, to be read on PCs or on portable book readers. Books need never go out of print, and new editions can be easily created. One can carry several titles at once on a portable reader and, over time, build a personal library. Features such as full text searching, changeable font size, markup, citation creation, and note taking will enhance usability. Print text can be integrated with multi-dimensional objects, sound, and film to create a whole new kind of monographic work.[12]

A February 11, 2005, article, entitled "Online Textbooks Fail to Make the Grade" in *The Chronicle of Higher Education*, did a particularly good job of exploring students' lukewarm response at best to online textbooks despite the inherent advantages cited above. The concerns students raised over electronic textbooks seem applicable to other electronic books as well. Their concerns include the following:

- There are too many restrictions placed on use.
- You have to be where there is an operating computer.
- The Internet is distracting, so it is harder to stay focused.
- You can't give it to friends, sell, or keep on shelf for later reading.
- Some passwords expire within a year.
- Some only allow access through a particular computer.[13]

These shortcomings echo earlier ones by students at Ball State University.

> Navigating through digital texts was one of the e-book users' biggest complaints. They found moving from page to page "tedious." They also found it difficult to find specific chapters in texts and to find particular words.
> With certain e-book devices, users were easily able to change settings, like font size and screen contrasts, but most students didn't

find those features terribly useful. The researchers found that the students were most interested in features that let them use the e-books the same way they would use printed volumes—for instance, a convenient feature that allowed them to highlight text.[14]

The prediction of electronic book providers and some librarians that students' enthusiasm for and use of electronic books will grow is likely true, but the questions are how quickly and to what extent.

In terms of budget limitations, electronic resources do offer advantages. Both electronic journals and e-books provide much greater potential for collaborative purchasing and resource sharing than print collections do. Higher education systems and various consortia of institutions have entered into purchase agreements that have netted at least modest savings while providing their campuses with access to a far larger number of journals—something of particular value to smaller campuses.[15] However, initial efforts that focused on a "bundling" approach are now being closely reexamined.

Bundling started in the late 1900s as a way of getting discounts on electronic resources. Publishers offer a set price (based on current payments) for libraries to buy electronic access to all its journals, with capped annual increases for a specified number of years. The major objection to such arrangements is that individual journal subscriptions may not be cancelled in their electronic format. In times of budget cuts, both library and classroom faculty find it increasingly frustrating to be paying for journals not needed to support campus programs and research when journals that are needed cannot be purchased for lack of funds.

By spring 2001, Kenneth Frazier, director of libraries at the University of Wisconsin, Madison, was unequivocally telling colleagues not to sign on "to any comprehensive licensing agreements with commercial publishers." His rationale was "that the push to build an all-electronic collection can't be undertaken at the risk of: (1) weakening that collection with journals we neither need nor want, and (2) increasing our dependence on publishers who have already shown their determination to monopolize the information marketplace."[16]

These concerns are set within an environment of anger at what many see as continued price gouging by some publishers and fears of what those same publishers will do to keep increasing revenues with a captive marketplace. The sweet deals offered to get customers signed up are not likely to be as sweet when renewal times come up. What then should a campus do?

At a January 2003 executive seminar for directors of the Association of Research Libraries (ARL), OhioLINK Executive Director Tom Sanville offered the best advice. It is that every library and/or consortium needs to do its own assessment of the benefits to them of entering into such licensing agreements at the same time that they actively support new approaches to scholarly communications, such as promoting open access practices (which will be discussed later in this chapter). OhioLINK, for example, has a threefold objective in its purchase of comprehensive licensing agreements: (1) expand access to journals at more sustainable prices, (2) vastly improve costs per unit, and (3) "take advantage of the serendipity that the electronic medium provides which increases the dynamic of how much information can actually be consumed." By these measurements, Sanville believes bundling works well for the OhioLINK community.[17]

At the 2003 ARL seminar, much attention was given to the needed resolution of two problems: a reliable means for archiving electronic resources and the elimination of restrictions on use of materials for interlibrary loan or for certain user categories, such as alumni.[18] These issues need to be addressed even while exploring alternatives to the current heavy reliance on major commercial publishers.

ENHANCING ACCESS THROUGH INFORMATION MANAGEMENT

Just providing access to online journals and databases is far from enough. With so much information available online, priority must be given to organizing this information so that faculty and students can easily obtain quality information needed for specific assignments and research. These new responsibilities fall into two major categories: providing an attractive and effective Web page and orchestrating the large collections of campus online databases and journals into manageable arrangements that allow intuitive retrieval of needed quality information accessed through a single search engine. Just as important as the online resources themselves are the "resources that enable [users] to find the best information with the fewest barriers to access."[19] Not only do these organizational efforts pose new challenges for teams of librarians and information technology personnel, but they also require a great deal of customization to match the needs of particular faculty and students with the specific online resources available on that campus.

Library Web Sites

"One of the most important new elements in the electronic library environment is the library Web site,"[20] which is the virtual front door "to the university library for many distance education students and for those simply choosing to access the numerous resources available to them through the library from off-campus."[21] Carefully constructed Web sites provide a 24/7 service to faculty and students by providing easily understood links to on-campus and worldwide resources, tutorials, subject resource guides, operational details (e.g., library policies, library hours), user information (e.g., fines, materials checked out), means for asking reference questions, patron-initiated interlibrary loans, directions for making a donation to the library, and much more. The very richness of potential content can, however, result in hard-to-use sites with cumbersome linkages. Moreover, keeping Web sites up-to-date is an ongoing challenge. The lack of expert staffing and the absence of clearcut quality measurements add to the difficulties. When they are done well, library Web sites can significantly contribute to the ease of access to needed information even when library doors are closed. On smaller campuses especially, appropriate academic computer experts will be needed to supplement library staff in creating good Web sites.

Search Engines

"The library's complex information environment caters poorly to those who want fast, easy access to unlimited, full-text content using interfaces that require no critical thought or evaluation."[22] Today, students and faculty alike have come to expect and to use Google-style search strategies on every database they encounter, and all planning for campus-based search engines must start with that premise.[23] Indeed, in order to continue to serve as an effective center of knowledge and learning on campus, libraries must implement new research and discovery systems to improve searching capabilities for users. "Libraries are used to handling semantically dense, richly structured data. A major challenge will be to handle more unstructured data. Libraries need to find ways of leveraging their investment in structured approaches in relation to large amounts of unstructured materials on the Web that are being generated by research and learning activities."[24]

Expectations to search across all resources with a single, simple (i.e., Google-like) search tool can largely be realized with metasearching, also referred to as federated, or distributed, search technology. Metasearching allows a user to simultaneously search across multiple resources from a single interface. Such resources include catalogs, reference databases, digital repositories, and subject-based Web gateways. Faculty and students would use this search method when they need to efficiently conduct the same search in more than one database or want to identify the database most appropriate for the discipline. For example, one might search an interdisciplinary topic—like religion in public schools—in both religion and education databases at the same time.

Metasearching technology can be integrated with libraries' context-sensitive linking services to allow users to determine easily which resources are available in their own libraries or to initiate interlibrary loan options. In addition, the technology allows the offering of alert services, in which users can save and automatically rerun searches at specified intervals—a particularly useful function when one is doing long-term research. Finally, in recognition of the continuing need of advanced searchers for the specialized features available only in individual database search tools, metasearch tools provide links to each resource's native interface.

Metasearching is a tool whose time has come. Metasearching simplifies the process of searching diverse local and licensed resources and results in a useful, intelligible set of results. The technology allows campus resources to be in alignment with user expectations for a single search portal to scholarly material.[25] Such capabilities can result in specialized services to targeted campus groups.

> As an example of a specialized service, the University of Virginia's proposed American Studies Information Community will draw on harvesting protocols to bring together disparate types of information (text, data, media, images) for a *community*, defined as a group of scholars, students, researchers, librarians, information specialists, and citizens with a common interest in a particular thematic area. The project is being undertaken collaboratively with other institutions and content providers (e.g., Thomas Jefferson Foundation, Virginia Tech University, and the Smithsonian National Museum of American Art). The University of Virginia describes these information communities as "learning and teaching environments in which subject-driven websites are developed around print and digital versions of our collections and the teaching interests of our faculty members. . . . Information communities will foster interdisciplinary and collaborative research and publication amongst scholars with common interests."[26]

Other efforts are being made on many campuses to enhance the library's online catalog by incorporating features of services such as those offered by Amazon.com. This may include adding book reviews, cover images, and publisher blurbs, as well as seeking to make the catalog more user friendly. Such continuing enhancements, as well as the improved Web site, need to be effectively brought to the attention of various campus constituencies, starting with students and faculty, but also targeting alumni, emeritus faculty, off-campus students, and, as appropriate, community groups. However, no group is more important to target than faculty, to enhance their research productivity and to reach their students.

Interlibrary Loan and Document Delivery

There are three ways of supplying journal articles: purchasing subscriptions, providing document delivery services, and offering interlibrary loan (ILL) services. As the amount of information keeps expanding and inflationary rates stay high, acquisitions dollars increasingly fall short of what is needed to support campus programs and research. Thus, interlibrary loan and document delivery have become integral elements of information management, because purchasing materials is the most expensive of the three options. Incorporating these services into information management strategies, however, necessitates establishing user fees or redistributing acquisitions funds—both of which have drawbacks. User fees work a hardship on the students and departments that are "economically challenged"; moreover, free document delivery to faculty offices is often provided to compensate for hated journal cuts. On the other hand, reallocating acquisitions dollars to pay for such services further reduces campus library holdings.

The dividing line between interlibrary loan and document delivery is being blurred by the technology. Historically, interlibrary loans of articles involved library staff—on behalf of users—requesting articles and responding to requests by faxing photocopies of articles to other libraries. Photocopies were then sent to the requesting faculty member by campus mail or picked up by students. Now electronic delivery of the article to the requesting person's computer is becoming the preferred norm because of the shorter waiting time and ease of use once received.

Interlibrary loan services have also been enhanced through the use of technology coupled with collaboration among groups of libraries that can access each other's catalogs. Where they share the same online system and are geographically close together, patron-initiated ILL requests can speed up delivery time from library to library to a few days and with significantly less demand on staff time than with traditional ILL operations. For example, Link+, a patron-initiated ILL product of Innovative Interfaces, Inc. (III), as of February 2004 had thirty-one participating libraries among its California library sites. These multitype libraries collectively own 5.7 million unique titles and had 173,382 ILL requests in 2003, up from 47,000 over the previous year. Average time for delivery following a request is three days.[27] Of course, more labor-intensive traditional interlibrary loan services are still needed to locate and borrow resources not available within the participating libraries' collections.

Some words of caution are needed regarding resource sharing:

> In contrast with library philosophy and practice centuries ago, libraries today often acquire materials and offer services "just in time," rather than "just in case." The cost of access to information appears to be more affordable than the cost of ownership. The escalating cost and volume of publications over time, widespread adoption of technology, and reduced barriers to Internet access may account for the trends of licensing access, increased use of interlibrary loan, and speculation that the digital divide is disappearing. If the access model continues to offer more information at less cost to an increasing number of people, the worst-case scenario would reserve the ownership model for only high-cost, low-use materials. Though this worst-case is unlikely to happen (at least in our lifetime), the access approach to acquiring library materials is risky business. If no one purchases or preserves the materials, interlibrary loan is not viable. If no one archives and moves digital collections to the inevitable new formats and platforms that the future will bring, access to them will be lost when the hardware and software become obsolete. Libraries may have new measures to capture new inputs (for example, number of licensed databases, full text e-journal or e-book titles), but the measures do not capture the implications of the shift in library practice from purchased ownership to licensed access.[28]

QUESTIONS OF ACADEMIC LEADERS ON COLLECTIONS

Perhaps no library issue has been more questioned over the years by academic administrators than how much information does the library really need to support campus programs. This question is complicated by changing programs and the increasing emphasis on electronic resources, and often it can seem as if there will never be an end to growing collections that demand building expansions. There is no definitive answer to such concerns. However, some general principles regarding institutional accountability for providing adequate program support coupled with ongoing assessment of the quality of information management in the library can provide academic administrators with a workable framework for budgetary decision-making.

To assist in developing such a framework, answers to these three questions will be addressed: (1) how much information is enough? (2) is the library doing a good job of information management? and (3) what is a digital library?

How Much Information Is Enough?

Campus library holdings should meet the bulk of undergraduate and most master's-level instructional resource needs. In addition, as has already been discussed, campuses will need to participate in state and national library resource sharing to supplement campus holdings. Graduate and professional schools will require a greater dependency on resource sharing, and their campuses need to assume a share of the responsibility for maintaining the national scholarly network by developing some in-depth research collections.

Libraries can use the volume of materials borrowed through document delivery services or on interlibrary loan from other institutions as a rough measure of the adequacy and appropriateness of current holdings. If such statistics document heavy borrowing in a particular subject area, further investigation may indicate the need to adjust the information management policy to meet changing instructional or research demands. If statistics document heavy borrowing to support most areas of undergraduate instruction, chances are the acquisitions budget is inadequate. Of course, the better the information literacy instruction and the more integrated and active the learning process, the more extensive the resource demands of students will be. So this measure, while useful, must be weighed with other factors.

The percentage of the collection that circulates and the volume of materials placed on hold can also indicate areas of imbalance or particular need. For example, poor circulation statistics within a particular subject range of materials may be caused by a lack of research assignments or a collection so poor as to be unusable, or they may indicate a changing curriculum that should trigger changes in purchasing priorities. Such factors can be explored through faculty and student surveys and through ongoing dialogue between classroom and library faculty.

Beyond internal statistics, accreditation and program review reports may yield valuable feedback, and libraries can compare overall or program-specific holdings with collections at peer institutions or at institutions whose stature the campus is aspiring to attain. Such peer comparisons often carry credibility in setting funding levels, but without closer analysis of actual holdings, this approach only addresses size, not quality. Quality issues are better examined by reviewing nationally respected collections and key bibliographies; this approach is especially important in building areas of excellence and when developing new graduate or professional programs.

No single approach to determining the adequacy and quality of a collection will work for academic libraries. For example, formulas do not lend themselves easily to multidisciplinary databases and fail to incorporate start-up costs for new programs. They are not sensitive to variations among campuses with similar enrollments and programs that nevertheless have very different roles and missions. Campuses that feature highly media-oriented programs, offer extensive off-campus programs, or enjoy heavy local community use will have very different collection needs than those of more traditional institutions.

The best way to determine how much acquisition is enough requires academic officers to work with the library director to develop a multifaceted collection evaluation process that can be applied on a regular basis. Such a plan may involve some or all of the measurement techniques suggested in this section. The important first step is to agree on *what* to evaluate: size of collection in comparison to other schools or programs, adequacy of research support for faculty as measured by faculty evaluations and/or their research productivity, or level of support for undergraduate and graduate instruction as measured by faculty/student evaluations and/or quality of student research. The evaluation process should reflect campus priorities, provide more than one type of measurement, and enjoy support from and credibility with the administration, faculty, and the librarians before implementation.

In addition, when new programs are initiated, administrators should ensure that adequate and realistic provisions are made for library resources. Far too often, faculty plans for new programs are approved despite the lack of accounting for needed library or media resources. Sometimes new program library costs can be met through the freeing up of acquisition funds from eliminated programs. Whether or not this is possible, the library will likely need to purchase important older materials in building "retrospective" collections to support new programs. We suggest establishing a standard procedure, perhaps using an agreed-upon form that librarians complete in consultation with the program faculty. When existing course offerings are linked to form interdisciplinary programs or when new centers and outreach programs are developed, the planning committees could also employ this form to ensure that adequate consideration is given to online and print collection needs.

Is the Library Doing a Good Job of Information Management?

A consistent and carefully designed collection evaluation process will provide insight into how well acquisition funds are being distributed among academic programs and whether the library is purchasing the materials those program areas need. However, if you are concerned about how effectively the library is conducting information management planning, implementation, and evaluation, you will need to evaluate the process as well as the results. The following questions should be considered:

- Do librarians or classroom faculty control the allocation of acquisitions dollars?

- Who within the library has responsibility for coordinating information management? Is this person a competent administrator who is actively involved in information management committees and/or research work both on and beyond the campus? (Annual personnel evaluations should help answer these questions.)

- Does the acquisitions process encourage classroom faculty involvement in materials selection?

- Does the library have a written information management policy? Does it accurately reflect campus instructional and research priorities? Does the plan include procedures for weeding and evaluating the collection? Is the plan appropriately adjusted as programs are added and eliminated on campus?

- Does the library pursue cooperative information management efforts with other libraries?[29]

- Does the library use approval plans? (Under these plans, vendors send a selection of newly published materials directly to the library for evaluation and possible purchase.) If so, are the profiles of information management needs used by vendors in selecting materials updated frequently to reflect program changes?[30]

- How have academic program and accreditation reviews evaluated the collection? If problems were identified that transcend reasonable funding limitations, how is the library addressing these problems?

Answers to these questions should confirm whether campus management of information resources is in good hands. If a more detailed examination seems appropriate to address specific problems, the best alternative would be to bring in one or more outside consultants to review the current collection and electronic resources as well as the information management policies and procedures.

What Is a Digital Library?

Consideration of information management would not be complete without mention of the concept of digital libraries, if for no other reason than the seriousness of collection preservation needs that were raised in our earlier book. Indeed, in recent years, much has been written about the concept of the digital library, and the term means many things to many people. What it does not mean nor ever will mean is that a library's entire collection is digitized. For all practical purposes, we can say that all academic libraries are to some degree digital and that the percentage of the collection in digital format in any academic library will continue to grow.

One major value of digitization technology is to address the material preservation needs that in earlier years might have been microfilmed, especially for libraries that have unique collections that would contribute to the scholarly knowledge base if they were available in digital format. Although it is the large research libraries that are most aggressively active in such efforts, even small institutions may have collections—often of local history materials—that should be preserved and made more easily available through digitization. Criteria for determining what collections should warrant such treatment include the following:

- Does the item or collection have sufficient value and/or demand from a current audience to justify the digitization effort?
- Do we have the legal right to create a digital version?
- Do we have the legal right to disseminate it?
- Can the materials be digitized successfully?
- Does or can digitization add something beyond simply creating a copy?
- Is the cost appropriate?[31]

A 2002 survey by the Institute of Museum and Library Services found that only a minority of museums and libraries were involved in efforts to digitize any of their holdings. The most frequently mentioned determinants were a lack of money and the need for on-site expertise.[32] For those campuses wishing to undertake such projects, OCLC, a library service provider, has developed two software applications (OAIcat and OAI-Harvester) that "provide an open systems framework for repositories by supporting the Open Archives Initiative protocols for data storage and harvesting."[33] This software is being used to support a number of very diverse projects on university campuses, including Duke University's project with the Sheet Music Consortium, the Ohio State University Knowledge Bank to advance distance education, and the Archaeology Data Service at the University of York.[34]

Campuses undertaking such projects should consult publications of the Council on Library and Information Resources, which regularly addresses this topic through research within the Digital Library Federation, an international association promoting new research and scholarship and supporting a network of digital libraries.

THE ROLE OF ACADEMIC LEADERSHIP IN PRESERVING THE SCHOLARLY NETWORK

Academic leaders can help ensure access to information for all scholars by supporting networking and resource sharing by their libraries. Given the naturally competitive nature of academic institutions and the normal resistance of institutions to relinquishing autonomy, the president's role as a champion of such efforts is essential. Presidents and library deans must make key decisions based both on reasonable projections of the technological future and on an understanding of the future implications of current decisions.[35] How will a dollars-and-cents decision today affect access to scholarly information five or ten years from now? How much will a commitment to campus autonomy constrain future expansion and flexibility? Presidential support will be crucial to allow the library to pursue the best long-range solution rather than settle for a safe but limited option.

Presidents can work at the state and regional levels to encourage the development of standards, policies, and procedures that require adequate library support for off-campus instruction. Presidents must make sure their own campuses take this responsibility seriously. One approach for ensuring adequate academic support for off-campus courses would be for state policy to require sponsoring institutions to be accountable for providing library and media support for all off-campus courses or to justify why such support is not needed. Written agreements between the sponsoring institution and a local library could be developed to address library/media support for off-campus offerings. Arrangements with a public library could be made in areas that lack an academic library. Alternatively, publicly supported academic libraries could be reimbursed by their states for providing services and direct use of their collections beyond their own campus personnel.

Beyond local and state access issues, there are also ongoing and sometimes unexpected challenges to information building and access that are of national or global concern. These need attention not only from the library profession, but also from other higher education and scholarly groups as well. While these issues should be of concern to all academic leaders, they particularly deserve to be a matter of active concern and appropriate action at research-intensive institutions where the greatest need exists for research materials.

Independence from Commercial Publishers

Most importantly, a concerted effort of the entire academic enterprise is needed in the struggle to provide greater independence from leading commercial publishers. By this time, all academic leaders should be somewhat knowledgeable regarding the alarming and continuing high inflationary rate of subscriptions, which for the past decade or so have hovered in the range of 7 to 10 percent, before currency factors are applied.[36] When scientific, technical, and medical journals are looked at separately, the situation shows a 215 percent increase over the fifteen years ending in 2001.[37] "The British Office of Fair Trading characterized the international serials market in 2002 as not 'working well.'"[38]

To address this dysfunction, committees of both the U.S. Congress and the British Parliament recommended in 2004 that papers from government-sponsored research should be made available free.[39] Unfortunately, the British Parliament rejected most of the recommendations of its Joint Information System Committee amidst accusations of "kowtowing to industry."[40] This will not prevent government funding agencies in the United Kingdom from following the recommendations just as the U.S. National Institutes of Health (NIH) have done. In February 2005, NIH announced "a new policy designed to accelerate the public's access to published articles resulting from NIH-funded research. The policy— the first of its kind for NIH—calls on scientists to release to the public manuscripts from research supported by NIH as soon as possible, and within 12 months of final publication. . . . Authors are strongly encouraged to exercise their right to specify that their articles will be publicly available through PubMed Central (PMC) as soon as possible."[41] Already every article written by NIH employees is in the public domain.

Besides what government can do to promote free or open access to scholarly information, there is much that academic institutions can do as well. For example, "many university libraries now encourage open access by subsidizing a portion of the publication charges in open-access venues for authors affiliated with the university."[42] Increasingly, campuses are archiving and allowing free access to the publications of their own faculty. This is being made easier by publishers who are allowing their authors to self-archive, if not the publisher's copy, then pre-refereeing preprints and their refereed postprints.[43] For example, the University of California eScholarship Repository has a rapidly growing database of research and scholarship by faculty and units on campus, plus seminar series. (See http://repositories.cdlib.org/escholarship/.)

Experiences on other campuses have not been as successful. Massachusetts Institute of Technology (MIT), for example, launched its DSpace in November 2002, but when faculty participation fell far below targeted levels, campus leadership found it necessary to use advertising more common to retail business than to elite universities.[44] When the project was initiated, ninety professors were asked their concerns about participating in DSpace. Their biggest concerns were that they

- preferred that only formally published works be available for public consumption;
- worried that publishing a paper in MIT's archive might constitute prior publication and prevent submission of the work to journals; and
- were hesitant to assign distribution rights for scholarly works to MIT.[45]

As similar projects are initiated, such concerns should be addressed aggressively.

Indeed, the problem goes deeper. Faculty groups are wrestling with how to evaluate electronic publishing for promotion and tenure review. Electronic systems that allow direct input by scholars sometimes lack the quality controls inherent in traditional scholarly publishing of books and refereed journals. Electronic systems offer scholars the opportunity to share current research activities, but, since anyone can put anything online at any stage of development, it is difficult to differentiate completed and tested research from in-process efforts. At its worst, electronic publishing can become a cut-rate vanity press for the presentation of faculty work. While future expansion of the peer review process to include coverage of electronic publishing can address this concern, it should not be so comprehensive as to inhibit scholarly dialogue on current work.

Given these concerns, any successful open-access system will need to have the following characteristics:

- Peer review must be built into the open access model as firmly and deeply as it is in the print model. . . .
- Citation tracking and impact-analysis work have to develop in tandem with the publishing opportunities.
- Academic communities have to place at least equal value on work published in open access as they do on work published in prestigious journals.[46]

One of these challenges was met in spring 2004 when ThomsonISI, the company that compiles databases on the use of scholarly papers in print, announced that it would collect similar information on scholarly works that are available solely online. The new product, Web Citation Index, will list which scholarly works have cited papers published online.[47]

While a number of research libraries are undertaking unique and highly valuable initiatives to further open access, what all campuses can do is to actively support faculty in retaining copyright to their publications whenever possible,[48] or when not possible, to subsidize their buying rights to make their articles accessible online for free.

> Alternatives to current copyright management can be imagined. For example, universities could claim joint ownership of scholarly writings with the faculty they pay to produce them, then prohibit unconditional assignment to third parties, thus becoming important players in the publishing business themselves. Or universities could request that faculty members first submit manuscripts to publishers whose pricing policies are more consonant with larger educational objectives. Another possibility is that university-negotiated licenses grant unlimited copying to libraries and individual scholars and specify said permission in the copyright statement. All these proposals are extensions of the broader idea under current discussion, that universities should reclaim some responsibility for disseminating the results of faculty scholarship.[49]

In addition, all campuses can pursue having their libraries archive and digitally publish faculty writing and research. Such efforts are in keeping with scholarly organizations across the world that support the Budapest Open Access Initiative, the goal of which is "open access to peer-reviewed journal literature." The Initiative states that "self-archiving and a new generation of open-access journals are the ways to attain this goal."[50] Even more important, campuses can ensure that refereed open access publishing receives equitable standing with print publications, and they can provide appropriate acknowledgment of faculty service contributions in refereeing online journal articles in retention, tenure, and promotion reviews.

Access to Global and U.S. Government Documents

Besides the longstanding battle with commercial publishers, there are other access to information issues that warrant the attention and involvement of academic leadership. For example, in December 2004, "in an apparent reversal of decades of U.S. practice, recent federal Office of Foreign Assets Control regulations bar American firms from publishing works by dissident writers in countries under sanction unless they first get U.S. government approval . . . even if publishers obtain a license for a book—something they are loathe to do—they believe the regulations bar them from advertising it, forcing readers to find the dissident works on their own."[51] Learning in many disciplines will be negatively impacted if materials from countries like Iran, Sudan, Cuba, and North Korea are no longer published in the United States. In censorship challenges of this magnitude, it is essential that leaders in higher education and scholarly organizations support court efforts to overturn the regulations.

Another important area where academic leaders can exert influence is in public access to government documents. A few years earlier, the ability of federal agencies to distribute reports at no cost on the Web raised significant concerns because access safeguards of earlier years were slated to be removed. A report of the National Commission on Libraries and Information Science (NCLIS) pointed out the dangers.

> Public ownership of information created by the federal government is an essential right. It not only allows individuals to fulfill their civic responsibilities, but also contributes to an overall improvement in their quality of life. Current information technology not only brings with it expanded opportunities for using government information but also a number of difficulties, including adequacy of finding tools, technological incompatibilities, and sometimes just the overwhelming amount of information.
>
> Government agencies are trying to use the World Wide Web to ensure availability of information, and emerging efforts in develop-

ment of indexing tools and web portals offer some hope. However, not all needed information is available on the Internet nor do users of public information necessarily have the professional skills to use what is available in any format. Also, government information made available electronically can disappear as quickly as it has appeared. No policy is in place for long term or permanent public access to web-based public information.

Special populations, especially individuals with disabilities, but also those who, for whatever reason, find it difficult to use computers and computer networks, exist throughout the nation. Such populations clearly can benefit from information technology but special efforts need to be taken to guarantee the availability to them of appropriate information technology and government information content.[52]

As of this writing, there is still much uncertainty about ongoing access to electronic government documents; despite unanswered questions, by 2003 only 40 percent of the titles selected for inclusion in designated federal depository libraries were being made available in some tangible form (e.g., print, microform).[53] Concerns center on three major issues.

Authentication

What constitutes the official document? When updates occur, how will the library community (and the public) know what is the current official document?

Preservation

What organization will preserve electronic documents and will there continue to be free access?

- For example, when a legislator retires or loses an election or agencies are reorganized or eliminated, their Web sites and documents can disappear.
- In another example, the clearinghouses that served educators and librarians and were once supported by grants from the U.S. Department of Education are no longer supported by the Department, and these clearinghouses and their Web sites have been removed.

Security issues

Who is responsible for monitoring the removal of government information from Web sites? There is a protocol for putting documents into the classified category. However, there is now a new category, sensitive but not classified, that has no review process. Federal agencies are individually struggling with this issue.

> For example, on November 18, 2004, the National Geospatial–Intelligence Agency (NGA) posted a notice in the Federal Register that it will remove in June 2005 its Flight Information Publications (FLIP), Digital Aeronautical Flight Information Files (DAFIF), and related aeronautical safety of navigation digital and hardcopy publications from public sale and distribution. These materials have been published by the NGA since the late 1940s and have always been widely available to the public. Some of these maps were used to locate devastated areas after the December 26, 2004, tsunami struck south Asia.[54]

Academic and scholarly organizations are needed to aggressively support efforts to safeguard public availability of information in cases such as those cited above.

The best Web pages, search engines, or other library services will avail little where financial or political barriers hinder access to needed information. Just as library and classroom faculty need to form effective partnerships to ensure information-literate graduates, just so must professional organizations representing academic leadership—presidents, provosts, business managers, deans, and faculty—partner with library organizations to forge a workable future for our scholarly endeavors.

> Our development of networking is critical if we are to give improved service to users through new technologies. But our leadership in networking is crucial if we are to help ensure that our traditional values of freedom to access information, freedom from censorship, objective preservation of our cultural heritage, and the user's right to privacy, are to be protected as new information regulations and policies emerge for a network society.
>
> We must advance these causes in a network nation; the issues at stake are so vital and so basic a part of the citizen's information rights that we cannot divest ourselves of this responsibility. We cannot

continue to play games as we do at all levels with library network politics while others, for much higher stakes, are playing at the game of information control.[55]

NOTES

1. Katie Hafner and Jennifer Tanaka, "Wiring the Ivory Tower," *Newsweek*, 30 January 1995, 62.

2. Michael Gorman, "Laying Siege to the 'Fortress Library,'" *American Libraries* 17 (May 1986): 325.

3. Ward Shaw, "Resource Sharing and the Network Approach," in *Priorities for Academic Libraries*, ed. Thomas J. Galvin and Beverly P. Lynch (San Francisco: Jossey-Bass, 1982), 56.

4. Online Computer Library Center, *2004 Information Format Trends: Content, Not Containers* (Dublin, Ohio: Online Computer Library Center, 2004), 9. Retrieved 4 December 2004 from http://www.oclc.org/info/2004trends.

5. Dennis Dillon, "College Libraries: The Long Goodbye," *The Chronicle of Higher Education* 50 (10 December 2004): B5.

6. "From Inside the Library: A Perspective on IT," *The Edutech Report* 16 (January 2001): 3.

7. Andrew Richard Albanese, "Moving from Books to Bytes," *Library Journal* 126 (1 September 2001): 52.

8. Ibid.

9. Donald W. King and Carol Hansen Montgomery, "After Migration to an Electronic Journal Collection: Impact on Faculty and Doctoral Students," *D-Lib Magazine* 8 (December 2002). Retrieved 27 February 2003 from http://www.dlib.org/dlib/december02/king/12king.html.

10. Scott Carlson, "A University Library Painfully Cancels Hundreds of Journal Subscriptions," *The Chronicle of Higher Education* 48 (20 September 2002). Retrieved 3 March 2005 from LexisNexis Academic database.

11. Association of College & Research Libraries, *Environmental Scan 2002* (Chicago: Association of College & Research Libraries, 2003), 12.

12. Lucia Snowhill, "E-books and Their Future in Academic Libraries," *D-Lib Magazine* 7 (July/August 2001). Retrieved 21 July 2003 from http://www.dlib.org/dlib/july01/snowhill/07snowhill.html.

13. Scott Carlson, "Online Textbooks Fail to Make the Grade," *The Chronicle of Higher Education* 51 (11 February 2005): A35.

14. "Online" (sidebar), *The Chronicle of Higher Education* 48 (13 September 2002): A33.

15. Andrea L. Foster, "Second Thoughts on 'Bundled' E-Journals," *The Chronicle of Higher Education* 48 (20 September 2002): A31.

16. Kenneth Frazier, "The Librarians' Dilemma: Contemplating the Costs of the 'Big Deal,'" *D-Lib Magazine* 7 (March 2001). Retrieved 28 January 2004 from http://www.dlib.org/dlib/march01/frazier/03frazier.html.

17. Tom Sanville, "Reassessing Aggregate Licensing," in *Reassessment of Bundled Subscriptions to Electronic Journals* (Birmingham, Ala.: EBSCO Information Services, 2003), 5.

18. Initiatives addressing these issues include JSTOR (see http://www.jstor.org/) and Project MUSE (see http://muse.jhu.edu/).

19. Steven J. Bell, "Is MORE Always BETTER?" *American Libraries* 34 (January 2003): 45.

20. *Encyclopedia of Library and Information Science*, vol. 72, supp. 35 (New York: Marcel Dekker, 2002), 139.

21. Debra Engel and Sarah Robbins, "Improving Reference Services through a Library Website: Strategies for Collaborative Change," *The Reference Librarian* 83/84 (March 2003):157.

22. Steven J. Bell, "The Infodiet: How Libraries Can Offer an Appetizing Alternative to Google," *The Chronicle of Higher Education* 50 (20 February 2004): B15.

23. Ibid.

24. Online Library Computer Center, *The 2003 OCLC Environmental Scan: Pattern Recognition* (Dublin, Ohio: Online Computer Library Center, 2004), 15.

25. Information on metasearching was largely excerpted from a San José State University library working document prepared by Charity Hope and Judy Reynolds.

26. Wendy Pradt Lougee, *Diffuse Libraries: Emergent Roles for the Research Library in the Digital Age* (Washington, D.C.: Council on Library and Information Resources, 2002).

27. Jerry Kline, Link+ Directors meeting presentation, 3 February 2004.

28. Denise A. Troll, "How and Why Libraries Are Changing: What We Know and What We Need to Know," *portal: Libraries and the Academy* 2 (January 2002): 103.

29. Cooperative collection development models exist for intrauniversity systems and at the local/regional, state, and national levels. For an overview of the topic and some case studies, see *Coordinating Cooperative Collection Development: A National Perspective*, ed. Wilson Luquire (New York: Haworth Press, 1986).

30. Approval plans—which permit vendors to select and send new publications based upon detailed profiles of collection development needs—allow direct review of the books in making purchase decisions and eliminate the need for individual orders. For an article that outlines prerequisites to the effective and efficient use of approval plans in academic libraries, consult Karen A. Schmidt, "Capturing the Mainstream: Publisher-Based and Subject-Based Approval Plans in Academic Libraries," *College & Research Libraries* 47 (July 1986): 365–69.

31. Janet Gertz, "Selection for Preservation in the Digital Age," *Library Resources & Technical Services* 44 (April 2000): 98–99.

32. Scott Carlson, "Few Libraries or Museums Digitize Collections," *The Chronicle of Higher Education* 48 (2 August 2002): A29.

33. Tom Storey, "University Repositories: An Extension of the Library Cooperative," *OCLC Newsletter* (July 2003): 7.

34. Ibid.

35. Russell Ackoff et al., *Designing a National Scientific and Technological Communication System* (Philadelphia: University of Pennsylvania Press, 1976), 18.

36. Lee Van Orsdel and Kathleen Born, "Big Chill on the Big Deal?" *Library Journal* 128 (15 April 2003): 51–56.

37. Ibid.

38. Ibid., 52.

39. Andrea L. Foster and Lila Guterman, "American and British Lawmakers Endorse Open-Access Publishing," *The Chronicle of Higher Education* 50 (30 July 2004): A13.

40. Daniel Engber, "British Government Rejects Call to Support Open-Access Publishing," *The Chronicle of Higher Education* 50 (10 November 2004). Retrieved 30 June 2005 from LexisNexis Academic.

41. National Institutes of Health, *NIH Calls on Scientists to Speed Public Release of Research Publications*, National Institutes of Health press release, 3 February 2005. Retrieved 3 March 2005 from http://www.nih.gov/news/pr/feb 2005/od-03.htm.

42. Andy Gass and Helen Doyle, "The Reality of Open-Access Journal Articles," *The Chronicle of Higher Education* 51 (18 February 2005): B13.

43. Stevan Harnad, "Elsevier Gives Authors Green Light for Open Access Self-Archiving," Budapest Open Access Initiative Forum Listserv post, 27 May 2004. Retrieved 3 March 2005 from http://threader.ecs.soton.ac.uk/lists/boai forum/341.html.

44. Andrea L. Foster, "Papers Wanted: Online Archives Run by Universities Struggle to Attract Material," *The Chronicle of Higher Education* 50 (25 June 2004): A37–A38.

45. Ibid., A38.

46. Nancy Davenport, "Open Access Is the Buzz," *CLIR Issues* 42 (November/December 2004): 5.

47. Vincent Kiernan, "Company to Track Citations of Online Scholarship," *The Chronicle of Higher Education* 50 (19 March 2004): A31.

48. For more information on retaining copyright, see http://www.lib.berkeley.edu/scholarlypublishing/copyright.html and http://osc.universityofcalifornia.edu/manage/seven_points.html. For additional information regarding scholarly communication, see http://www.arl.org/scomm/.

49. Anthony M. Cummings et al., *University Libraries and Scholarly Communication* (Washington, D.C.: The Association of Research Libraries for the Andrew W. Mellon Foundation, 1992).

50. *Budapest Open Access Initiative*. Retrieved 22 April 2005 from http://www.soros.org/openaccess/read.shtml.

51. Scott Martelle, "Will Voices of Dissent Still Be Heard?" *Los Angeles Times*, 7 December 2004, E1.

52. *A Comprehensive Assessment of Public Information Dissemination, Final Report: Executive Summary* (Washington, D.C.: U.S. National Commission on Libraries and Information Science, 2001), 2–3.

53. Judith Russell, superintendent of documents, remarks before the Association for Research Libraries, Lexington, Ky., 15 May 2003. Retrieved 21 April 2005 from http://www.gpoaccess.gov/about/speeches/052003_kentucky.pdf.

54. Susan Kendall, e-mail correspondence to Patricia Breivik, 7 March 2005.

55. Barbara Evans Markuson, "Revolution and Evolution: Critical Issues in Library Network Development," in *Networks for Networkers: Critical Issues in Cooperative Library Development*, ed. Barbara Evans Markuson and Blanche Woolls (New York: Neal-Schuman, 1980), 306–7.

CHAPTER 9

Leadership for the Changing Library

At the beginning of chapter 7, "Libraries in Transition," we explored the rapid transformation of libraries in the context of technological changes in society. Inherent in the continuing rapid changes to which libraries must respond is the need for an ever-changing set of workplace skills for both librarians and library staff.

Commercial publishers and information aggregators play a more active role in collecting, organizing, and preserving information in the digital environment than they did in the print environment. As the work of librarians in this arena declines and new technologies change relationships among libraries, publishers, authors, and artists, the role of libraries is shifting. Libraries are publishers when they digitize collections, host journals that are "born digital," or assemble student or faculty works online. Librarians are politicians when they lobby faculty authors not to sign away copyright to a print publisher, who then requires them or the library to pay for use of their own works. They are teachers when they help users develop information retrieval and evaluation skills in the digital environment and assume greater responsibility for the learning and research outcomes of their institution. They are researchers when they conduct user studies to assess user needs and expectations or the usability of their digital resources and websites. Librarians are expected to employ a greater variety of research methods in the digital environment than they did in the print environment (for example, user protocols, card-sorting studies, cognitive walk throughs, heuristic evaluations, and paper

prototyping), and to collaborate with a wider range of people than
in the past, including computer scientists, graphic designers, pedagogy experts, archivists, and museum curators. The core competencies required to perform these new tasks are different from those
required of librarians in the traditional print environment.[1]

Such changes require constant updating of job descriptions, frequent rethinking of organizational structure, and provision for ongoing staff development opportunities.

SHORTAGE OF LIBRARIANS

Another significant change since our earlier book is the current shortage of librarians, which will only worsen in the coming decade or so. An
excellent analysis of this situation is given in an American Library Association 2002 task force report, *Recruitment, Retention and Restructuring:
Human Resources in Academic Libraries*.[2] The shortage is caused by a number of factors, including an unusually high percentage of the librarian
workforce that will reach retirement age between 2015 and 2019, according to research conducted in 2004.[3] With fewer library schools and
greater competition for librarian skills by agencies and organizations outside traditional library settings, it is unlikely that even the $10 million
initiative in 2002 of President George W. Bush to recruit and educate librarians will significantly impact the shortage.[4] That this challenge is
even greater for academic librarians is documented in an Association of
College & Research Libraries environmental scan that found "fewer individuals are entering the library profession and fewer still are choosing
to go into academic librarianship even though college enrollments are
projected to increase by 15% over the next 10 years."[5] Of the 90,000
M.L.S. librarians, 45 percent will reach age sixty-five in the decade beginning in 2010.[6]

Not only will there be an insufficient pool of recruits for general library faculty positions, but it will be even harder to recruit librarians with
"more specialized skills"[7] and librarians for middle management and leadership positions. An increasing number of librarians, who are finding satisfaction in partnering with classroom faculty in developing and
implementing information literacy programs and in doing research, are
not attracted to positions requiring responsibility for personnel, fiscal
management, public relations, and fundraising.

While the library profession itself is aggressively seeking to recruit
more people to the field, on the campus level, recruiting and retaining

talented librarians in the future may require a rethinking of salary levels and benefits. Market and pay equity studies of campus librarians, though not frequently documented in the literature, have consistently resulted in the need to raise salaries. For example, "during the 1995/1996 academic year, the University of Colorado Boulder Libraries received market equity for librarian salaries. However, the University administration stipulated that equity increases were to be position specific rather than divided equally. Moreover, individual increases were to be based partly on past merit."[8] In 2003, the American Library Association established the Allied Professional Association as a separate entity to address issues aimed at improving salaries. This organization maintains a growing database on practical and recent materials that can be of value on campuses considering pay equity studies.

Beyond salary issues, serious consideration needs to be given to staffing levels that will facilitate all but library administrators holding ten- rather than twelve-month appointments. Shortages of librarians may also need to be addressed by hiring more professionals who do not hold M.L.S. degrees but do have the expertise in needed areas such as IT, human resource management, fiscal management, outreach services, and fundraising. Another approach would be to offer incentives for library faculty to continue to work past normal retirement age. But it all starts with having the right leadership. And to forge the library into a strong tool of empowerment for the campus first requires ensuring proper leadership that is appropriately positioned.

LIBRARY LEADERSHIP

Throughout this book, we have emphasized the concept of partnership—partnership between the president and the library dean, the classroom and library faculty, and the community and the library. The strength of these relationships depends on the individuals involved, and the library dean is a crucial link. Presidents who want to use their libraries more fully and creatively will need to work with and, as needed, recruit a library dean who shares their visions for the library; the library dean, in turn, must be effective in recruiting and retaining library faculty who will actively support those visions. Presidents and library deans will need to structure a framework both for their partnership and for partnerships between library and classroom faculty. One key area, for example, to benefit from the partnership between a library dean and university leaders is in fundraising. Since it is unlikely that there will ever be adequate funding for all that a campus would wish to do, fundraising abilities are increasingly needed in library deans, and here again the key element is leadership.

> There is little doubt the libraries that will be most successful at raising money in the future are those who are led by librarians whose vision, leadership abilities, and personal qualities will enable them to communicate the special qualities and merits of their libraries. Libraries need to take advantage of their unique collections and position themselves within the community. By explicitly carving out a niche and promoting the library as being the authoritative source for material and programming, a library can build a fundraising and development program that will allow for the institution to grow and prosper.[9]

Evaluating the Library Dean

How should the head of the library be evaluated? Performance reviews should be thorough, regular, and geared specifically to the demands of the position. Even when the head of the library carries the title of dean, the procedures and forms used for evaluating college deans are probably unsuitable. The competitive standard normally applied in higher education among, for example business colleges, is inappropriate for librarians who must emphasize cooperation and resource sharing to ensure access to materials beyond campus holdings and to reap savings from collaborative purchasing. This will be increasingly true in the future. Besides this major difference between academic programs and libraries, libraries also have a proportionately higher number of support staff than academic programs; offer relatively few if any credit-bearing courses; produce no alumni; are regularly involved with all academic programs on campus; and provide a wide range of services seven days a week during long hours throughout the entire calendar year. Clearly, college deans and heads of libraries alike must be committed to affirmative action, represent their units effectively, and budget responsibly, but the substantial differences in responsibilities dictate a substantively different evaluation procedure and form for the head of the library.

In reviewing the library dean's performance, administrators should seek feedback from a somewhat different cast of colleagues. Most academic deans can evaluate the performance of other college deans more effectively than they can evaluate the performance of the library dean since they know firsthand the intricacies and challenges fellow college deans face. Program support staff will also provide more valuable evaluations of academic deans than the support staff in a large library can provide for their dean, because in large libraries many staff members will have little opportunity to see—much less work with—the dean. In contrast, the limited number of support staff in many academic programs generally allows most college staff members some firsthand knowledge of their deans. Library faculty evaluations of the dean should be sought, as well as those of classroom faculty who have regular contact with the dean—for example, those serving on the library faculty advisory committee. There are, of course, no alumni or students of the library "program" to solicit for evaluations. Given the importance of resource sharing, on the other hand, the perception of other library deans in the state can contribute a valuable perspective during the evaluation process—an extramural element that is inappropriate under a competitive model. Finally, in cases where the library is an intrinsic part of campus outreach strategies, evaluation by appropriate community members is also desirable.

As is already the case on some campuses, comprehensive reviews should allow realistic appraisals of performance, relate performance to library outcomes, and provide information that can be used to enhance performance. Outcomes of strategic planning efforts should also be considered in reviewing a dean's performance and should serve as a basis for deans and their supervisors to agree upon annual performance objectives. Progress in fulfilling objectives could then serve as the basis for the annual salary review.

Annual, comprehensive reviews, while both important and necessary, cannot replace the honest, ongoing dialogue between the president or academic vice president and the head of the library that marks an active and effective partnership. Too much depends on their shared visions for the library and a close linking of their implementation strategies to allow in-depth communication to occur only once a year. Problems should be dealt with as they occur. The more formal evaluation procedures allow for a valuable overall assessment of accomplishments and an opportunity to make broader course corrections to reflect evolving campus priorities.

In summary, the evaluation process for library deans should be tailored to the unique responsibilities of the head of the library. Tailoring the evaluation process should emphasize the leadership role of the dean in integrating the library into the mainstream of campus activities.

Choosing a New Library Dean

Potential library deans consider the same kinds of factors that attract other academic deans to a particular campus: the perceived prestige of an institution, the perceived quality of its library and library personnel, the total compensation package, and the location of the institution. Library deans, like their college counterparts, also consider the importance the administration seems to place on their area of responsibility—in this case, the library instead of a specific college. To appeal to innovative candidates, presidents and academic vice presidents who want more than a traditional library should clearly articulate their visions and goals for the library. They need not spell out plans for implementation, but they should present the conceptual framework for the type of library they want and then evaluate the candidates' ability to respond meaningfully to their ideas. Outstanding candidates will appreciate a campus leadership that demonstrates personal knowledge of and commitment to the library's active involvement in pursuing campus goals and priorities, for far too many administrators have neglected their responsibility for the administration of campus libraries.[10] Knowing that the president is personally interested in the library may be threatening to some candidates, but candidates who can provide strong and creative leadership will appreciate evidence of firm administrative support for the library.

Given a commitment to the overall academic enterprise and the campus mission this book advocates, titles such as "University Library Dean," "Dean of Library Services," or, depending on the position's scope, "Associate Vice President" or "Vice President for Academic Information Resources and Services" seem more appropriate than "Library Director." Presidents committed to integrating their libraries into the curriculum might consider a title change as a symbol of the expanded role they expect the head of the library to serve. A title of dean or vice president would emphasize the president's commitment, add credibility in the recruiting process, and smooth the way for repositioning the head of the library in the administrative structure.

Most search processes, in fact, do not produce a particularly rich pool of candidates for the position of library dean, whatever the title. This is particularly true for campuses seeking candidates who can provide dynamic leadership and bring about change. Search committees frequently concentrate on inappropriate criteria for the library dean because they only have a hazy idea of what the modern library does. They are not familiar with the changes driven by the information explosion, the subsequent need for resource sharing, and the new opportunities possible through computers and other new information technologies such as those discussed throughout this book. Faculty or administrators who lack a realistic understanding of what it takes to provide access to information are poorly equipped to determine which qualifications they should seek. Search committee members could visit campuses with dynamic libraries to overcome this problem or use consultants in developing an appropriate job description and establishing evaluation criteria.

Not only is it important to understand the general knowledge and abilities search committee members should look for in a person to oversee the library, but care needs to be taken to determine the specific needs of the campus and its library for the position at that particular point in time. A 2004 article in *Change* makes this point very clear in relation to all campus dean searches.

> The role of a dean calls on a person to use, in varying proportions and at various times, five different sets of skills. Every dean must be something of a *prophet, promoter, provider, politician,* and *police officer.* There is not much correlation between commonly used selection criteria, which are publishing success and length of comparable administrative service, and the five P's that describe a good dean.[11]

Beyond assessing these abilities in candidates, the authors urge campuses to determine which of the abilities are most needed by the campus at this particular time. For example, the type of leadership needed to integrate library resources and services into the curriculum will vary significantly from the leadership needed to enable the library to position itself as a major tool in building external bridges to the surrounding community or in consolidating campus departmental libraries.

Search committees may also limit the pool of candidates unnecessarily by overemphasizing similarity of institutional background. Small to medium-size liberal arts colleges, for example, will frequently pass over middle-management-level librarians from large institutions in favor of librarians from a seemingly more "compatible" institutional background. In a column discussing library leadership, Herbert S. White, dean of the University of Indiana School of Library and Information Science, comments on the dangers of this conformist approach:

> Probably the most obvious example of the "get along by not rocking the boat" syndrome is found in the very closed system of research library administration. Major research library directors emerge from a candidate pool of directors of smaller research libraries, or of assistant directors of still larger libraries. It is of course possible for unique and distinctive leaders to rise to the top in this process because we have examples of it, but they are really swimming upstream. The system is geared to protect the collegial and the conformists.[12]

This closed shop tends to stifle creative leadership, as ambitious librarians usually find it advantageous to please their administrators to facilitate internal rewards.

The ultimate criteria for evaluating candidates should be determined by the kind of library a campus wants,[13] not by conformity to traditional search practices. For a library that will be dynamically involved in addressing campus goals and priorities, we would suggest the following criteria for prospective directors:

- Solid administrative experience (not necessarily at a similar institution);
- Demonstrated commitment to networking and resource sharing;
- Demonstrated commitment to service;
- Demonstrable interpersonal and communications skills;
- A master's degree from an American Library Association-accredited library school and a second master's degree or (preferably) a doctorate;
- Indications of professional innovation and creativity; and
- Strong publication and professional service records, especially when they evidence a candidate's ability to function beyond librarianship or unite librarianship with other disciplines.

If a candidate has no prior record of innovative involvement in higher education beyond librarianship per se, he or she is unlikely to be the dynamic leader who can integrate a campus library into the mainstream of institutional priorities. A careful checking of references should clarify whether the person has a real commitment to networking with other institutions to expand access opportunities for the campus. Scheduling candidates to meet with library directors in the community and eliciting the latter's input for the screening process may also provide insights into how likely a candidate will be to support local resource-sharing efforts.

Commitment to service is also highly important. No matter how active their role, libraries remain essentially service agencies. For libraries to reach their potential, they cannot be "self-centered,"[14] and the directors of libraries should thus be committed to a role of "servant leadership."[15] A dean who cares more about the national fame of a library's special collections than about student mastery of information literacy skills is not the right leader to integrate the library into the curriculum, for integration requires not only leadership but also the ability to be a team player. These qualities are more important than the size of the candidate's current library or whether the institution is private or public, urban or rural.

Organizational Placement of the Library Dean

The majority of academic libraries today are located organizationally within the campus academic affairs unit. In this arrangement, library deans report to academic vice presidents or provosts and serve on the campus deans' councils. Certainly, this makes sense in integrating the library into academic planning. Moreover, as library deans keep abreast of pending changes in academic policies and programming, they can prompt timely involvement of library faculty in curriculum development and subsequent fine-tuning of collection development policies and library services. This arrangement also allows the library dean to support a campuswide perspective on issues and to encourage the use of pertinent information in academic decision-making. (See chapter 6 for more information on library support of the administration's information needs.)

This traditional organization may also have its limitations. Where, for example, are the heads of faculty development and academic computing placed? Does the existing arrangement promote close interaction among these leaders? If media operations are not already part of the library, does the organizational arrangement facilitate close coordination of these academic support functions?

Finally and most important, does the existing placement facilitate or hinder ongoing interaction between the president and the library dean? Is the dean sufficiently involved with the president's administrative team to ensure good access to information for decision-making and planning? Given the complexities and campuswide nature of library operations and the external affairs/service potential of the library, would it make sense to have the library director report directly to the president? If all academic support services are combined, to whom should the head of such a unit report? (See chapter 7 for more information about integrated services.) If the head of the library reports to the president, how will ongoing dialogue with the deans and the academic vice president be ensured? How will the arrangement facilitate interactions between faculty development and the library?

The best solution will depend upon the structure and needs of a particular campus. Yet, we would suggest that a dean who has responsibility only for the library report to the academic vice president and sit as a peer among the deans, while also serving as a resource person for the president's management team. This arrangement preserves the integral ties of the library to the academic programs while facilitating full use of the library in addressing administrative planning and external affairs goals and objectives.

LIBRARIANS AND FACULTY STATUS

The president and academic vice president need not be directly involved in recruiting most library employees, although if they normally interview prospective faculty members, they should also interview prospective librarians. The key point of involvement for the president and academic vice president relates instead to academic policy. The core question is generally whether or not librarians should have faculty status, and the answer to this relates to the role and responsibilities given to librarians on particular campuses. At one time, librarians were primarily concerned with purchasing and cataloging books. But automation and networking have altered the responsibilities of librarians, transferring many former responsibilities to the paraprofessionals or classified staff, who, along with student workers, now make up 78 percent of the workforce in U.S. academic libraries.[16] Before cataloging systems went online, librarians across the country spent vast amounts of time cataloging the same materials being cataloged in hundreds of other libraries. Now, cataloging librarians are needed for staff training and supervision; for analysis, design, and evaluation of online systems; for quality control; and for only a little original cataloging.[17] Increasingly, paraprofessionals carry primary or full operational responsibilities for acquisitions, interlibrary loans, preservation, and even supervision of circulation, shelving, periodicals, and other service units. Due to the lack of formal educational programs for support staff, however, most libraries must run ongoing in-house staff training programs, which are usually coordinated and taught by librarians. If librarians delegate higher-level clerical activities to support staff, a one-to-four ratio of librarians to support staff is a reasonable rule of thumb.

These changes have freed librarians' time for more aggressive involvement in the instructional, research, service, and other priorities of the campus, and, as a result, librarians on most campuses have responded accordingly, particularly by assuming greater involvement in the teaching/learning process. An increasing emphasis has also been placed on the research being done. (See chapter 4 for more information on research by librarians.) In addition, librarians are well prepared for campus service responsibilities. Their organizational skills and commitment to student learning make them productive members of faculty task forces and committees.

Why, then, are some faculty so suspicious of granting librarians faculty status? Ignorance may be the answer. Because of their own teaching, classroom faculty members know in general what goes on in other faculty members' classrooms, but few have had much exposure to the inner workings of libraries. Casual exposure to library operations will have brought them in contact mainly with support staff and student employees at circulation and reserve desks. Those with such limited library experience, may be more likely to show indifference, condescension, or even hostility toward librarians. One liberal arts college librarian has suggested that faculty who base their teaching on library resources and services understand better the contributions of librarians:

> [they] will have a realistic sense of the problems librarians confront in introducing research techniques and the organization of the bibliographic record to young people who typically have had little or no training in library resources or techniques in secondary school. They will also understand that library usage does not involve only narrow technical skills but has a substantial intellectual dimension, and that bibliographic organization is a complex matter which requires patience and systematic effort to master.[18]

But when librarians begin to function more like classroom faculty, they see two potentially major problems with faculty status: they are asked to meet two distinct sets of performance criteria for promotion and tenure (librarian and faculty),[19] yet they lack the time and support for research that classroom faculty enjoy. "An almost universal complaint of librarians is lack of time for research."[20]

If librarians have mixed feelings about faculty status, so do other academic administrators, and these feelings have not substantially changed since a 1984 survey of universities whose libraries were members of the Association of Research Libraries and where, even today, faculty status is less frequently part of the academic culture than at state universities and colleges. In that study, administrators shared their views on the advantages and disadvantages of faculty status for librarians.

> In listing their perceived advantages to the institution, administrators focused on chiefly psychological factors, with a good deal of conjecture about the probably (desirable) influence of faculty status on librarian conduct and performance. The result was a rather idealized portrait of the librarian as a faculty member. Analysis of the statements revealed the following: (1) faculty status allegedly attracted a "better qualified, more academically oriented professional to library service"; (2) faculty status was believed to improve the morale and self-esteem of librarians, giving them "a closer feeling of belonging to the institution, rather than second-class citizenship"; (3) faculty status was purported to prompt the acceptance of librarians "as professional peers by faculty members in other disciplines"; (4) faculty

status was thought to motivate librarians to "act responsibly," exhibit a "professional attitude toward the position," and to "develop research programs"; and (5) faculty status was believed to open the way for librarians "to participate on university committees," to "participate in all faculty curricular deliberations, and thus understand the course and direction of university academic policy."

Statements of perceived disadvantages to the institution for granting librarians faculty status were nearly uniform in singling out the unsuitability for librarians of the traditional faculty requirements for tenure-demonstrated effectiveness in teaching and research. These traditional tenure requirements were thought by administrators to be inappropriate for librarians because (1) librarians have "different basic responsibilities" from the regular teaching faculty; (2) their "work and traditions are different"; and (3) "the degree of freedom and independence afforded librarians is much less than for the faculty."[21]

Librarians and administrators seem to agree that it is both unrealistic and bad management to hold librarians in a double bind, particularly if they are asked to match classroom faculty levels of research on twelve-month appointments.

In our earlier book, we made the case for faculty status and salary equity for librarians despite the obvious fiscal implications. We argued that if the gap between the classroom and the library was to be bridged and if the library was to become an integral part of undergraduate learning, then counting librarians among the ranks of faculty is both practically and symbolically important. The increasing involvement of librarians in the learning process on so many campuses since that time strongly supports our recommendation.

The double bind that concerns both librarians and administrators can be avoided by developing a set of criteria specifically for library faculty. We see no real reason to hold librarians accountable for fulfilling two sets of evaluative criteria. The great majority of our faculty are not highly productive researchers and writers. Academic disciplines such as architecture and planning have terminal degrees other than doctorates, and their faculty do far more applied than basic research. Scholarly and teaching activities vary significantly among such academic programs as law, fine arts, and microbiology. Colleges and universities easily accommodate this diversity. What is important is that clear performance criteria for academic programs and academic libraries be developed and administered equitably.

Let us look at the model of faculty members who are performers. They are not expected to do traditional research; they are expected to perform and to teach. Most frequently, they perform with other artists. They pass their mastery on to others, and some of them may create or compose artworks. Librarians also "perform" by supporting the research activities of other faculty. They pass their research mastery on to others, and some of them may "compose" their own research.

To take another example, clinical law or medical professors pass their mastery on to students in a working situation; such faculty seldom do research of their own, although they use the research of others. Peer evaluation procedures for performing and clinical faculty may provide a fertile source of ideas in developing faculty evaluation models for librarians. And, of course, some campus faculty concentrate on research and do little or no teaching, so teaching per se is clearly not a prerequisite for faculty status. As the gap between the classroom and the library closes, the distinct role of library faculty will seem no more different than the music faculty's difference from the chemistry faculty, and issues of pay equity may become easier to address on many campuses.

Performance expectations for library faculty must take into consideration the work responsibilities that the seven-day-a-week, twelve-month-a-year, on-call service demands of libraries entail. Flexibility in personnel evaluative criteria should acknowledge the differences between classroom and library faculty. Librarians also have different educational patterns; most begin work immediately after receiving their M.L.S. degree and afterward pursue a subject area master's or a doctorate.

The model within the California State University (CSU) provides a good practical model that can be adopted or adapted to the appointment, retention, tenure, and promotion (ARTP) processes of other academic institutions. CSU librarians are full-fledged members of the faculty and have the option of working ten (a close equivalent of an academic year appointment) or twelve months each year. ARTP standards are the same as for classroom faculty except that librarians' primary job functions (i.e., reference, collection management, and information literacy activities) are evaluated in place of the classroom function of teaching faculty. Like their classroom colleagues, librarians have experienced higher research expectations as their campuses have progressed from their original focus, often as state normal schools that primarily educated teachers, to their current classification as comprehensive master's institutions.

Library faculty have served ably in a wide range of campus and system faculty committees and other faculty responsibilities—including, at one point, a librarian serving as head of the CSU statewide faculty union bargaining team. To support their activities and particularly their research, librarians are eligible for sabbaticals, research grants, competitive lottery funds, travel money, and all other benefits available to CSU faculty.

PRESIDENTIAL LEADERSHIP

Academic leaders should recognize the sources of tension between librarians and classroom faculty where they exist.[22] Classroom faculty may have very definite opinions about how the library can best serve their students, yet library faculty are usually in a better position to assess the broad needs of the academic community. As one university dean of humanities underscored, "the more serious the problems of knowledge and the library grow, the more depends on an effective spirit of understanding and collaboration between librarians and the users of knowledge."[23] The tone and style set by the president in determining the library dean's proper place in the university and acknowledging the library's value to the campus goals and mission can be crucial to integrating librarians quickly and effectively into the mainstream of the campus. Of all the service academies, the Air Force Academy incorporated women into its student body most expeditiously and with the fewest problems. The reason? General James Allen, who was superintendent when President Gerald Ford signed the bill extending admission to women, made it very clear he was committed to the law of the land and that integration would be successfully accomplished at the Air Force Academy. In an academic environment, the leadership of the president can be equally effective in setting the tone for the campus. In like fashion, later scandals at the Air Force Academy document what can happen when such leadership is lacking.[24]

The basic controversy surrounding faculty status and pay equity issues for academic librarians stems from an unrealistic perception of the librarian's proper role. Must librarians teach in the classroom and conduct their own research to qualify as faculty? It seems unreasonable to force librarians into a model that is not even serviceable for many academic disciplines. The literature of higher education continues to call for more flexibility in the overriding emphasis on research in our universities, and it urges that faculty become facilitators of learning rather than simply lecturers. Both trends support the case for faculty status for librarians.

Besides supporting the library dean's efforts to encourage independent research by librarians, presidents and academic vice presidents who wish to expedite the integration of classroom and library faculty at a very practical level should promote the following agenda:

- Encourage the inclusion of designated librarians in program faculty meetings. This is particularly valuable if the librarian is involved in providing information literacy learning opportunities to the students and overseeing collection management for the program.

- Request that the faculty governing body establish a committee to advise the library dean on issues of mutual concern.
- Include a department's liaison librarian when entertaining departmental faculty.
- Ensure that all faculty grants and awards are open to librarians.
- Include librarians on all appropriate committees and task forces.
- Facilitate librarians' pursuit of advanced degrees by providing flexibility in scheduling to accommodate course offerings, and, if possible, provide tuition waivers or discounts.

We concur with the former president of the Education Commission of the States, Frank Newman, who considers the "ideal librarian" to be someone who empowers students to learn by teaching them how to draw upon sources of information, knowledge, and ideas. In this sense, Newman sees classroom faculty and librarians as sharing a "common function," although they operate in different contexts.[25] Not all librarians see their role in this way, but we feel it is time for campus leaders, beginning with the president, to encourage librarians sympathetic to this vision to become more active facilitators of both student learning and faculty research. If campus structures obstruct rather than support this development, academic leaders will need to adjust campus personnel policies and practices accordingly.

NOTES

1. Denise Troll, "How and Why Libraries Are Changing: What We Know and What We Need to Know," *portal: Libraries and the Academy* 2, no. 1 (2002): 103.

2. Ad Hoc Task Force on Recruitment and Retention, ACRL Personnel Administrators and Staff Development Officers Discussion Group, *Recruitment, Retention and Restructuring: Human Resources in Academic Libraries* (Chicago: Association of College & Research Libraries, 2002).

3. Mary Jo Lynch, "Retirement and Recruitment: A Deeper Look," *American Libraries* 36 (January 2005): 28.

4. Ad Hoc Task Force on Recruitment and Retention, *Recruitment, Retention and Restructuring*.

5. Association of College & Research Libraries, *ACRL Environmental Scan 2002* (Washington, D.C.: Association of College & Research Libraries, 2002).

6. Mary Jo Lynch, "Retirement and Recruitment: A Deeper Look," *American Libraries* 36 (January 2005): 28.

7. Jennifer Jacobson, "A Shortage of Academic Librarians," *The Chronicle of Higher Education* 48 (14 August 2002). Retrieved 2 September 2004 from http://chronicle.com/jobs/2002/08/2002081401c.htm.

8. Scott Seaman et al., "Market Equity Tempered by Career Merit: A Case Study," *The Journal of Academic Librarianship* 26 (July 2000): 225. Available at http://www.ala-apa.org/salaries/payequitybib.html.

9. Frank Cervone, "A Long-Term Strategy for Library Funding," *Library Administration & Management* 19 (winter 2005): 15.

10. Herbert S. White, "Reactions to Defining the Academic Librarian," *College & Research Libraries* 46 (November 1985): 476.

11. Ray Maghroori and Charles Powers, "How to Choose the Right Dean for Your University," *Change* 36 (March/April 2004): 53.

12. Herbert S. White, "Oh Where Have All the Leaders Gone?" *Library Journal* 112 (1 October 1987): 68.

13. At the third national conference of the Association of College and Research Libraries in Seattle in 1984, a panel presentation by three presidents underscored just how divergent academic officers' views of the role of campus libraries could be. For more detail, see "Academic Libraries: Myths and Realities," *Library Journal* 109 (August 1984): 1419–20.

14. Harvie Branscomb, *Teaching with Books: A Study of College Libraries* (Chicago: Association of American Colleges and the American Library Association, 1940), 89.

15. Robert K. Greenleaf, *Servant Leadership: A Journey into the Nature of Legitimate Power and Greatness* (New York: Paulist Press, 1977).

16. Association of College & Research Libraries, *ACRL Library Data Tables 2003; Summary Data: Personnel and Public Services.* Retrieved 30 August 2004 from http://www.acrl.org/ala/acrlbucket/statisticssummaries/2003a/B12.pdf.

17. Lizbeth J. Bishoff, "Who Says We Don't Need Catalogers?" *American Libraries* 18 (September 1987): 694, 696.

18. William A. Moffett, "What the Academic Librarian Wants from Administrators and Faculty," in *Priorities for Academic Libraries*, ed. Thomas J. Galvin and Beverly P. Lynch (San Francisco: Jossey-Bass, 1982), 17.

19. Thomas G. English, "Librarian Status in Eighty-Nine U.S. Academic Institutions of the Association of Research Libraries: 1982," *College & Research Libraries* 44 (May 1983): 199–211.

20. Kee DeBoer and Wendy Culotta, "The Academic Librarian and Faculty Status in the 1980s: A Survey of the Literature," *College & Research Libraries* 48 (May 1987): 218.

21. Thomas G. English, "Administrators' Views of Library Personnel Status," *College & Research Libraries* 45 (May 1984): 189–95.

22. Mary Biggs, "Sources of Tension and Conflict Between Librarians and Faculty," *The Journal of Higher Education* 52 (March/April 1981): 182–201.

23. K. J. Weintraub, "The Humanistic Scholar and the Library," *Library Quarterly* 50 (January 1980): 34.

24. Judith Graham, "Air Force Leadership Blamed for Sex Scandal; Academy's Climate of Abuse Traced to Officers' Inaction," *Chicago Tribune*, 23 September 2003, 1. Retrieved 20 July 2004 from ProQuest Newspapers database.

25. Frank Newman, "Academic Libraries and the American Resurgence," in *Libraries and the Search for Academic Excellence*, ed. Patricia Senn Breivik and Robert Wedgeworth (Metuchen, N.J.: Scarecrow Press, 1988), 180.

CHAPTER 10

Funding Alternatives

B eing of practical minds, we have acknowledged cost considerations and cost tradeoffs throughout this book. Without a more in-depth look at library funding issues, however, we feared our suggestions for change would have little impact, for most of the opportunities we suggest for making libraries strategic tools for accomplishing learning and administrative goals require increased funding. While we shall be narrowly focusing on library funding issues, these concerns are set within an emerging danger that threatens the very viability of higher education as it exists today. Private institutions struggle to meet funding needs, and many believe that "universities have to recognize that public funding for public higher education, as the dominant source of support, has come to the end of its cycle. As we move forward, public universities will have to look to fundraising, entrepreneurial ventures, partnership agreements and tuition fees to find the money for their operating costs."[1] This shift in funding patterns is another good reason, we believe, for carefully considering the cost/benefit ratio of current and potential campus library resources and services.

Clearly, inadequate library funding is seriously impacting the very foundations of academe. *The Chronicle of Higher Education* described this danger in its September 20, 2002, cover story regarding how "budget cuts for libraries, university presses, journals, and culture combine to threaten the infrastructure on which professors and students depend."[2] The article goes on to explain: "This imperiled infrastructure is interconnected. As libraries buy fewer books, the university presses—already hurting from a shifting publishing landscape—see their balance sheets getting redder and redder. . . . As presses cut back on titles or, like the University of California, cancel a respected series on philosophy, professors and graduate students will find it harder and harder to get published, and get tenure."[3]

Even assuming that better funding days are ahead, many believe that the budgets supporting libraries, the intellectual foundation of our campuses, will not be able to bounce back. Certainly, if we are to believe history, this fear is well founded. In 2001, a report of the California State University Academic Senate, *The California State University at the Beginning of the 21st Century*, acknowledged that "cuts in expenditures for library collections were greater than cuts in general fund expenditures. Expenditures for library collections began to recover later and more slowly than general fund expenditures as a whole."[4]

It is within this troubling context that this book is being written. If libraries are continually an "easy hit" to the extent that they cannot adequately meet their most fundamental roles, there is little hope that they can fulfill their potential as strategic tools for their institutions. This chapter will assume, however, an adequate base budget for the library. Then, once presidents take a hard look at how their libraries can help achieve campus goals and objectives, they can decide what dollar-and-cents financial value they place on the accomplishment of those goals and objectives and determine what percentage of that amount is best invested in the library.

THE CURRENT FUNDING PICTURE

There are three reasons why determining resource levels for libraries—whether from general funds or as part of campus advancement efforts—is particularly problematic. These reasons should be consciously reviewed by any administrator or resource advising committee involved in setting the library budget. These issues to be reviewed concern (1) the fundamental differences between the library and the college funding model with which most campus personnel are familiar, (2) recent and significant changes in the management and costs of information resources, and (3) the continuing information explosion.

In the chapter on collections and access, we noted that traditional criteria for ranking research libraries based on number of holdings is no longer valid. With the increasing number of resources being purchased electronically (in 2001–2002, members of the Association of Research Libraries spent 7 percent of their total budgets on electronic resources[5]) and with electronic access being the preferred method of most faculty and students, other measurements of quality are needed. Moreover, the cost of the traditional library model is no longer financially possible. "While there may be a sense of nostalgia for the self-contained library on campus, it is a luxury that is no longer affordable economically or intellectually if our libraries and educational systems are to survive."[6] However, care must collectively be taken to ensure the preservation of knowledge for future generations of scholars and to understand that electronic alternatives do not equate with dollar savings.

At the same time, the general competitive environment of higher education makes those campuses with the prize collections uneasy in moving away from the traditional model, yet most chief academic and budget officers understand, even with some degree of uneasiness, that far more money could be well spent on the library than will ever be available. The onslaught of the information explosion has only exacerbated the situation. As discussed in chapter 2, not only is more information being published every year, but it is also being produced in more formats than ever before. For many years, inflation rates for library materials have consistently increased faster than the consumer price index so that maintaining even current acquisitions levels requires an awesome annual increase in funds—particularly for those institutions that purchase many foreign periodicals. Additional consideration must also be taken for support for new or expanding programs.

This situation has gotten so desperate that even the general press is raising concerns. A March 28, 2004, *San Francisco Chronicle* article on "the staggering price of [the] world's best research . . ." begins: "An alarm bell is ringing in the ivory tower. Something's gone terribly wrong, frustrated scholars say, when scientific journals cost as much as new cars and diamond rings."[7] Meanwhile, research libraries across the country have been forced to cut back on journal subscriptions despite significant increases in acquisition dollars. At Vanderbilt University, for example, an 11 percent increase is required simply to maintain current journal subscriptions for a single year.[8]

Even when buying is restricted, libraries still eventually overflow with materials, computers, and (as enrollments grow) students. Existing space is quickly exhausted, and the library soon needs more expansion space or a new building. Some academic officers and state officials have looked to the newer information technology to halt this continual expansion. Their wishful thinking, based on unexamined myths, generates predictably unrealistic conclusions. They reason that since we now have the Internet, library expansion and large acquisition budgets can be eliminated; or that the need for more materials can be met through coopera-

tive acquisitions, more active use of interlibrary loan, and the introduction of telefacsimile devices, none of which will require additional funds
(or so they believe).

A good illustration of the results of such thinking occurred during our
Colorado days. New facilities construction and library expansion requests
were held up for a number of years while the state approved new library
space guidelines, developed largely by the academic library professional
community. By the time the new guidelines were approved by the Colorado Commission of Higher Education (CCHE) in the fall of 1984, over
$75 million in capital requests for new and expanded library facilities had
accumulated for approval by CCHE staff. Since the state allocates only
approximately $12–$20 million annually to higher education for new
capital construction, this amount was seen as clearly unreasonable. For
two years, no solution was forthcoming.

Then, in 1986, CCHE established a task force, consisting largely of
business administrative personnel from some of the academic institutions,
to explore solutions to the library space problem. Initial correspondence
from the task force chair proposed such solutions as off-site storage facilities and increases in interlibrary loan services and telefacsimile devices. Nobody at the state level appeared interested in whether Colorado
had an adequate information resource base or whether funding practices
were designed to encourage resource sharing. This ignoring of basic academic policy issues and existing state funding practices could have created a situation in which the tail (facilities) was wagging the dog (library
resources and services). In fact, the eventual outcome was an innocuous
report that provided no real practical solution to the facilities dilemma.
It required institutions to provide documentation that they had explored
alternatives to new construction as part of their capital construction request. In this case, Colorado reacted to a significant library funding issue
in a manner similar to that throughout the country: Not enough money?
Have libraries cut back on services or acquisitions or, in this case, on
space needs, and never mind the impact on instruction or scholarship.

This Colorado example is important for underscoring the need for
well-thought-out state and national information policies and accompanying budget guidelines. The day of the "lone ranger" library is over, and
leadership is needed to establish reward systems that promote collaboration and resource sharing. Certainly, the technology now exists to facilitate information sharing, and plenty of examples illustrate the
economies of collaborative purchasing. Brian L. Hawkins, president of
EDUCAUSE, suggests that the larger the collaboration, the better for
scholarship.

The leveraging of our library resources is clearly called for, with the best solution being at the largest system-level possible—an international group of cooperating libraries. While associations of campuses, consortia, and other groupings will alleviate the problem, the best solution is found when no system or national boundaries are limiting factors, but where information is maximally available.[9]

Of course, not all academic libraries can be part of an international consortium, nor can libraries control the expanding world information base, the high inflationary rates for information resources, or the increasing labor costs required to place the information explosion into a meaningful framework for access by researchers and scholars. Libraries are on the front lines in tackling these problems, but without reinforcements, the best they can hope for is a stalemate or controlled retreat. Presidents need to recognize the problems as endemic to the information age, and academic leaders need to work with librarians to seek realistic solutions that include, for example, alternatives to ongoing expansion of libraries for housing collections, especially "when one takes into consideration the conventional wisdom that only 10% of the collection is heavily used, while 90% of the collection is used infrequently, and the vast majority of the collection never circulates."[10] The good news is that these solutions do not all depend directly on out-of-pocket dollars; the bad news is that the more far-ranging solutions will require a serious time and energy commitment by college and university presidents at both state and national levels.

Currently, funding decisions for libraries largely ignore the realities of the information age. In comparing how much colleges and universities actually spend per student versus how much they should spend, economist H. R. Bowen concluded that costs are determined not by need but by the funds available.[11] This general observation is equally true for libraries, which have received a remarkably consistent percentage of their institutions' budgets, no matter how library costs or the demands placed on libraries have changed. Staggering increases in journal costs and the introduction of major new services such as electronic reserves and document delivery, for example, have had little or no effect on most library budgets, which since 1968 have averaged around 3.8 percent of their institutions' general and educational budgets.[12] The range among academic libraries varies significantly, however.

In the United States, libraries generally spend between 2.5 and 7.5 percent of total university expenditures. The 1983 median for ARL libraries was 3.6 percent. It is difficult to explain the wide range of support from parent institutions. In the United Kingdom, a study prepared for the Standing Conference of National and University Libraries (SCONUL) recommended that 6 percent of the university's budget be allocated to the library. New universities spend more funds to create adequate library resources. Large universities with diverse graduate programs require large library budgets to satisfy the demands of their research and scholarly communities. Yet some smaller universities with modest graduate programs have library budgets that consistently exceed those of larger institutions. This anomaly needs further study.[13]

What should campuses that are serious about building and maintaining their intellectual capital, target in funds for their library resources and services? There is no clear-cut answer to this question, nor do the 2000 Standards for Libraries in Higher Education established by the Association of College & Research Libraries suggest any guidelines.[14] Libraries have in the past largely been evaluated by the numbers: "numbers of volumes held, number of volumes added, number of current serials received, total operating expenditures, and number of professional plus support staff."[15] These criteria determine eligibility for membership in the esteemed Association of Research Libraries (ARL), and every year *The Chronicle of Higher Education* reports changes in ratings among the largest research libraries (approximately 100 are members). However, even among these elite libraries, there is a growing feeling that these criteria perpetuate an outmoded set of values. Because of the differences in campuses and the different levels of expectations they have regarding the contributions their libraries should be making, no guideline or rule of thumb could be meaningful. Instead, the challenge before each campus is to define and measure its library's impact on campuswide outcomes and fund to the level of impact desired.[16]

What is clear is that historically almost all libraries' budgets have come from their parent institutions rather than external sources. A study done in the late 1970s showed a range from a high of 97 percent of budgets in southern public universities coming from the parent institutions to a low of 83 percent in northern private institutions.[17] Because of this very high percentage of funding by the parent institutions, library deans have concentrated on internal library operations and paid little attention to external relationships within and beyond the academic community.[18] This situation is currently in flux on many campuses. Increasingly, libraries are being called upon to undertake serious fundraising efforts and/or to charge fees for services; both issues are discussed in this chapter.

If, historically, funding of collections has been the key budgetary concern, increased expectations of libraries as strategic tools to accomplish campus priorities require a closer consideration of staffing levels. Here is one area where experience in schools and colleges does not prepare one well enough to fully understand library staffing issues. For example, in times of tight budgets, traditional academic practice is to close low-enrolled sections and increase class size as much as possible before turning students away. There is no library equivalent to closed sections. Doors of the library cannot be closed after a certain number have been admitted on a particular day, nor can every fifth student be refused service at the reference desk. Indeed, longer library hours are often demanded by students, who increasingly want 24/7 electronic and/or phone reference support, whether or not they attend classes on campus.

Even with efficient management of library operations and elimination of little used services, insufficient staffing in the library can only lead to staff burnout and, even more important, poorly served students across the board. Moreover, while students may suffer from their inability to take a needed course at a particular time, closing sections does not jeopardize the overall quality of the program. However, insufficient library staffing can deprive students of the resources they may need for academic success.

Significant technology costs must also be added to growing collections and staffing expenses. Who would question the value of current Web-based library systems, of having thousands of journals and databases available at home or in the office, of 24/7 reference support from on or off campus, or tools that effortlessly link bibliographic citations to full text? Yet all of these come with costs in hardware, software, and staffing. Many of these are so new that costs are not even known as yet.

> Usage statistics and cost analyses of these services are not readily available, but even a simple change in service can have significant impact on library operations. For example, the shift to providing email notices of overdue books and enabling online renewals resulted in a significant drop in revenue from fines in Carnegie Mellon University libraries. According to a survey conducted by the Digital Library Federation, several libraries experienced a significant decline in revenue from fines and photocopying when electronic reserves were implemented. Again, traditional measures do not—because they were not designed to—capture these changes or their implications.
>
> Whether the fundamental mission of libraries has changed may be a matter of interpretation or local policy, but the environment and

circumstances in which libraries pursue their mission is dramatically
different from the environment and circumstances of the past.[19]

Research at Drexel University, for example, indicates that, while "its
subscription costs are lower for electronic journals," "there are substantial costs in maintaining an electronic journal collection that more than
offset the savings from eliminating the clerical chores associated with
maintaining a print journal collection."[20] Nor is there any expectation
that publishers may be willing to share savings resulting from the lower
costs of electronic publications.[21] What is clear is that libraries are constantly in the forefront of using technology to harness the information
explosion to the service of learning and research and that there are significant costs associated with doing that.

> The application of information technologies has both modernized
> and transformed libraries. As one of four identified infrastructures of
> a modern library, information technology has increased the efficien-
> cies and effectiveness of staff productivity and increased the acces-
> sibility and availability of information resources and related services
> for library users. As a result of the increasing importance over the
> past two decades of information technology, its application has con-
> sumed a greater percentage of a library's operating costs for which a
> library must be accountable to prove its fiscal responsibility.[22]

WHAT CAN PRESIDENTS DO?

In the face of these realities, how can presidents hope to engage their
libraries more effectively as tools of empowerment? First, presidents can
make sure they and other campus leaders have good information available for making decisions about the library. Given the differences in functions of schools and colleges versus those of libraries, it is especially
important that libraries thoroughly document service and collections options within budgetary considerations, as well as provide a clearly documented framework in which budget decisions can be wisely made.
Budgetary decisions should be made knowing what the impact will be of
various scenarios and how what is being contemplated on one campus
compares with what is happening on sister campuses and peer institutions. To do this well and to ensure credibility requires a strong library
faculty committee working with library staff. Once a good basis of documentation is accepted and in place, annual updates should be provided
by library staff. It is also quite appropriate to expect the library to pro-

vide planning and assessment documentation to ensure that the library is meeting the information needs of its users while containing costs (i.e., that it is being efficient in its operations and/or that areas of inefficiency are the result of campus mandates or other acknowledged priorities).[23]

In similar fashion, when new or expanded services or roles are to be assumed by the library, there needs to be up-front agreement on funding sources or on what will be eliminated or curtailed to fund the new endeavor. This need is most often ignored by new program proposals that do not require a serious review of necessary library resources. In times of expanding programs, Peter can be robbed so often to support Paul that eventually no program has adequate library resources.

Second, there is always some flexibility for projects of importance to the future of the institution, in spite of the large percentage of fixed costs in campus budgets. Presidents and other academic leaders could, if they wished, make more dynamic use of their libraries. By determining in conjunction with their librarians and other campus leadership, what they really want from their libraries, they could then work from those goals and objectives to set appropriate funding levels. They could decide to fund their campus libraries on the basis of agreed-upon objectives and expectations.

Third, academic leaders need to examine some longstanding assumptions about libraries. It is time for institutions and their libraries to confront the funding problem directly and realize that, with very few exceptions, acquisitions levels of the past cannot realistically be sustained. The academic community—especially the faculty—needs to acknowledge this limitation and understand its consequences for users. This shared acceptance would permit the library to act in more imaginative ways. The need to emphasize access over possession is understood by most librarians, and this awareness is becoming part of the operating philosophy of other campus leaders as well. If libraries are to remain relevant to the academic enterprise, they must be free to seek workable solutions to the problems that confront them. Academic leadership in changing campus expectations to emphasize access over possession can, in turn, allow libraries more internal flexibility.

Fourth, presidents, development officers, and library deans alike need to start thinking more seriously and more creatively about securing supplementary funding for their libraries through fund raising and other outreach efforts.

Finally, leadership by presidents and educational organizations at the state and national levels is crucial in shaping information policy and controlling journal and database pricing. All of these possibilities will be explored in this chapter. All demand a clear vision by presidents of what they want their libraries to accomplish.

CAMPUS PLANNING AND REALLOCATIONS

Reminding us that budget cuts are not new, the authors of a 1983 article addressing the problem of retrenchment in higher education stress the need "for seriously considering alternatives to the business-as-usual efficiency response to retrenchment."[24] We would urge presidents to apply this advice in planning and budgeting for libraries. Old images and beliefs about campus libraries must give way to a fresh examination of the library's capabilities. Library deans and campus leadership should creatively explore what the library could offer in empowerment to accomplish both short- and long-term campus goals. In the initial stages, cost considerations should be ignored. The first step should be to identify desired outcomes; only then should action plans and cost figures be developed.

If the campus has a strategic plan, an initial first step might be to establish a task force of librarians, administrators, and faculty to explore point by point how the human and informational resources of the library could be more effectively used to obtain outcomes specified in the plan (e.g., if improved student writing is a priority, what does and what could the library contribute to this goal?).

While academic program and college planning need to focus outward on changing job market demands, libraries should focus on overall campus priorities. Their planning priorities should match campus efforts in teaching/learning, scholarly, and outreach efforts and should reflect both the campus mission statement and emerging campus priorities. Such a campus support role will require flexibility so that annually reviewed strategic initiatives will work better than a three- to five-year planning cycle. This process assumes, of course, that campuses have reasonably well-articulated mission statements and priorities.

To be effective, the library planning process should regularly involve classroom faculty and other appropriate people. Ideally, there will be the active and ongoing involvement of a faculty library advisory committee. Working through its advisory group, librarians should alert campus leaders to larger funding issues: the spiraling costs of library materials, which outstrip rates of inflation in the consumer price index; the impact of new information technologies on services and library costs; external funding sources for libraries; and the benefits and limitations of interinstitutional cooperation. Academic leaders should also be aware of the possible payoffs.

Review at appropriate stages by other key stakeholders should also be instituted. Having such campus involvement can bring a number of advantages. It can help expand campus awareness of the library's current level of resources and effectiveness. It can articulate the advantages and disadvantages of potential library efforts in support of campus priorities and suggest areas to be targeted. The library staff can then develop an action plan for each project and determine resource needs for implementation. If the list is long, initial review and endorsement of the priority list by the president as well as the advisory group can allow library staff to concentrate on developing action plans for those projects most likely to be implemented in light of identified campus priorities. Once the elements in the action plans are deemed desirable by the administration, then and only then should resource issues be addressed. The timing for implementation can be adjusted to meet financial constraints if need be.

Such planning as we have suggested should also result in regular assessments of overall library performance. In the same manner in which academic programs regularly undergo program review, there should be a parallel process to review how well the library is meeting agreed-upon objectives, how efficiently it is using its resources, and whether those resources are adequate. The outcomes of these reviews should be shared campuswide and set the foundation for future planning efforts. Not to have such reviews is almost a guarantee that, over time, impossibly high expectations will exist for library resources and services.

Once plans for integrating the library into the various campus priority efforts have been agreed upon, a number of possibilities can be explored for providing needed resources. One approach is to reallocate existing funds.

Reallocation of Campus Funds

To determine whether campus reallocation of funds will have an overall beneficial effect for your campus, have budget and library personnel work together to develop needed cost estimates. They should start by estimating the value of each proposed initiative in terms of anticipated time saved, increased productivity, or improved quality of performance by the various departments or offices that will receive new services or other support from the library. That amount should be translated into dollars to be transferred to the library for increased staffing or other expenses related to the new activity. For example, if the library is going to assume responsibility for a campus records–management program or for the systematic collection and organization of current information of concern to the campus, budget and library staff should determine what current procedures are costing, then estimate the additional value of having a centralized operation organized for easy access by the entire campus. If the library cost estimates for taking over this function exceed or equal current costs, a judgment should be made as to whether the transfer would result in significantly better service. If not, the operation should not be transferred. The library can proceed instead with another activity that better and/or more efficiently supports campus priorities.

Campuses that become more sophisticated in integrating their libraries will find some advantages in responding effectively to changing enrollments or tight budgets. In response to an earlier time of budget cutting, Franklin W. Wallin, former president of Earlham College, made an argument for library funding that remains true today.

> Libraries can offer academic administrators a cost-effective means to support quality education and provide an important area of flexibility for the tight budget years that lie ahead. While a position added to one school or department of the institution will only increase program quality within that one unit, he commented, the addition of one librarian at an instructionally active library like Earlham's can support faculty in many areas, increasing the overall efficiency of faculty efforts and program quality. This cost-effective placement of a position also allows for flexibility in meeting changing student needs in the future. If a position is placed in a school or department which later suffers a significant drop in enrollment, it is difficult to shift and retrain the faculty member to contribute effectively in another academic area. It is much easier for librarians to adjust their instructional efforts to accommodate fluctuating student demands.[25]

Joint faculty appointments between the library and various academic programs can produce similar benefits.

Internal Library Reallocations

Libraries, like their parent institutions, have budgets consisting largely of fixed costs. Faculty expectations for continuing acquisitions levels, materials inflation rates, and mandated salary increases more than consume annual budget increases and make budget cuts all the more challenging. Technology is essential to respond to the expanding universe of information and to expand service capacities, yet the high costs of technology must often be entirely or partially covered by already badly stretched library allocations. However, the situation varies significantly from state to state and institution to institution. A 2003 survey of Colorado academic library directors found that:

- While 70% of the library directors agreed that their libraries were affected by significant budget cuts, a surprising 26% of the directors managed libraries that faced no budget cuts at all. . . .
- The budget reductions were a recent phenomenon; before 2002–2003, 72% of the directors managed budgets that were actually rising, flat, or decreasing only slightly.[26]

Contrast that with the 2002 report in *The Chronicle of Higher Education*, in which it was noted, that some libraries faced severe hardships:

> [at the] University of Massachusetts at Amherst's library, as at others, the talk is of "inventing a new library." The library lost about 20 percent of its staff and saw its acquisitions budget shrink by more than $1-million. It canceled 1,000 journal subscriptions and cut back on buying books.
>
> "We're trying to make choices," says Margo Crist, director of library services. "What are we going to invest in and what are we going to downsize or eliminate?"[27]

The elimination of print journal subscriptions in favor of online versions is increasingly easier to "sell," since most faculty and their students prefer the ease of accessing online journals from on or off campus and whenever desired. Indeed, students prefer the ease of access even when there is a noticeable loss in quality, such as in art journals. A good interim step is a careful review of journal use and the elimination of print subscriptions in favor of online journals for moderately used print journals.[28] For those with little or no use, cancellation with a document delivery service for the seldom-consulted journal is appropriate. Research has provided the following information:

> that nonsubscription costs are lower, on a per-title basis, in electronic than in print format. The per-title effect is more pronounced at smaller libraries, mainly because they license relatively large collections of electronic titles in comparison to the size of their print collections. Relative to collection size, however, the cost advantages of the electronic format exist across the board. These findings sug-

gest that, other things being equal, an electronic collection should achieve lower nonsubscription costs than a print collection.[29]

The real challenge is to have faculty well-informed in advance as to the need for cuts, the targeted savings level, and how the process will be conducted. Active library faculty advisory committees can be invaluable for ensuring that the process seems logical and evenhanded across the disciplines.

Indeed, as budget challenges continue and worsen, strategic retrenchment tactics are needed. In a 2002 article, Susan Curzon, CSU dean of the university library at Northridge, describes a number of low-risk strategies that enable librarians to retain their positive commitment to the library's primary services and mission in order to move forward during difficult times of budget cutting. For example, she recommends library staff focus on what to preserve, not cut, and to set long-term goals. When library staff is proactive and positive in outlook, and users are informed about potential changes, damaging losses of services, staff, and support from the library's community of users can be avoided or reduced.[30]

Where campus planning has resulted in integration of the library into the campus mainstream, traditional retrenchment approaches should give way to a more positive and creative analysis of library objectives and subsequent use of allocations. The president and library dean can use times of financial restrictions to initiate a special library review that can expand campus awareness of the changing information environment and the consequent need to reevaluate the traditional role of the campus library. From this review, guiding principles for making budget cuts can be developed and shared campuswide. (For a sample of such a set of guiding principles, see Appendix F.)

Presidents and academic vice presidents can also provide leadership by encouraging institutional research and budget personnel to work creatively with librarians. They can encourage institutional research officers to work with librarians to collect data on the benefits of library services and systems to campus priorities. Measuring benefits is difficult, and little literature is available, but a few models do exist, such as the use of activity-based costing in two Australian universities.[31] However, even where inventories of benefits must be based on empirical or anecdotal evidence, the assessment process can help expand campus awareness as well as provide a working tool in developing future plans. The best assessment of benefits will incorporate the judgment of library users,[32] and models for emulation can be obtained from campus units that experience high satisfaction with library services.

Changes in budgeting procedures should reflect the realities of today's information technologies, and hard questions need to be addressed regarding what costs, if any, should be placed on library users, to what degree fundraising can supplement institutional dollars, and how dependent the campus should be on cooperative resource sharing. What are the costs involved, and how should these be budgeted? What should be reported to faculty as acquisitions expenditures? There are no right or wrong answers to such questions, but adhering to a narrow definition of acquisitions and campus pressure to maintain library materials allocations around 30 percent of the budget (the current rule of thumb) will hamper libraries' ability to make optimal use of their limited financial resources. More flexible budgeting procedures for the library can support new library priorities of access over ownership and can allow libraries to respond more creatively to campus needs and priorities. Developing and maintaining reasonable regional, state, and national information bases depends upon adequate overall funding for acquisitions; and, of course, no library can expect other libraries to accord it free borrowing privileges if its research collections have nothing to offer. Libraries must provide a workable balance.

A special word needs to be added here about the potential, in some cases, of collaborative efforts—often made possible by new technology— to actually improve services and/or expand access to information without increasing expenditures. For example, "the eleven university libraries of the University of California (UC) annually achieve a 30 percent efficiency by avoiding at least $80 million in costs on a total combined budget of approximately $240 million."[33] While many of the UC strategies for avoiding costs concern collection-related activities, some also address service needs such as the following:

> Several years of user-needs analyses tell us that Google-like interfaces for information relevant to particular research or teaching needs are in high demand. The problem is that research and teaching needs vary across disciplines and, for individuals, across time. The challenge is to build tools that enable the ready development of highly configured search interfaces. The approach adopted at UC is a layered one. The California Digital Library (CDL) is creating a suite of tools that campus library staff will use to build online portals serving specific user communities. With these tools, campus library staff will also be able to integrate information resources that are available globally (e.g., via the World Wide Web), regionally (e.g., via the online collections that the libraries license consortially), and locally (e.g., via the campus library collections) and to

tailor user interfaces so that they integrate appropriately with local online environments. The service model is hardly new—it mimics the model characteristic of any utility provider. It drives infrastructural costs down by spending once and sharing widely. The model is entirely new for libraries, however, and requires them to relinquish reliance on systems that are independently developed and locally controlled. It demands a new degree of collaboration and trust, as well as a new generation of technologies.[34]

For the most part, such efforts are less money savers than collection enrichers and/or service enhancers. Unfortunately, many libraries that are not part of major higher education systems may not have such opportunities available to them.

In like fashion, often new technology—once installed—may not save dollars but can result in a much more efficient use of staff time and, therefore, result in better services. Self-checkout machines, for example, are increasingly popular with library users and staff alike. RFID technology can produce significantly higher staff efficiencies and speed up checkout processes, security checks, and even inventorying.[35] These can be cheaper alternatives to adding more staff.

Ultimately, the burden lies on the library dean to develop a long-term strategy that will effectively utilize available resources to promote campus priorities. Most likely these efforts will include technology-based efforts and changes in staffing patterns that will take a number of years to implement. Continued administrative support will be particularly important during the interim years, when disruptive changes are more evident than long-term benefits.

FEES FOR LIBRARY SERVICES

In our earlier book, we suggested that one way of increasing funding levels for libraries is to have libraries charge individual faculty members and students for selected information-related services. Both experience and ethical considerations have proven us wrong on this point. The reality is that there will always be haves and have-nots among students and academic programs, and any fee structure for access to information can only serve to negatively impact those who can least afford it. If, however, the only way a desired service could be made available is fee-based, provision should be made to waive these fees for economically disadvantaged students and/or for "poor" academic programs.

The only point at which campus user fees could be legitimately considered is as a management tool to avoid unnecessary use of resources or to drive down use of services not intrinsic to student learning or research. The most obvious services for which a fee may be not only reasonable but desirable is in printing services, which, given the growing number of electronic resources, must now be offered by libraries. Besides the considerable costs involved in print services, "most of the literature discusses printer abuse as a major concern"[36] when there is no required fee. However, there is as yet no consensus across campuses on this issue.[37] Employing fees for room rentals or other non-learning/research-related services needs to be balanced against the costs of collecting and managing the limited amount of income such services will produce. But, again, as a means of driving down use, such fees may be desirable.

The one common exception to the above is when student fees are designated for library use on an ongoing basis. These funds are frequently earmarked for specific library purposes—most often for longer hours, but not always exclusively for that. Certainly, such fees are as appropriate as fees that support athletics or childcare centers. Indeed, library fees inherently benefit all students, unlike most other student fees, which have fewer beneficiaries. Where library fees exist, students have the right to be assured that their fees are actually enhancing services and/or resources of particular interest to them rather than replacing general fund dollars. It is advantageous for deans of libraries to annually report on the use of such funds to student government officers, as well as to appropriate campus offices. Increasingly, library deans are finding time invested in building relationships with student leadership groups to be particularly beneficial when fees are considered. Practicing such good stewardship lays the groundwork for fee increases in the future as well as library-happy alumni who may be future donors to the library.

Whereas service fees for students and/or faculty should be avoided except under special circumstances, fees for services to external groups are a different matter. Some campuses, as discussed in chapter 5 on services to the community, are quite successful in creating services for which people are willing to pay. Though usually not major moneymakers, these services reap other benefits as well. Such benefits include the following: "(1) the new technologies developed by fee-based services can be expanded to the library's primary clientele, (2) the specialized reference tools and databases required by a fee-based service expand the resources available to all library users, (3) service to the community can mean an increase in donations, cooperation, and networking between the library and its external clientele, and (4) the value of libraries and information is enhanced by fee-based services."[38]

GRANTS AND CONTRACTS

In seeking an alternative to user fees or simply to increase the funding base for the library without affecting allocations elsewhere on campus, one of the best sources of untapped additional funds for libraries is through the regular grants-and-contracts processes. Although some funding/contracting services specifically exclude library resources, most do not. Most grant proposals could well include a budget item for resource materials and/or library services. When funds for acquisitions are received, the library could order and catalog the materials and then lend them to the department or professor involved for the duration of the project, after which they would become part of the regular collection.

Funding requests should also be built into many grants proposals for research by librarians, document delivery, and media production for publications and presentations. If these items are funded for full cost recovery, grants could produce a steady, ongoing flow of funds into the operational budget of the library, thus increasing the library's capacity to respond to service demands and opportunities. Also, building in money for librarians as research consultants could increase research productivity.

Exploiting the normal grants/contracts process to secure enrichment money for the library seems like an ideal approach, yet campuses seldom pursue this alternative because of the logistics involved. Faculty seldom think of including library resources in proposals, and rushed deadlines frequently mean that even those who think of this may feel they do not have the time to investigate and include library items.

Another way to supplement existing library funding, which is employed on some campuses, is to earmark a percentage of the overhead dollars from grants for the library. While this approach is one good way to bring more funding into the library and is far easier to implement than including library resources and services on individual grants, it does not increase the total dollars coming to the campus.

Presidents and academic vice presidents should find it well worth their time and effort to modify the operations of their grants offices to ensure additional funding for their libraries. The effort should start with an academic policy requiring that library items be included for funding in all proposals unless specifically excluded by the funding source. Faculty development efforts will be needed to minimize psychological resistance. Many faculty see library support as "free," so they have little incentive to consult with a librarian to determine what would be a reasonable amount to include for library support. An ongoing awareness campaign will be needed to educate faculty—and in some cases, staff in the grants office—about how they can play an important part in achieving campus priorities by consistently including library budget items in their proposals. In addition, administrators will need to implement a support system that is not cumbersome to faculty.

Grants routing sheets should provide sufficient information to ensure consideration of the full range of library and media services and resources appropriate for inclusion in the proposals. Grants office staff need to encourage such inclusions as a matter of academic policy and priority. Library personnel, in turn, must be prepared to respond promptly to faculty inquiries about appropriate inclusions, without necessitating a trip to the library. A telephone call from a faculty member, briefly outlining a proposal and the range of funding being sought, should elicit concrete suggestions with dollar figures and short statements of justification within twenty-four to forty-eight hours at most.

Entrepreneurial Activities

Additional funds can be obtained for both collection building and for enhanced services by aggressively seeking funding alternatives. Yet as individual campuses and their libraries across the country move toward incorporating such efforts into the mainstream of their operations, care must be taken to safeguard longstanding commitments to quality service and support of scholarship, or instruction and research will suffer.[39] Entrepreneurial activities always require a significant amount of staff and/or volunteer time, which needs to be evaluated against the potential gains. Some of these possibilities were discussed in chapter 5 as services to the business community. To be successful, efforts targeted at off-campus markets must be understood as a natural complement to library services to faculty and students. The successful development of entrepreneurial activities requires that staff understand how services marketed off campus complement library and campus priorities; that there is sufficient staffing to meet both campus and community needs; and that library staff know how the funds generated by such services are expended.

If an "entrepreneurial attitude" among library faculty and staff can be cultivated and rewarded, they are apt to "discover" new avenues of both one-time and ongoing support. For example, what incentives are there for staff to seek equipment donations from their associates in the public sector, or to think of services that could profitably be marketed to the business community? Annual awards to library faculty and staff who provide the best ideas for improved services and resource avenues can help encourage an entrepreneurial attitude.

Whenever possible, services and projects undertaken to secure additional resources should also either enhance the library's visibility on campus or in the community or complement campus and library priorities. The offering of research and document delivery services to the business community was discussed in chapter 5. Other income-producing activities might include the following:

- *Incorporating a professional library from the business community.* The University of Nevada at Las Vegas, for example, is now the home for the International Gaming Collection.

- *Foreign language collections.* Foreign companies and ethnic or cultural organizations could be approached to donate money for materials in their language or about the country they represent. They may also be open to funding enhanced library services for appropriately targeted foreign students (for example, information literacy programs).

- *Book sales.* Some libraries operate a year-round bookstore or have regular books sales to sell materials discarded from the collection or donated materials that are unsuitable for addition to the collection. The University of Florida Smathers Library is one of a half dozen or so academic libraries where it has been found that "once established a small bookstore is easier to manage than a large book sale, and far more profitable and efficient in the long term."[40]

- *Merchandising.* Everything from book bags to mugs to cookbooks to note cards can be sold as moneymakers for the library. The Smathers Library bookstore at the University of Florida sells greeting cards, bookmarks, and small prints, all showcasing images of its unique Florida history materials, as reported by Steven Carrico, associate university librarian, and will consider selling mugs and T-shirts if a coffee/gift shop is included in a pending renovation project.[41]

- *Special events.* Though such undertakings are time-consuming, they could benefit the library both financially and in public awareness, which can be helpful later in approaching potential donors. The key to success is finding the right event and building on its success year after year. Other events are needed to acknowledge, honor, and cultivate donors.

- *Marketing teleconferencing or media production services.*

- *Marketing of library services and/or resources, databases, or online systems to other agencies.*

FUNDRAISING

In comparison with other library administrative issues, not much has been written about fundraising over the years. Often, the building of a new library facility or a major expansion of an old one is the first cause for fundraising efforts. Yet, while larger research libraries have been seen over the years to be the domain for ongoing fundraising, the need is increasingly important for small specialized libraries and every size in between![42]

> At the outset, it needs to be emphasized that successful development depends on the leadership and participation of the library director because it requires visionary leadership. Not everyone can be an effective fundraiser. A library undertaking a major gifts fundraising program must be willing to take risks in an entrepreneurial way. That kind of activity can only occur under the direction of a visionary and entrepreneurial leader—typically a library director—who understands that a good development plan balances the wishes of a donor and the needs of a library. . . .
>
> There is little doubt the libraries that will be most successful at raising money in the future are those led by librarians whose vision, leadership abilities, and personal qualities will enable them to communicate the special qualities and merits of their libraries.[43]

Presidents seeking expanded roles for their librarians need to look for such qualities in the library deans they hire.

Generally speaking, the more time and resources invested in fundraising, the more money will be raised.

> Serious seeking of funds beyond regular budgetary sources and/or income from services rendered is similar in many respects to other major library operations. First of all, to be accomplished successfully it requires that there be general acknowledgment of the need for fund raising, and placing it among the other operational priorities of the library. Fund raising requires outlays of time and money, and unless there is a reasonable commitment by the staff and governing bodies actively to seek funds, there is little or no chance of success.[44]

After an adequate commitment of resources, the next most important thing is clear-cut goals.

More than process and techniques, what library fund-raising needs most is a rationale that guides thinking, planning, and action. That rationale begins with the selection of the goals to be achieved through fund-raising. Fund-raising goals should convey a vision or a sense of how the institution pictures itself in the future. They should be compelling enough to generate excitement about what that future will be. The goals should also require the institution to reach but should not be so unrealistic as to be beyond its grasp. Finally, the goals should be timely in order to communicate some urgency to the need for assistance from potential donors.[45]

Libraries should be integrated into campus fundraising efforts. They should have their own advisory boards, and membership should reflect their locations and fundraising opportunities. The board of urban campuses would properly be made up almost exclusively of local business people. Flagship campus libraries have historically had boards made up of faculty and/or faculty spouses. This model is less appropriate as external fundraising demands increase. A 2002 survey report of eighty-six academic libraries identified the factors for success in academic fundraising. While some of the following factors are true for all campus fundraising efforts, the list provides some library-specific insights.

- Age of the program. The most statistically significant factor was the age of the library fund-raising program. . . . It takes time and cultivation of prospects to raise money and, as a result, the number of years engaged in fund-raising efforts is a critical factor of success. . . . Average funds raised are insignificant for the first two years of a program and seem to remain quite low until the sixth year. . . .

- Size of the donor pool. The next significant indicator was the number of donors in the database . . . libraries with the largest donor pools have the greatest success.

- Involvement of the library dean. Another success factor was the involvement of the library director in the fund-raising effort. Involvement could loosely be defined as any type of hands-on fund-raising, including developing donor strategies, setting fund-raising goals, donor cultivation, campaign planning, and gift solicitations. . . . Those institutions with the highest dollars raised had directors who were involved in fund-raising, on average, 50 percent of the time. . . .

- Time on task. Another indicator of success is the amount of time devoted to fund-raising activities. . . . Library development directors . . . who spend the largest percentage of their time on fund-raising raised the most funds. . . . The number one priority, according to survey results, is major gifts. Historically, time spent on cultivating major gifts has the most significant impact on fund-raising success. However, major gifts require much time and energy over an extended period of time before results start to show. Time on task also allows the development director to focus energy on fewer big gifts rather than on a larger number of small gifts. The overall benefits to the program are increased dollars for specific programs with less cost per dollar raised.

- Types of institutions. The survey results showed that private institutions are raising more funds annually than public institutions. . . . The survey also showed that research universities far surpass all other types of institutions in raising funds. The average for these institutions is $1,100,000 raised annually as compared to community colleges at an average of $100,000.

- Friends groups that are a part of the annual giving programs raised substantially more funds than Friends groups that are not.

- Programs with the highest fund-raising goals raised the most. . . .

- Programs that are connected to the central advancement effort raise substantially more funds. . . .

- Development directors with four or more years in fund-raising raise more funds.[46]

We would also emphasize the importance of finding the right development officer to spearhead—with the dean—library fundraising efforts. Securing someone who appreciates the unique challenges of fundraising for the library is only half the battle. It is also necessary for the officer to be able to articulate the differences between fundraising for the library and for academic programs *and* to create a synergy between the two. Take, for example, the question of access to the alumni donor base.

> Several institutional barriers exist for academic libraries wishing to raise external funds. Access to the institution's alumni and supporters is critically important to the library, yet in some instances these people, who potentially have more interest than any other group, are off-limits to the library, usually unless they "self-identify," or come forward on their own as supporters of the library.
>
> These barriers are foolish. No college or university is able to tap all of its alumni, neighbors, and other supporters. Identifying the library as another possible attraction for the university's community should be regarded as a positive asset. At the very least, the library should be given access to those alumni who are nondonors by presenting them with other options for supporting their alma mater. Indeed, when several members of a family have attended a university, they might be alumni of different schools or colleges, and can there-

fore contemplate a family gift to the library rather than trying to determine which of their schools should be the beneficiary of a family
donation. Similarly, alumni of a reunion class all used the library, no
matter what their major or school was; they can all support a gift to
the library.[47]

The library can also be an effective first ask for groups of disaffected
alumni, for example:

those classes that graduated during the Vietnam War era when the
campus may have been in chaos or perhaps women who were among
the first classes of coeducation in formerly male institutions. These
alumni are now of an age to be ready to give something back to their
university, but their experiences prevent them from identifying
closely with a school, a department, or even the university as a
whole. The library is often able to present itself as a positive force,
and one that was a presence during those earlier years on campus.[48]

A good example of the potential value of libraries in attracting new
donors occurred at the University of Illinois at Chicago. Joan Hood, now
retired, "convinced the administration that a library ask was a good first
ask for alumni. The university was just beginning to ask its alumni for
funds, and was not sure where to start. Obviously the library, said Joan,
and she made the library the theme for the university's early annual appeals. That strategy raised $600,000 a year for the library."[49]

Given this situation, particular care must be given to how the relationship is established between the advancement office and the library.
"The Library's goals should be seen as key University goals, and . . . the
Library's function as Information Provider/Trainer/Broker/Pioneer
[should] be seen as an overarching theme in fundraising, much as 'scholarship' is seen as a theme."[50] To this end, the library development officer
needs to work constantly to get the other development officers and advancement leadership to partner in fundraising activities that can benefit both the academic programs and the library. To be successful will take
some thoughtful reflection on the campuswide benefits of the library (i.e.,
it supports all academic programs, all students, and all faculty).

Given this universality of library benefits and particularly if the library
is truly becoming a strategic tool in accomplishing the campus's mission
and priorities, a case can be made for the president's being the natural
partner with the library dean in soliciting major gifts. Certainly, the president should be the one person who can be counted on to have a comprehensive campus viewpoint and, therefore, be the best positioned to
advocate for library donations. Undergirding any presidential involve-

ment should be a sound fundraising program that includes a multifaceted approach to a sustained and growing fundraising program—starting with annual funds.

Annual Funds

Annual fund efforts for the library have taken many different forms on campuses. Parents of graduating students and/or those participating in parents' days make donations in honor of their children whose names will be put on bookplates. "A number of academic libraries have developed well-publicized fundraising partnerships with their institution's athletic department or with an outstanding coach. The Pennsylvania State University Libraries' long collaboration with football coaching legend Joe Paterno and the Indiana University Libraries' relationship with Hoosier basketball coach Bob Knight are just two of these well-known efforts. Such partnerships can provide academic credibility to athletics and visibility and excitement to libraries."[51]

Annual mailings to donors can parallel mailings to alumni or be incorporated in them. In fact, incorporating library asks into the annual fund activities of the schools and programs can be a win-win situation. In planning their annual funds, schools and programs might highlight donations to the library in one mailing and/or telethon, with alumni being allowed to earmark donations to the subject field of their choice. The donor's name or the name of a person in whose memory the gift is made could be inscribed on a bookplate or, if a journal, acknowledged in the online catalog. Donors can also be told the name of the book or subscription purchased with their funds when the gift is acknowledged. Of course, to be meaningful, the materials purchased through such funds must be in addition to what would normally have been purchased for the designated program.

Besides collection improvement, there are some side advantages to the academic programs that integrate libraries into their annual funds. Asking alumni more frequently for gifts usually results in more money being received, so extra requests for library support should increase the total dollar response.[52] Donors can also be encouraged to increase their usual donation to match the cost of a book, journal subscription, or other specific library item. Once donors increase their giving level, they tend to stay at the higher level or make further increases. In this way, schools can gain ground in overall funding for their programs. As referred to earlier, because libraries have a special appeal for some alumni, targeted efforts can elicit first-time gifts from alumni who have as yet not made a gift. San Diego State University (SDSU) is a good example of this. Leslie DiBona, SDSU Library's director of development,

> devised a simple, yet effective, plan from which the library and par-
> ticipating colleges benefited. Deans from the colleges of Arts and
> Letters, Engineering, and Sciences gave permission for their nondo-
> nating alumni to be called on behalf of the library. Gifts received
> were placed in a library materials endowment fund restricted to the
> donor's college. Both the library development officer and the college
> development officer received a report listing these new donors.
> Donors from this campaign were treated as LYBUNTs (donors who
> made a gift last year but not this year) for the college and were so-
> licited by the college the following year. In a one-year period, the
> SDSU [San Diego State University] Library received gifts from well
> over 300 alumni who had previously been nondonors to the insti-
> tution, with the average gift around $25.[53]

In part because of this very respectable showing, the SDSU Library has since been included in all aspects of the institutional annual fund program. The library now appears as an option on all annual fund direct mail appeals and is offered as a choice for those contacted by the telefund program.

On most campuses, the library dean has primary responsibility for fundraising, but an increasing number of larger libraries, such as the SDSU library, now have a full- or part-time development officer. There is also a national organization for those involved in library development. The Academic Library Advancement and Development Network (ALADN) can serve as a support and idea source for such personnel; the URL for the organization's Web site is http://www.library.arizona.edu/aladn/. Other sources for library fundraising efforts include the Development Officers of Research and Academic Libraries (DORAL) and Friends and Fund-raising Section–Library Administration and Management Association of the American Library Association (FRFDS–LAMA, http://www.ala.org/ala/lama/lamacommunity/lamacommittees/fundraisingb/fundraisingfinancial.htm).

A lot more could be written about fundraising for campus libraries. The library-specific aspects of fundraising are few and include things like the following:

- Some academic libraries have friends groups, and the good ones are
  development-oriented. They can raise endowments, form part of the annual giving base, host special events, and recruit other volunteers.[54]
  Such organizations, however, are time-consuming to sustain.

- For donors who like public recognition, libraries can offer a wide range of naming opportunities, from plaques on walls and bookplates to credit on the online catalog for books or journals purchased with their donations.[55]

- Special collections are often attractive for gifts of materials and cash donations. As with gifts of books to the general collections, gifts in kind should only be accepted when they match campus needs. "The lure of obtaining something for free often results in the relaxing of normally applied selection criteria. Not only does this lead to the addition of materials that would not typically be added, it can be detrimental to the collection as a whole."[56]

However, for the most part and whether dealing with capital campaigns or annual funds, fundraising basics for libraries remain the same as fundraising for any other campus unit.

As is the case for all deans, fund raising is no longer an option but rather an essential part of the job. Success will come to library deans who stay in tune with donors and campus priorities, know how to make successful connections,[57] and can articulate with passion the library's expertise and resources to the campus and its community.[58]

NOTES

1. C. D. Mote, Jr., "The Graceful Decline of Higher Education," *The Sun Herald*, 7 July 2004. Retrieved 13 October 2004 from http://www.sunherald.com/mld/thesunherald/news/editorial/9094170.htm.

2. Scott Smallwood, "The Crumbling Intellectual Foundation," *The Chronicle of Higher Education* 49 (20 September 2002): A10–A13.

3. Ibid., A10.

4. California State University, *The California State University at the Beginning of the 21st Century: Meeting the Needs of the People of California* (Long Beach, Calif.: California State University, 2001), 18. Retrieved 30 March 2005 from http://www.calstate.edu/AcadSen/Records/Reports/CSU_21stCentury.pdf.

5. Online Computer Library Center, *2002 Environmental Scan: Pattern Recognition* (Dublin, Ohio: Online Computer Library Center, 2002), 24.

6. Brian L. Hawkins, "The Unsustainability of the Traditional Library and the Threat to Higher Education," in *The Mirage of Continuity: Reconfiguring Academic Information Resources for the 21st Century*, ed. Brian L. Hawkins and Patricia Battin (Washington, D.C.: Council on Library and Information Resources, 1998), 150.

7. Charles Burress, "The Staggering Price of World's Best Research—Bay Area Universities Leading Charge against Publishers, Arguing the Knowledge

in Academic Journals Must Be Kept within Reach," *San Francisco Chronicle*, 28 March 2004. Retrieved 24 April 2005 from http://www.sfgate.com/cgi-bin/ar ticle.cgi?f=/c/a/2004/03/28/BAGQE5SL3I1.DTL.

8. Paul Gherman, e-mail correspondence to Patricia Breivik, 20 July 2004.

9. Hawkins, 149.

10. Ibid., 139–40.

11. H. R. Bowen, *The Costs of Higher Education: How Much Do Colleges and Universities Spend Per Student and How Much Should They Spend?* (San Francisco: Jossey-Bass, 1980), 17.

12. Richard J. Talbot, "Financing the Academic Library," in *Priorities for Academic Libraries*, ed. Thomas J. Galvin and Beverly Lynch (San Francisco: Jossey-Bass, 1982), 35.

13. Martin M. Cummings, *The Economics of Research Libraries* (Washington, D.C.: Council on Library Resources, 1986), 14.

14. Association of College & Research Libraries, *Standards for Libraries in Higher Education*. Retrieved 3 November 2004 from http://www.ala.org/ala/acrl/acrlstandards/standardslibraries.htm.

15. Association of Research Libraries, *2002–03 ARL Membership Criteria Index (Principal Component Scores)*, 2. Retrieved 27 April 2005 from http://www.arl.org/stats/index/index03.pdf.

16. Bonnie Gratch Lindauer, "Defining and Measuring the Library's Impact on Campuswide Outcomes," *College & Research Libraries* 59 (November 1998): 546–70.

17. Jacob Cohen and K. W. Leeson, "Sources and Uses of Funds of Academic Libraries," *Library Trends* 28 (summer 1979): 29.

18. Paul Metz, "The Role of the Academic Library Director," *Journal of Academic Librarianship* 5 (July 1979): 149.

19. Denise A. Troll, "How and Why Libraries Are Changing: What We Know and What We Need to Know," *portal: Libraries and the Academy* 2, no. 1 (2002): 103.

20. Carol Hansen Montgomery, "Measuring the Impact of an Electronic Journal Collection on Library Costs," *D-Lib Magazine* 6 (October 2000): 13. Retrieved 21 July 2003 from http://www.dlib.org/dlib/october00/montgomery/10montgomery.html.

21. Richard W. Meyer, "Session #7, Multi-Institutional Cooperation: Consortial Access Versus Ownership" (Andrew W. Mellon Foundation conference on Scholarly Communication and Technology, held at Emory University on 24–25 April 1997). Retrieved 20 April 2004 from http://arl.cni.org/scomm/scat/meyer.html.

22. Robert E. Dugan, "Information Technology Budgets and Costs: Do You Know What Your Information Technology Costs Each Year?" *The Journal of Academic Librarianship* 28 (July 2002): 243.

23. E. Stewart Saunders, "Cost Efficiency in ARL Academic Libraries," *The Bottom Line: Managing Library Finances* 16, no. 1 (2003): 14.

24. Hugh G. Petrie and Daniel Alpert, "What Is the Problem of Retrenchment in Higher Education?" *Journal of Management Studies* 20 (1983): 118.

25. Patricia Senn Breivik, *Planning the Library Instruction Program* (Chicago: American Library Association, 1982), 5.

26. David Gleim, "The Shape of Our Lean Years: A Survey of Budget-cutting Strategies Used by Colorado Academic Librarians," *Colorado Libraries* 29, no. 3 (fall 2003): 24.

27. Scott Smallwood, "The Crumbling Intellectual Foundation," *The Chronicle of Higher Education* 49 (20 September 2002): 10. Retrieved 8 June 2005 from LexisNexis Academic database.

28. See, for example, how one campus did such a review: Marisa Scigliano, "Serial Use in a Small Academic Library: Determining Cost-Effectiveness," *Serials Review* 26 (April 2000): 43–52.

29. Roger C. Schonfeld et al., *The Nonsubscription Side of Periodicals: Changes in Library Operations and Costs between Print and Electronic Formats Executive Summary* (Washington, D.C.: Council on Library and Information Science, 2004), 1.

30. Susan Carol Curzon, "Budget Shortfalls," *Library Journal* 128, no. 9 (15 May 2003): 34–35.

31. Jennifer Ellis-Newman and Peter Robinson, "The Cost of Library Services: Activity-based Costing in an Australian Library," *The Journal of Academic Librarianship* 24 (September 1998): 373–79.

32. Cummings, 36.

33. Daniel Greenstein, "Research Libraries' Costs of Doing Business (and Strategies for Avoiding Them)," *EDUCAUSE Review* 39 (September/October 2004). Retrieved 14 September 2004 from http://www.educause.edu/pub/er/erm04/erm04510.asp.

34. Ibid.

35. Laura Smart and Louise Levy Schaper, "Making Sense of RFID," *Library Journal* 129 (15 October 2004): special section, 7–14. Retrieved 27 April 2005 from Expanded Academic ASAP Plus database.

36. Beth Ashmore and Sara E. Morris, "From Scraps to Reams: A Survey of Printing Services in Academic Libraries," *College & Research Libraries* 63 (July 2002): 342–52. Retrieved 30 June 2003 from Wilson Web database.

37. Ibid.

38. Helen B. Josephine, "Intrapreneurship in Fee-Based Information Services," *Journal of Library Administration* 10, no. 2/3 (1989): 151–58.

39. James F. Govan, "The Creeping Invisible Hand: Entrepreneurial Librarianship," *Library Journal* 113 (January 1988): 35–38.

40. Steven B. Carrico, "The University of Florida Smathers Library Bookstore," *Library Collections, Acquisitions, & Technical Services* 25 (spring 2001): 46.

41. Steven Carrico, e-mail correspondence to Patricia Breivik, 14 February 2005.

42. Frank Cervone, "A Long-Term Strategy for Library Funding." *Library Administration & Management* 19 (winter 2005): 7–15.

43. Ibid., 7, 15.

44. Patricia Breivik and E. Burr Gibson, *Funding Alternatives for Libraries* (Chicago: American Library Association, 1979), 11.

45. Robert Wedgeworth, "Donor Relations as Public Relations: Toward a Philosophy of Fund-Raising," *Library Trends* 48 (winter 2000). Retrieved 27 February 2003 from Expanded Academic ASAP database.

46. Reprinted with permission from Irene M. Hoffman, Amy Smith, and Leslie Dibona, "Factors for Success: Academic Library Development Survey Results," *Library Trends* 48, no. 3. (winter 2000): 540. Copyright © 2000 The Board of Trustees of the University of Illinois. Retrieved 9 May 2003 from Infotrac database.

47. Allen Kent, ed., "Academic Library Fund-Raising," *Encyclopedia of Library and Information Science*, vol. 72, supp. 35 (New York: Marcel Dekker, 2002), 6–7.

48. Susan K. Martin, "Academic Library Fund-raising: Organization, Process, and Politics," *Library Trends* 48, no. 3 (winter 2000). Retrieved 27 February 2003 from Expanded Academic ASAP database.

49. Adam Corson-Finnerty, "Pitching the Powers-That-Be: How do Librarians 'Sell' Library Projects to Their Campus Fundraisers?" *The Bottom Line: Managing Library Finances* 15, no. 3 (2002). Retrieved 8 May 2003 from Emerald database.

50. Adam Corson-Finnerty, "The Illogic of Academic Library Fundraising (Draft, intended for comment)" (prepared for ALADN Conference, 27–29 March 2004, Miami, Florida). Retrieved 24 March 2005 from http://www.library.pitt.edu/aladn/plenarysessionMon29.doc.

51. Jennifer Paustenbaugh and Lynn Trojahn, "Annual Fund Programs for Academic Libraries," *Library Trends* 48 (winter 2000): 579–96. Retrieved 27 February 2003 from Expanded Academic ASAP.

52. Keith Jesperson, "How to Get More Money from Your Donor File," *Fundraising Management Magazine* 17 (November 1986): 52.

53. Paustenbaugh and Trojahn, "Annual Fund Programs for Academic Libraries," 586.

54. Victoria Steele and Stephen D. Elder, *Becoming a Fundraiser: The Principles and Practice of Library Development* (Chicago: American Library Association, 1992).

55. Rebecca Martin and Mark A. Williams, "Current Methods of Donor Recognition for Library Development," *Illinois Libraries* 82 (fall 2000): 236–38.

56. Rob Kairis, "Comparing Gifts to Purchased Materials: A Usage Study," *Library Collections, Acquisitions, & Technical Services* 24 (fall 2000): 351.

57. Steele and Elder, *Becoming a Fundraiser.*

58. Wendy Pradt Lougee, *Diffuse Libraries: Emergent Roles for the Research Library in the Digital Age* (Washington, D.C.: Council on Library and Information Resources, 2002).

CHAPTER 11

Making a Difference within the Information Society

Sometimes ending a book can be far harder than starting it. How does one bring to closure a topic as broad as the role of campus libraries as strategic tools in accomplishing campus priorities—especially within the rapidly changing environments of information and technology? Then Google came to our rescue with its December 14, 2004, announcement of its plans to digitize books from the collections of five major research libraries and then to make them available for online searching. Amidst much media attention, a full range of responses from pleasurable excitement to significant misgivings were raised in the weeks following. This project, we believe, is a prime example of the challenges facing campuses' provision for the information needs of their faculty, students, and other communities.

THE GOOGLE CHALLENGE

We can start by examining the pros and cons of this undertaking. Proponents point out the following benefits:

- The dream of making an incredible array of research materials available to every one, if not at home then through even the smallest school or public library, will finally be realized.
- Materials will be digitized at no cost to the libraries.
- Materials—many of which may be physically at risk—will be preserved in digital form.

- Academics and other scholars will save time and money by not needing to travel to other libraries and/or not laboriously borrowing through interlibrary loan services.
- For those who only use a Google search approach, this project will allow them to access more scholarly material than previously.
- Publishers hope the service will increase sales.

While not against the idea of having these collections digitized, many have raised cautionary voices around three areas of concern:

- Quality of the digitizing process:
  - Will materials, especially fragile ones, be susceptible to damage?
  - Will technical standards be adequate for future technologies?
  - Will scanning be of high quality?
  - How long will the project take to complete?
  - How long will digitized formats last?
- Quality of the content:
  - Will access only be provided in full text for items published before 1923 because of copyright restrictions?
  - Will agreements with publishers over copyright ever permit full text of later materials?[1]
  - What about copyright restrictions in the United Kingdom and Europe?
  - Who will pick the excerpts to be displayed from copyrighted materials?
  - Will there be a bias toward English-language materials and Anglo-Saxon publications?[2]
  - What kind of advertising will appear alongside scholarly material?
  - Will scholarly material be listed among top choices presented for a search since top positioning now goes to items that are most popular with users?
- Other issues of concern:
  - What will happen if the project is not profitable to maintain?
  - Will libraries discard all print versions?
  - What impact will it have on the promotion of reading?
  - How will libraries financially handle the anticipated enormous increase in printouts of materials?

All of the above must also be set within the larger economic environment. Google exists to make a profit, and there is a competitive playing field. For example, in spring 2004, both Google and Yahoo began working with librarians to be able to link to research libraries' holdings that currently cannot be picked up by the scanning of search engine servers. In November of that year, Google Scholar was announced, a version of its popular search engine that limits its results to scholarly materials. Google Scholar does not, however, allow searchers to limit or customize the results they receive as most scholarly databases do.[3] Other organizations offer similar services. For example, Elsevier has operated Scirus since 2001, and the American Chemical Society is, at the time of our writing, suing Google for violating the Society's trademark for its Scifinder Scholar.[4] Microsoft announced its plans to build a new search engine around the same time. Other contenders are also emerging.

> Experts say the reason for the sudden interest in academic content by search-engine makers is simple: competition. Google's addition of features to its search tool coincides with the initial public offering. . . . "These search engines are now in competition for quality content" rather than just quantity in their search results, says Herbert Van de Sompel, a researcher at Los Alamos National Laboratory who has designed software to help search engines find academic materials.[5]

The day after Google announced its project with research libraries, "the Library of Congress and a group of international libraries from the United States, Canada, Egypt, China and the Netherlands announced a plan to create a publicly available digital archive of one million books on the Internet.[6] The group said it planned to have 70,000 volumes online by next April."[7] Some of the significant differences in this project, which involves the Internet Archive,[8] a nonprofit organization dedicated to building online archives with libraries and archives, are as follows:

> Where the Internet Archive offers storage, digitizing technology, and R&D in processing and access, the partner libraries drive collection development and cataloging. As far as possible, the Text Archives will provide whole books and sets of books, in context, not just access to pages through a web interface. In this way people can discover the physical books they might want, download books, or do computer analyses, all of which may open new doors of access to not only those inside and outside physical libraries, but to computational scholarship.[9]

It will be sometime before the outcome of this juggling for position works out, and at this time, it is difficult to predict whether these players can succeed where others with equally lofty goals have failed.

> Four other companies have tried to do just the sort of digitization that Google is undertaking, and they have had problems. One of them, NetLibrary, filed for Chapter 11 bankruptcy and became, in much-scaled-down form, a subsidiary of the Online Computer Library Center. A second, Questia, remains independent, but it has reduced its workforce significantly and is on shaky legs. Each company began with over $80-million in venture capital; neither found that to be enough. The third company, Project Xanadu, is little more than a Web presence now.
>
> Project Gutenberg has done better than the other companies, but it still begs for dollars on its Web site from would-be users, foundations, and anyone else who might lend an ear, and a dime.[10]

THE CHALLENGE TO LEADERSHIP

The point to be made by this Google saga is that today's academic libraries must exist, operate, and serve our campuses in a time of unparalleled change and confusion—largely the product of continuing breakthroughs in the management of information technology. No faculty committee or academic administrator—not even presidents—can hope to keep abreast of the information arena. James J. Duderstadt, president emeritus of the University of Michigan, spoke compellingly to this challenge before the House Science Subcommittee on Basic Research. In his testimony on "The Future of the University in the Digital Age," he addressed the issue of libraries:

> The preservation of knowledge is one of the most rapidly changing functions of the university. The computer—or more precisely, the "digital convergence" of various media from print to graphics to sound to sensory experiences through virtual reality—will likely move beyond the printing press in its impact on knowledge. Throughout the centuries, the intellectual focal point of the university has been its library, its collection of written works preserving the knowledge of civilization. Today such knowledge exists in many forms—as text, graphics, sound, algorithms, and virtual reality simulations—and it exists almost literally in the ether, distributed in digital representations over worldwide networks, accessible by anyone, and certainly not the prerogative of the privileged few in academe.
>   The library is becoming less a collection house and more a cen-

ter for knowledge navigation, a facilitator of information retrieval and dissemination. In a sense, the library and the book are merging. One of the most profound changes will involve the evolution of software agents, collecting, organizing, relating, and summarizing knowledge on behalf of their human masters. Our capacity to reproduce and distribute digital information with perfect accuracy at essentially zero cost has shaken the very foundations of copyright and patent law and threatens to redefine the nature of ownership of intellectual property. The legal and economic management of university intellectual property is rapidly becoming one of the most critical and complex issues facing higher education.[11]

What, then, can and should presidents, provosts, and other academic leaders seek to do to address such a critical and complex issue? Key to the answer is the hiring and adequate support of well-qualified professional librarians, starting with the dean of libraries. William R. Brody, president of the Johns Hopkins University, captures the importance of this very well in the December 26, 2004, issue of the *JHU Gazette*:

> Then the light went on! Full of Google-envy, I suddenly realized that we already have the ultimate information search engine right here at Johns Hopkins. It's one that is readily accessible and highly trusted. And it can be used to locate important references from credible sources, without getting a lot of extraneous garbage. Just think of what this Hopkins search engine would command on the NASDAQ market.
>
> Therefore, any day now, two prominent New York investment banks will announce the initial public offering for JHUSL.com, the newest and most powerful search engine yet—better than Google, Yahoo, MSN and AskJeeves by a long shot. Already traders have lined up across the world to purchase shares. Why this excitement? It's all in the discernment. What is so great about JHUSL.com is that when you perform a search, say on "16th-century weapons of mass destruction," you will get only one or two dozen references—the ones that are really meaningful and helpful—rather than the 50,700 that came up in the Google search I tried.
>
> What is this great technology, you ask? Well, JHUSL stands for the Johns Hopkins University Sheridan Libraries. You see, our library has the most effective search engines yet invented—librarians who are highly skilled at ferreting out the uniquely useful references that you need. Rather than commercializing the library collections, why not export to the public market the most meaningful core of Hopkins' intellectual property—the ability to turn raw information into useful knowledge.

> I hope by now you realize that any talk of taking our library pub-
> lic is simply to emphasize the point missing in all this Google mania:
> Massive information overload is placing librarians in an ever more
> important role as human search engines. They are trained and gifted
> at ferreting out and vetting the key resource material when you need
> it. Today's technology is spectacular—but it can't always trump a
> skilled human.[12]

Such respect and encouragement of the contributions library personnel
make and could offer toward accomplishing campus priorities will certainly be appreciated and will bring greater benefits to the campus.

There are many cases in which academic programs do a good job—albeit unintentionally—of making sure their libraries remain empty and that
students remain information illiterate. For example, the business library of
a prestigious university experienced little use despite the good intentions
of the librarians. During a visit to the San José State University library, the
business school librarians expressed an interest in ideas about how to make
their library more inviting as a way to increase student use. When it was
pointed out that the most effective means of ensuring student use of library
resources is for faculty to create assignments that require use of those resources, the visiting librarian acknowledged the source of their challenge.
Students had no incentive to use the business library, because the entire
business curriculum is based on self-contained case studies.[13]

WHEN CHANGE IS NEEDED

We would like to share a recent story from Vanderbilt to underscore
the profound difference one academic leader, who takes seriously the potential role a library can play in promoting academic quality, can make.
In this case, the leader is Vanderbilt's Dean of Education and Human Development Camilla P. Benbow.

We would like to believe that very few academic libraries are as dysfunctional as the one that existed in the Vanderbilt Peabody College of
Education and Human Development in 1998 when a new college dean
came on board. Dean Benbow quickly set about improving the quality
and status of the College—including its library. We asked her to reflect
on how and why the library has been transformed and to describe some
of the benefits the Peabody Library now brings to the College. While few
libraries are in as bad shape as this library was when she arrived, we do
believe that this Vanderbilt success story is equally applicable to situations where the contributions of libraries have been far less than their

potential because of the lack of adequate attention and active partnering with academic leadership outside the library.

As you read this story of how one campus library changed "overnight" from being considered for elimination by college faculty to being a highly used and appreciated intellectual center for the college, keep several questions in mind.

- How could campus leadership so neglect its library as to allow it to become so dysfunctional?
- When was the last time campus leadership at your institution undertook a serious assessment of your library's contribution to your mission and goals?
- How good are the relations among classroom and library faculty and between the president, provost, and the library dean?
- How good is the leadership in your library?

"The Peabody College of Education and Human Development: A Library Case Study"

Camilla P. Benbow
Dean, Peabody College of Education and Human Development
Vanderbilt University

When I arrived in 1998 as the new dean of the eminent Peabody College of Education and Human Development at Vanderbilt University, eager to make a great school even greater, it struck me as odd to learn how disconnected its library appeared to be from the life of the College. The building was beautiful from the outside (a Carnegie Library). Yet no one ever thought of it, let alone went in there. Even I had found no reason to venture inside after several months on the job. A couple of incidents sparked my curiosity to investigate further.

- A staff member expressed concerns about the safety of our buildings and students. Students were breaking in to our academic buildings after hours (or even hiding as doors were locked) and then took over empty classrooms for places to study. (We could see the effects in the morning.) They would go to all this trouble to find a good place to study but they would not walk across the quad and use our "beautiful" library.
- A faculty member relayed to me, in an attempt to be humorous, how, when the accreditation team came in and wanted to see the library, she just escorted them to the door of the library. She let them see for themselves the library as she was too embarrassed to go in with them.
- Another faculty member told me that they didn't use our curriculum lab because the one shared with other universities and off-campus (much to the inconvenience of our residential students with no cars) was so much better and the materials in our curriculum lab were so dated.

- And, people were suggesting that we address our budget short-fall by just getting rid of the library!

Well, my curiosity became piqued. Nothing, I thought, could be that bad. People must be exaggerating. So, I took a stroll down our beautiful quad to the library with a faculty colleague. And, to my dismay, I discovered that the library was much worse than reported. People must have gotten used to the sorry state of affairs, I concluded. When I walked in, I thought that I had entered a time machine and returned to the 1950's. The furniture and collections appeared to be all from that era. No wonder no one ever went there. We had a museum on our hands! So, I decided to check how many patrons ever came to the library, only to discover that our library was the least used in the whole Vanderbilt system. It even fell behind the specialized library in the music school with just about 200 students. Peabody had about 10 times that many students. When I mentioned this number to the library staff and made a suggestion for improvement, the response I received was: "If we do that, more people will come to the library." I knew right then that we were not just in serious but deep trouble.

It was tempting to take the suggestion of closing the library. We were short of funds at the time and sorely needed more space. Yet, that course of action did not feel right. Here we are in the information age and we were contemplating shutting down the library, which should be the source of information and of assistance with evaluating and accessing it. And, people kept bemoaning our lack of community. Shouldn't the library be the center of our intellectual community?

After much discussion, we decided that we would "rebuild" our library and that radical change was in order. There was no tinkering towards utopia. To get the library's attention, because they thought they were doing just fine and it was the potential patrons who were the problem, I cut the budget severely and established a library advisory committee to develop a strategic plan. This committee was made up of faculty members only as the library staff were too resistant to any change. They truly believed that they were doing fine and that we were the problem and took on a bunker mentality. After a year of deliberations, the committee, led ably by Professor Ann Neely, came up with an excellent and forward-looking plan, only to discover that a similar plan had been drafted 17 years earlier but never acted upon! Given how resistant the library staff was, I was not surprised.

Now, we had to implement the plan and, despite everyone's hard work, the library staff resisted and continued to blame others. They thought the plan was wrong. So, we decided to bring in a consultant. We did, after all, lack expertise in library science. John Collins, the director of the Education Library at Harvard, came down to review the library and presented a set of recommendations. Most importantly, he affirmed the faculty report. It was on target, he concluded. This surprised the library staff as they thought that he would put us in *our* place. And, still they resisted the needed change. At that point, we decided that new leadership was necessary and immediately. We also decided to forge ahead and renovate the first floor, turning it into a reading room for our students with a "Starbucks" feel to it. We needed to do something for our students. And, the Vanderbilt Student Affairs Division decided to partner with us, paying half the cost!

New Director

We hired Sharon Gray Weiner in 2002 to be the new Director of Peabody Library, after a year of an excellent interim director (Flo Wilson). The library had just been renamed from the more specific "Education Library" so that it better reflected the range of programs offered by Peabody College. It became immediately clear to the new director that she needed to make a strong and immediate impact on the Peabody faculty and administrators. The library was in worse shape than anyone had realized. From her first day of work, her approach to the transformation of the library was dual-faceted: to address the internal organization and personnel issues in the library; and to convince the faculty, administrators, and students that the library was a valuable resource for their work. Her leadership, as it turned out, was critical in the transformation of the library. We would not be where we are today without her vision and courageous leadership.

Faculty and Administrators

The Director met individually with each administrator of the College and many of the faculty. The purpose of the meetings was to become visible, listen to concerns, and identify ways that the library could facilitate their priorities. Any concerns they expressed were addressed immediately. Often, their complaints were easy to remedy. For instance, faculty who had requested in the past that the library purchase books, journals, or videos, had been told that the library did not have the money to purchase the materials they needed. The Director assured them that the library would now purchase any materials they needed for their teaching or research. She changed the policy on purchasing materials so that faculty and student requests had the highest priority. Other complaints pointed to the need for customer service training and to have the main library desk staffed by the regular staff rather than student assistants.

The library, we learned, had routinely placed barriers in the way of the faculty, students, and administrators when they needed to obtain information. So the library's primary constituency developed "work-arounds" and found other ways of fulfilling their information needs. Professors pointed to walls in their offices that were filled with books and videos that they bought because the library had refused to purchase them. They subscribed to journals using their own personal or departmental funds. They or their teaching assistants taught their students the information literacy skills they thought were important. Research assistants conducted literature searches for professors. And, of course, students studied in the other libraries on campus that were more attractive and welcoming or in classrooms.

The faculty could not envision how the librarians could work with them as partners in their teaching and research because they had no experience of the professional capabilities of librarians or of a service-oriented philosophy. It became increasingly clear how the library had not been proactive, innovative, or strategic and had become isolated from all functions that mattered to the College.

Moreover, the building and the collection suffered from long-term neglect. Recent refurbishing of the main floor of the library showed that the historic building had the potential to be a beautiful, inviting place. But until then, the building had commonly been described as dingy and unwelcoming. The collection had not been weeded in a long time. Because of this and the presence of duplicate copies of many old books, the collection appeared out-of-date. Faculty complained that there were "no new books" because the new books that were purchased were selected without knowledge of the College's programs or research areas. There were many uncataloged materials.

There was no specific strategic plan, vision, or mission for the library, so there was no context for organizational prioritizing and decision-making.

The Transformation: Strategic and Data-Driven

Within the library, the Director worked tirelessly to understand and revitalize librarians and staff and to address long standing personnel issues. For example, in addition to staff meetings and team meetings, the Director met with each staff member every other week. Although time-intensive, this ensured that the Director would have direct knowledge of the daily issues and concerns of the staff. It also ensured that the staff would have information from the Director herself about her expectations. A strategic plan, vision, and mission statements were developed. Within two years, the staff had accomplished an impressive 69% of their objectives.

Externally, the Director immediately took advantage of every opportunity to speak to faculty, students, and administrators at meetings and informally. She worked to persuade them that the library now had a vision that was congruous with the priorities of the College. She listened for information needs that they expressed and translated them into new programs and services provided by the library. One of those involved the new Office of Research Enhancement. This Office was established to increase the amount of grant funding awarded to faculty in the College by providing support services. There were two obstacles to accomplishing this: difficulty in finding out what the research interests of the faculty were and difficulty in finding out which agencies and organizations were soliciting proposals. The library created a database of faculty research interests with information obtained during the Director's meetings with individual faculty. The librarians assumed responsibility for monitoring requests for proposals and forwarding them to the professors who might be interested. This increased the visibility of the library and showed that the library could have a key role in supporting a goal for the College.

The Curriculum Materials Center and Test Collection had outdated materials, were infrequently used, and occupied almost an entire floor of the building. The Director established task forces of faculty and librarians to determine whether the library should support these functions. The task forces were asked to make recommendations. As a result, the collections have been honed to include only current and relevant materials. Through internal reallocation of resources, the Director doubled the budget for the Curriculum Materials Center. The addition of a "Curriculum Design Studio" provided all of the equipment, software, and resources the students need to create curriculum materials for their student teaching and coursework. One professor said she almost cried when she saw the improvements that had been made!

When professors at the College learned that the Vanderbilt Census Information Center would no longer be supported by its home department, they recommended to the Dean that the Center relocate to the library and be supported by the College. The GIS mapping services that were provided by the Center were unfamiliar to the library staff. However, the staff welcomed the addition of the important service. The Center creates maps of data for the faculty and for nonprofit organizations in the community. Among the clientele are area school systems. By providing this service, the library helps with the College's desire to maintain positive and supportive relationships with the school system administrators.

Today

Two years later, the library is an integral part of Peabody College. Further renovations have resulted in a physical space that is elegant and welcoming. A French café, outdoor terrace with picnic tables, and sculpture garden provide a conducive environment for scholarly discussions and informal networking. The successful reading room concept of the main floor was expanded to the first floor and connected to the café. The top floor was renovated beyond just the curriculum lab and the design studio. The renovation included the youth library and the beginnings of a learning commons. And to top things off, the beautiful skylight that was broken and covered up for 60 years, was restored. A grand "reopening" celebration was hosted in fall 2004 along with an alumni reunion for graduates before 1979 when Peabody merged with Vanderbilt University.

The library staff interacts daily with faculty, students, and administrators. They have a reputation for providing outstanding service and for being open to new roles and responsibilities. The faculty relies on the library now. The information literacy program is growing and the collection of books, journals, videos, and other materials is completely focused on the needs of the students and faculty. There is an array of new services. Staff meetings, professional development activities, and informal gatherings provide ample opportunity for communication and resolution of issues. The number of people entering the library tripled from 2000 to 2002; then tripled again from 2003 to 2004! There is no more talk about getting rid of the library. It has become the center of our intellectual community.

THE FOCUS FOR LEADERSHIP'S EFFORTS

As illustrated in Dean Benbow's story, there are three essentials in freeing libraries to become empowerment tools: vision, partnership, and facilitating change. The first two may be the easiest to accomplish. The third may take months or years of raising questions; targeting faculty development opportunities; presenting white papers for campus discussion; encouraging librarian involvement in key committees; influencing academic policies and procedures; upgrading library personnel, resources, and technology; and—most important of all—setting a personal example of an effective partnership with a librarian.

Beyond this general leadership role, we would suggest that there are areas of such vital concern to the future of our graduates and, therefore, to the future of our communities and our country that involvement of top academic leadership is imperative. Already discussed at the end of chapter 8 is the need for leaders at research institutions to actively support a robust global scholarly network. But there are two areas that require the attention of academic leaders on all campuses. They, too, have been discussed in earlier chapters, but they deserve to be emphasized once more.

First and foremost, ensure that information literacy learning is institutionalized throughout the curriculum and that student learning outcomes are regularly assessed, with information literacy program adjustments being made as appropriate. The value of such learning is already clear to graduates.[14] However, far too many faculty overestimate the information literacy abilities of their students, and, as documented in a study at UC–Berkeley, so do many students themselves.

> The most fundamental conclusion that can be drawn from the University of California–Berkeley Teaching Library surveys is that students think they know more about accessing information and conducting library research than they are able to demonstrate when put to the test. Sadly, in five of the eight groups studied between 1994 and 1999, the median score for graduating seniors was a failing score. As indicated in other studies of student library research skills, the UC–Berkeley experience confirms that students continue to be confused by the elementary conventions for organizing and accessing information. Why is this so? There are many possible reasons for this, including the fact that the state of California ranks close to the bottom nationally on funding for school libraries. In 1994, the entire state had only 850 school librarians. Seven out of eight schools in the state have less than half-time professional library staffing; and although the national ratio of library media specialists to students is 1:882, in California the ratio is 1:5342. With this very evident lack of support for school libraries within California, where the majority of UC–Berkeley students reside, is it any wonder that students arrive at the university without information literacy skills? The Information Literacy Surveys focused primarily on the most fundamental and easiest-to-measure information competencies, described as lower-order thinking skills, considered basic to accessing information resources. It is upon these skills that the higher-order information literacy skills of analysis, synthesis, and evaluation are built.[15]

The situation is no better at other campuses than it is at Berkeley.

This leads directly to the second area that requires top-level and campuswide academic involvement. Campuses both public and private need to repeatedly make clear to feeder schools and to students once they come to campus that information literacy is a required core competency as important today as math and reading.

There is a good body of research that documents the payoff from investments in school library media programs in terms of student academic success. One Scholastic publication summarizes such research across the states of Alaska, Colorado, Florida, Iowa, Massachusetts, Michigan, Minnesota, Missouri, New Mexico, North Carolina, Ohio, Oregon, Pennsylvania, and Texas.[16] Other local research tells the same story. For example, one community college campus studied the comparative abilities of students coming from three different high schools—only one of which has librarians—in mastering research skills. The "study demonstrates that student achievement is substantially higher for students who come from high schools that have librarians and library programs."[17] There is also documentation that introducing resource-based learning through information literacy programs such as Big6™[18] results in significantly higher achievement. For example, students in an American history class who took the New York State Regents exam on that topic had a pass rate of 53 percent in 1996–1997. A year later with the introduction of an information-centered approach to learning (the only change in the course), students achieved a 91 percent pass rate.[19]

The research clearly indicates that strong school library media programs headed up by professional librarians lead to better overall academic performance, as well as leaving students better prepared for college-level research. Moreover, it is not an unreasonable assumption to think that dynamic school library programs might have a positive impact on current concerns that Americans in general are reading less literature than ever. The National Endowment for the Arts documents "the steepest decline—and the one that the report notes with the most alarm—has occurred among young adults. In 1982, respondents age 18 to 34 were the group most likely to report recreational reading of literature. Over the intervening decades, they have become the group least likely to do so (except for some segments of the population over 65)."[20] Unfortunately, many states besides California are quick to cut school library support in times of tight budgets, and few school districts appreciate the relative importance of this investment against priorities such as smaller class sizes.

Soon the Educational Testing Service information and communication technology (ICT) test will be widely available. If not before, once the hard data available regarding students' ICT abilities is documented, institutions of higher education must make clear statements as to their expectations that high schools will ensure students acquire reasonable levels of information literacy skills before coming to college. This is not a library issue. In today's information society, it is an essential learning issue.

IN CLOSING

The preface to our 1989 book documents the impetus for our collaboration first on library efforts at the University of Colorado and then in joint authoring of the book. Although our backgrounds provided very different motivations, we both found a common cause in the belief that quality education in the information age requires that students become effective information consumers who are able to locate and evaluate pertinent information for any need in their personal or professional lives. We believe quality education means an active education that helps students develop a pattern of lifelong independent learning. Then as now, our book is one of advocacy. It is not, however, a book of advocacy for libraries per se, but rather of advocacy for the quality of learning, research, and service that can occur on campuses where more imaginative use is made of academic libraries.

This concept is emphatically expressed in the words of Sterling Professor Emeritus of History at Yale University and Past President of the American Academy of Arts and Sciences Jaroslav Pelikan. In his book, *The Idea of the University: A Reexamination*, Dr. Pelikan makes the following observation:

> This reexamination of the university can be said to consist of three interrelated stages: the advancement of knowledge through scholarly investigation; the extension and interpretation of knowledge through teaching, including professional training; and the diffusion of knowledge through scholarly publication. At each stage, the vocation of the university depends absolutely on the library.
>
> Such a dependence implies the need for the university library to be involved as a genuine and full partner of the other components of the university in both short-range decisions and long-range planning.[21]

In these words, Dr. Pelikan clearly articulates the message of this entire book. We fully agree with his statement that "no single institution in the contemporary world of scholarship has a greater bearing on the future of the university than the library."[22]

We hope that the case has been made that academic libraries on the smallest to the largest campuses can be effective tools in the hands of presidents and other academic leaders in achieving the mission and goals of their institutions. When that is true, the ultimate beneficiaries will be our students, their families, and communities.

NOTES

1. Jeffrey R. Young, "Publishing Groups Say Google's Book-Scanning Effort May Violate Copyrights," *The Chronicle of Higher Education* 51 (18 February 2005): A3.

2. Aisha Labi, "Google Library Project Is Culturally Biased, Says French National Librarian," *The Chronicle of Higher Education* 51 (4 March 2005): A35.

3. Jeffrey R. Young, "Google Unveils a Search Engine Focused on Scholarly Materials," *The Chronicle of Higher Education* 51 (3 December 2004): A34.

4. Jeffrey R. Young, "Chemical Society Sues Google," *The Chronicle of Higher Education* 51 (7 January 2005): A40.

5. Jeffrey R. Young, "Libraries Aim to Widen Google's Eyes," *The Chronicle of Higher Education* 50 (21 May 2004): A31.

6. For more information on this project, see http://www.library.cmu.edu/Libraries/MBP_FAQ.html. Retrieved 29 March 2005.

7. John Markoff and Edward Wyatt, "Google Is Adding Major Libraries to Its Database," *New York Times*, 14 December 2004, A1.

8. For more information about the Internet Archive, see http://www.archive.org/about/about.php.

9. "Straight Answers from Brewster Kahle," *American Libraries* 36 (February 2005): 22.

10. Mark Y. Herring, "Don't Get Goggle-Eyed Over Google's Plan to Digitize," *The Chronicle of Higher Education* 51 (11 March 2005): B20.

11. House Science Subcommittee on Basic Research, *The Future of the University in the Digital Age: Hearing before the Subcommittee on Basic Research*, 106th Cong., 2nd Session, 9 May 2000. Retrieved 27 April 2005, from LexisNexis Congressional database.

12. William R. Brody, "Thinking Out Loud: A Billion-Dollar IPO for Johns Hopkins," *The JHU Gazette* 34 (6 December 2004): 2. Retrieved 9 December 2004 from http://www.jhu.edu/gazette/2004/06dec04/06brody.html.

13. Patricia Senn Breivik, "21st Century Learning and Information Literacy," *Change* 37 (March/April 2005): 20–27.

14. Barbara J. Cockrell, "Talking with Faculty and Administrators: Using Numbers to Demonstrate the Value of Bibliographic Instruction," in *Integrating Information Literacy into the College Experience*, ed. Julia K. Nims et al. (Ann Arbor, Mich.: Pierian Press, 2003).

15. Patricia Davitt Maughan, "Assessing Information Literacy among Undergraduates: A Discussion of the Literature and the University of California–Berkeley Assessment Experience," *College & Research Libraries* 62 (January 2001): 10.

16. *School Libraries Work!* (Danbury, Conn.: Scholastic Library Publishing, 2004). Retrieved 29 March 2005 from http://www.scholasticlibrary.com/download/slw_04.pdf.

17. Topsy N. Smalley, "College Success: High School Librarians Make the Difference," *The Journal of Academic Librarianship* 30 (May 2004): 193.

18. See the Big6 Web site (http://www.big6.com/) for more information.

19. Michael B. Eisenberg and Robert E. Berkowitz, *The Big6 Collection: The Best of the Big6 Newsletter* (Worthington, Ohio: Linworth, 2000), 127.

20. Scott McLemee, "Americans Found to Read Less Literature Than Ever," *The Chronicle of Higher Education* 50 (16 July 2004): A16.

21. Jaroslav Pelikan, *The Idea of the University: A Reexamination* (New Haven, Conn.: Yale University Press, 1992), 117.

22. Ibid., 13.

APPENDIX A:
Selected WASC Criteria for Review and Accompanying Guidelines

The following text was excerpted from two standards, which deal with information literacy skills among students and the correlation with library use, in the 2001 WASC *Handbook of Accreditation*.

From "Standard 2: Achieving Education Objectives Through Core Functions"

2.2. All degrees—undergraduate and graduate—awarded by the institution are clearly defined in terms of entry-level requirements and in terms of levels of student achievement necessary for graduation that represent more than simply an accumulation of courses or credits.

Baccalaureate programs engage students in an integrated course of study of sufficient breadth and depth to prepare them for work, citizenship, and a fulfilling life. These programs also ensure the development of core learning abilities and competencies including, but not limited to, college-level written and oral communication; college-level quantitative skills; information literacy; and the habit of critical analysis of data and argument. . . .

Guideline: Competencies required for graduation are reflected in course syllabi for both General Education and the major.

2.3. The institution's expectations for learning and student attainment are clearly reflected in its academic programs and policies. These include the organization and content of the institution's curricula; admissions and graduation policies; the organization and delivery of advisement; the use of its library and information resources; and (where applicable) experience in the wider learning environment provided by the campus and/or co-curriculum.

Guideline: The use of information and learning resources beyond textbooks is evidenced in syllabi throughout the undergraduate and graduate curriculum.

2.13. Student support services—including financial aid, registration, advising, career counseling, computer labs, and library and information services—are designed to meet the needs of the specific types of students the institution serves and the curricula it offers.[11]

In addition, WASC also addresses library resources, services, and technology under "Standard 3: Developing and Applying Resources and Organizational Structures to Ensure Sustainability."

3.6. The institution holds, or provides access to, information resources sufficient in scope, quality, currency, and kind to support its academic offerings and the scholarship of its members. For on-campus students and students enrolled at a distance, physical and information resources, services, and information technology facilities are sufficient in scope and kind to support and maintain the level and kind of education offered. These resources, services and facilities are consistent with the institution's purposes, and are appropriate, sufficient, and sustainable.

Finally, "Questions for Institutional Engagement" that are raised for each standard, and those asked regarding library resources and service are ones worthy of asking on any campus.

To what extent does the institution provide an environment that is actively conducive to study and learning, where library, information resources, and co-curricular programs actively support student learning?

How does the institution assess the continuing adequacy of its fiscal, physical, and information resources and plan for the future to ensure that they are appropriately renewed and (if necessary) altered in size and character?

How does the institution ensure that its members develop the critical information literacy skills needed to locate, evaluate, and responsibly use information? How does it utilize the special skills of information professionals to support teaching, learning, and information technology planning?

To what extent do the institution's resources, services, and information technology respond to faculty needs with respect to scholarly activity and curricular development?

APPENDIX B:
Prologue and Major Recommendations of the Carnegie Foundation's Report on Colleges

This section of the Carnegie Foundation's report from 1986 (excerpted from *The Chronicle of Higher Education* 33 [5 November 1986]: 21) addresses the importance of the library and its resources as critical to the mission of a college.

IX. RESOURCES FOR LEARNING

The quality of a college is measured by the resources for learning on the campus and the extent to which students become independent, self-directed learners. And yet we found that today, about one out of every four undergraduates spends no time in the library during a normal week, and 65 percent use the library four hours or less each week.

The gap between the classroom and the library, reported on almost a half-century ago, still exists today.

- The college library must be viewed as a vital part of the undergraduate experience. Every college should establish a basic books library to serve the specific needs of the undergraduate program.
- All undergraduates should be introduced carefully to the full range of resources for learning on a campus. They should be given bibliographic instruction and be encouraged to spend at least as much time in the library—using its wide range of resources—as they spend in classes.

- Support for the purchase of books should be increased. A minimum of 5 percent of the total operating budget of the college should be available for library support.

- The undergraduate college should work closely with surrounding schools and with community libraries to help strengthen library holdings, and provide continued training for school and community librarians.

- The undergraduate college also has a special obligation not only to support adequately the library, but in a larger sense to sustain the culture of the book. Colleges should celebrate the book and schedule activities each year that feature books and reading-bringing authors to the campus, for example—or they can have seminars in which faculty talk about works that were influential in their lives.

In the past, technological revolutions bypassed education because teachers were bypassed in the process.

This time it may be different. Today, on many campuses we found teachers more actively involved in the use of computers, and with their help, programming has improved.

- To improve the undergraduate experience—and strengthen the community of learning—the challenge is to build connections between learning resources on and off the campus. The strategy we have in mind is to link technology to the library, to the classroom, and, in the end, to college goals.

- To achieve such integration, we propose three specific recommendations.

First, computer hardware should not be purchased before a comprehensive plan has been developed, one that covers personal computers, information services, and the use of technology by the institution.

Second, we urge that every college have a high-level faculty committee to plan for the integration of learning resources on the campus.

Third, to broaden their services, we recommend that every college and university also link its library to one or more computer-based networks.

While using technology, students also need to understand how society today is being reshaped by our inventions, just as tools of earlier eras changed the course of history. There is a danger that greater credibility will be given to data than to ideas and that scholars will mistake information for knowledge. The challenge is not only to teach students how to use new technology but also to encourage them to ask when and why it should be used.

APPENDIX C:
Selected Resources for Incorporating Information Literacy into the Curriculum

The four resources referenced here offer models or information useful in planning information literacy curricula in the college and university setting.

ACRL WEB SITE

The Association of College and Research Libraries (ACRL) maintains an extensive information literacy Web site that provides a gateway to a wide range of resources, including examples of best practices, links to bibliographies, standards, and information on important initiatives. It is available at http://www.ala.org/ala/acrl/acrlissues/acrlinfolit/information literacy.htm. Through ACRL's best practices initiative, a set of characteristics of programs that are hallmarks of the most effective programs for undergraduates in both two- and four-year institutions provides good guidance and can be found at http://www.ala.org/ala/acrl/acrlissues/ acrlinfolit/professactivity/iil/bestpractices/bestpracticesproject.htm.

CSU INFORMATION COMPETENCE INITIATIVE

A document entitled "Integrating Information Competence into the Disciplines" was compiled by Ilene Rockman, manager of the Information Competence Initiative, California State University, Office of the Chancellor. The document is a bibliography of relevant articles listed by

subject matter and is available at http://www.calstate.edu/LS/integrating
_2005july.doc.

INFORMATION FOR THE INSTRUCTION OF
DIVERSE POPULATIONS

ACRL's Instruction for Diverse Populations Committee has produced
a bibliography available on the Web at http://www.ala.org/ala/acrlbucket/
is/publicationsacrl/diversebib.htm. The definition of "diverse populations" for this bibliography includes groups such as students of color, international students, disabled students, non-traditional or adult learners,
and students who are the first members of their family to attend college.
Print and electronic resources are included.

LOEX CLEARINGHOUSE FOR LIBRARY INSTRUCTION

Easy access to existing models is available through many state and regional clearinghouses and through Library Orientation Exchange
(LOEX) (http://www.emich.edu/public/loex/loex.html), a long-existing
national depository of library instruction materials located in Ypsilanti,
Michigan. LOEX also sponsors annual conferences on library instruction
at various locations in the United States.

APPENDIX D:
Promoting Information Literacy through Class Assignments: How Faculty Can Help

This document was first created by librarians Sarah Blakeslee and Kristin Tefts at the Meriam Library, California State University Chico, 23 September 1999. It is now available online on the University of Louisville's Web site at http://www.louisville.edu/infoliteracy/promotinginformationliteracy.htm. More information is also available at http://www.csuchico.edu/lins/assignments/assigncelt.html.

IMPORTANCE

Let students know that the assignment has a specific, understood purpose and communicate why learning how to find information is important to their success in class, in college, and throughout their careers. If they're not interested in scholarly research, point out that information exists on any topic, from buying a new stereo to planning a trip to Europe. If you have a personal story that illustrates the power of information, tell it.

GOALS

Think about what you want students to gain from the assignment. Just as you cannot teach a semester course in one day, information literacy cannot be achieved in one assignment. For anything other than a large research paper, consider focusing on a particular collection, research tool, or skill, such as finding reference books on a topic, using a specific periodical database, or evaluating information.

EXPECTATIONS

Don't assume students know how to use the library, even if they tell you they do. The majority of students have never been presented with the number of information choices they find in a university library. They also do not enter college understanding the organization of information within a discipline, how to search computerized databases, or how to evaluate information.

RELEVANCY

Try to tie information seeking into class assignments or to some area of student interest. Assignments asking students to find things for no particular reason (i.e., the scavenger or treasure hunt) are often considered "busy work" by the students, are actively resented, and have been proven to be ineffectual.

REALITY

Don't ask your students to do something that can't be done. An impossible assignment frustrates a student and turns them against the library. Try doing the assignment yourself to test its feasibility and see if there are enough books and periodicals available in the library to sufficiently cover the assignment requirements. For additional help on determining the feasibility of an assignment as it relates to the library's collections and holdings, check with your department's librarian liaison, or with one of the reference librarians.

CLARITY AND ACCURACY

Be specific in what you want the students to do and how you direct them to do it. If you want them to use scholarly articles, be sure they are clear about what distinguishes a scholarly journal from a popular journal. If you want the students to look for articles in PsychInfo, don't tell them to go to a library computer and find it on the internet. Instead, direct them to the Library's Web page/All Databases/PsychInfo. Provide a list of appropriate resources to give students a starting point.

TOPIC

Choosing a topic is often difficult for students. Although everybody writing on the same topic creates difficulty in keeping materials on the shelf, too wide a choice of topics paralyzes many students and often finds them researching inappropriate subjects for which they can find very little information. Consider offering your students a list of possible choices that you have pre-researched and know will result in a successful research experience. If it is necessary to have students write on one topic, consider putting items on reserve at the Circulation Desk.

CRITICAL THINKING

Create an assignment that requires the student to think about the information they are retrieving. Often, students will take the first things they find on a topic if not given a reason to be more discriminating.

PACE THE ASSIGNMENT

For large research assignments, break the assignment into smaller chunks so you can ascertain whether or not the student understands the research process and is finding appropriate sources. Looking at a draft of a bibliography a month before a paper is due can help direct student research and also gives students time to use the Interlibrary Loan services, if necessary. Additionally, pacing the assignment discourages procrastination.

INTERNET

Explain to students the difference between public web documents found through search engines (like Yahoo, Google, and Dogpile), and structured scholarly information databases available via the web like (ERIC, Medline, and Philosopher's Index). Students are often told by their instructors NOT to use the internet for a class assignment, when in reality the majority of our periodical databases are only accessible via the internet.

TECHNOLOGY

Make sure students understand the technology required and have reasonable access to the computers and software necessary to complete assignments.

GETTING HELP

It is helpful to the librarians, if you provide a copy of your students' assignment. This allows us to support your educational goals and be additional resources for your students. If you have questions, or would like a librarian to look over an assignment for potential problems, collaborate on an assignment, or talk with your class, please contact Anna Marie Johnson in our Office of Information Literacy at x1491 or annamarie @louisville.edu.

APPENDIX E:
The Prague Declaration:
Towards an Information Literate Society

We the participants at the Information Literacy Meeting of Experts, organized by the U.S. National Commission on Library and Information Science and the National Forum on Information Literacy, with the support of UNESCO, representing 23 countries from all of the seven major continents, held in Prague, the Czech Republic, September 20–23, 2003, propose the following basic Information Literacy principles:

- The creation of an Information Society is key to social, cultural, and economic development of nations and communities, institutions and individuals in the 21st century and beyond.
- Information Literacy encompasses knowledge of one's information concerns and needs, and the ability to identify, locate, evaluate, organize and effectively create, use and communicate information to address issues or problems at hand; it is a prerequisite for participating effectively in the Information Society, and is part of the basic human right of lifelong learning.
- Information Literacy, in conjunction with access to essential information and effective use of information and communication technologies, plays a leading role in reducing the inequities within and among countries and peoples, and in promoting tolerance and mutual understanding through information use in multicultural and multilingual contexts.
- Governments should develop strong interdisciplinary programs to promote Information Literacy nationwide as a necessary step in closing the

digital divide through the creation of an information literate citizenry, an effective civil society, and a competitive workforce.

- Information Literacy is a concern to all sectors of society and should be tailored by each to its specific needs and context.
- Information Literacy should be an integral part of Education for All, which can contribute critically to the achievement of the United Nations Millennium Development Goals, and respect for the Universal Declaration of Human Rights.

In the above context, we propose for the urgent consideration of governments, civil society and the international community the following policy recommendations:

- The September 2003 Prague Conference Report should be studied and its recommendations, strategic plans and research initiatives implemented expeditiously as appropriate (the report will be disseminated in December 2003).
- The progress in, and opportunities for implementation of the above should be assessed by an International Congress on Information Literacy, which could be organized in the first half of 2005.
- The possibility of inclusion of Information Literacy within the United Nations Literacy Decade (2003–2012) should be considered by the international community.

This document, as well as other information pertaining to the 2003 Prague Information Literacy Meeting of Experts, is available at http://www.infolit.org/International_Conference/index.htm.

APPENDIX F:
Guiding Principles for Budget Reductions

These principles were developed by Harold Schleifer, dean of the university library at California State Polytechnic University, Pomona, and the library faculty and staff.

The library selects programs (resources and services) based on quality, cost, coherence, and centrality to our mission. We carefully evaluate programs to avoid duplication within the Library. The focus of our activities is in support of the teaching and learning mission of the University. We acknowledge that the most likely source for needed resources will be the reallocation of existing resources. In addition to these standing principles, we will apply the sublisted guidelines during this period of budgetary exigency.

CORE SERVICES

- To provide access to scholarly resources that support the curriculum.
- To provide assistance with information retrieval.
- To provide instruction for information competence.
- To provide technology to enhance access to library resources and services.

METHODOLOGY

- Consult with the dean's Budget and Policy Advisory Group.
- Seek input from library faculty, staff, and patrons.
- Survey peer libraries.

OBJECTIVES

- To achieve a strategic balance between funding and programs.
- To ensure that scarce resources will be responsibly allocated, measured, and reported.
- To ensure that unique and essential services are preserved.
- To arrive at decisions that are mission-driven and data-based.

GUIDELINES

(No priority is implied in the position on this list.)

- Select programs (i.e., resources/services) based on costs, quality, coherence, and centrality to our mission.
- Focus on facilitation of learning and teaching rather than supporting research.
- Favor programs that provide the greatest good for the greatest number.
- Implement vertical rather than horizontal "across-the-board" cuts.
- Maintain awareness of future needs when making decisions.
- Curtail or defer programs where future recovery is feasible.
- Ensure that the programs we can continue to offer are of high quality.
- Choose the least cost alternative for providing comparable resources and/or services.
- Eliminate duplication of resources and services within the library and between the library and other campus entities.
- Ensure that proposed reductions do not merely shift the burden for that expenditure from one unit to another.
- Provide self-service to the maximum extent possible with sensitivity to patrons' needs.
- Acquire leading-edge products and services by phasing out legacy activities that no longer provide value or enable the library to meet its mission, if budget permits.
- Invest in infrastructure rather than peripherals.
- Protect and develop staff; avoid layoffs.
- Value flexibility and responsiveness.

INDEX

Abell, Angela, 120
Academic administrators: attitudes toward libraries, 2, 217; and campus planning, 2–3, 119; and collection development, 217–220, 222–223, 228; and knowledge management, 122–123; need for vision, 62; and resource-based learning, 46; the scholarly network, 222–228; support for research partnerships with librarians, 85–86
Academic libraries: administrators' attitudes toward, 2, 217; business and industry use of, 29, 93–94, 99, 103–105; changing facilities, 181–183; and civic engagement, 105–107; collaborations and consortia, 168, 190–200; collection development, 207–220, 222–223, 228; and community service, 2, 92–93, 103–104, 108–111; and digital libraries, 167; and educational quality, 53–54; effects of technology on, 173–186; faculty attitudes toward, 1–2, 41; fee-based services, 95–98; funding for, 251–258; and fundraising, 271–275; as information management, 207–208; instructional role, 4, 126, 128; and integrated learning, 49, 53–54; integrating with computer centers, 169–173; library-based learning, 41, 47–48, 54; library-based services, 80, 98, 108–109; programs for special student groups, 151–155; and public libraries, 65, 66, 159–160; and research support, 2, 74–79; resource sharing among, 192–193, 208, 218; roles and responsibilities of, 1, 4, 34–35, 66, 167–169; as social gathering places, 144–145; special uses of, 145–148; staffing, 234–235; as strategic tools in achieving campus goals, 2; and student recruit-

About the Authors

PATRICIA SENN BREIVIK served as the Dean of the University Library at San José State University, before retiring in June 2005, where, in collaboration with the San José Public Library, a merged library opened in 2003 and serves as the Silicon Valley's twenty-first-century information hub. Dr. Breivik's previous experiences included Library Dean at Wayne State University; Associate Vice President for Information Resources at the Towson State University Campus of the University of Maryland; and Director of the Library and Professor, University of Colorado, Auraria campus in Denver, Colorado. Dr. Breivik founded and served as the first chair of the National Forum on Information Literacy, an umbrella group of over ninety national and international organizations concerned with the need for people to be able to access and use information effectively. Dr. Breivik holds a B.A. from Brooklyn College, an M.L.S. from Pratt Institute, and a D.L.S. from Columbia University. She can be reached via e-mail at breivikp@bellsouth.net.

E. GORDON GEE, one of the most experienced chief executives in higher education, has served as president of Brown University, Ohio State University, the University of Colorado, and West Virginia University. A joint degree recipient in law and education from Columbia University, Dr. Gee completed a federal judicial clerkship, after which he served as an Assistant Dean for the University of Utah College of Law.

After holding this position, Dr. Gee served as a Judicial Fellow and Senior Staff Assistant for United States Supreme Court Chief Justice Warren Burger. He then became Associate Dean and Professor at J. Reuben Clark Law School of Brigham Young University. After his appointment at West Virginia University, he made the transition from law school administrator to university president. He is currently Chancellor of Vanderbilt University in Nashville, Tennessee. He can be reached via e-mail at Gordon.Gee@Vanderbilt.edu.